Special Praise for *My Grandmother's Hands*

"*My Grandmother's Hands* is a gripping journey through the labyrinths of trauma and its effects on modern life, especially for African Americans. In this important book, Resmaa's penetrating insight into trauma is profoundly impactful, but even more powerful and useful are his strategies for addressing it—for healing. A brilliant thinker, Resmaa is able to bring a multitude of research and experience together to guide us in our understanding of how trauma affects our lives; how trauma is a part of all of our lives; and of how the history and progression of trauma has produced a culture in which no one is immune. This is essential reading if we are to wrest ourselves from the grips of trauma and discover the tropes in which our bodies and our minds are free of it."

Alexs Pate, author of *Amistad* and *Losing Absalom*

. . . . .

"Resmaa Menakem cuts to the heart of America's racial crisis with the precision of a surgeon in ways few have before. Addressing the intergenerational trauma of white supremacy and its effects on all of us—understanding it as a true soul wound—is the first order of business if we hope to pull out of the current morass. As this amazing work shows us, policies alone will not do it, and bold social action, though vital to achieving justice, will require those engaged in it to also take action on the injury, deep and personal, from which we all suffer."

Tim Wise, best-selling author of *White Like Me: Reflections on Race from a Privileged Son* and *Dear White America: Letter to a New Minority*

. . . . .

"As a career peace officer, I entered this noble profession to serve my community, but I had never received any instruction in the police academy or been issued a piece of equipment that prepared me to recognize or examine community trauma . . . or my own. *My Grandmother's Hands* gave me a profound and compelling historical map tracing law enforcement's role as sometimes unknowing contributors to community trauma. The book gives peace officers tools that can help in the healing of their communities and emphasizes self-care so that the men and women entrusted to be guardians and protectors of our communities are taken care of as well."

Medaria Arradondo, Acting Chief, Minneapolis Police Department

. . . . .

"*My Grandmother's Hands* invites each of us to heal the racial trauma that lives in our bodies. As Resmaa Menakem explains, healing this trauma takes courage and a commitment to viscerally feel this racial pain. By skillfully combining therapy expertise with social criticism and practical guidance, he reveals a path forward for individual and collective healing that involves experiencing the sensations of this journey with each step. Are you willing to take the first step?"

Alex Haley, Assistant Professor at the University of Minnesota's Earl E. Bakken Center for Spirituality & Healing

. . . . .

"Dr. W. E. B. Du Bois put his finger on African American consciousness when he wrote, 'One ever feels his twoness—an American, a Negro; two souls, two thoughts, two unreconciled strivings; two warring ideals in one dark body.' But even Du Bois never addressed the process of healing the psychological wounds of the 'two-ness.' In *My Grandmother's Hands*, Resmaa offers a path of internal reconciliation for a person enduring the generational trauma of American racism and gives us all a chance to dream of a healing from it."

Keith Ellison, Member of Congress and Deputy Chair of the Democratic National Committee

. . . . .

"Offers a well-needed paradigm shift on how we think, dream, and strategize against white supremacy in our bodies, cultures, and institutions. A must-have for anyone interested in advancing racial justice and healing."

Chaka A. Mkali, Director of Organizing and Community Building at Hope Community and hip-hop artist I Self Devine

. . . . .

"*My Grandmother's Hands* is a revolutionary work of beauty, brilliance, compassion and ultimately, hope. With eloquence and grace, Resmaa Menakem masterfully lays out the missing piece in the puzzle of why, despite so many good intentions, we have not achieved racial justice. Yes, we need to understand white supremacy, but as Menakem so skillfully explains, white supremacy is not rational and we won't end it with our intellect alone. White supremacy is internalized deep into our bodies. We must begin to understand it as *white body supremacy* and go to the depth of where it is stored, within our collective bones and muscles. To this end, *My Grandmother's Hands* is an intimate guidebook toward racial healing, one that achieves that rare combination for its readers; it is deeply intellectually stimulating while also providing practical ways to engage in the process of repair, even as we read. I believe this book will change the direction of the movement for racial justice."

Robin DiAngelo, Racial Justice Educator and author of *White Fragility*

. . . . .

"Forget diversity. Forget teaching tolerance. Forget white guilt. With clarity and insight, Resmaa offers a profoundly different approach to healing racism in America."

John Friel, PhD, and Linda Friel, MA, directors of ClearLife Clinic and *New York Times* best-selling co-authors of nine books, including *Adult Children: The Secrets of Dysfunctional Families*

. . . . .

"A fascinating, must-read, groundbreaking book that offers a novel approach to healing America's long-standing racial trauma."

Joseph L. White, PhD, Professor Emeritus of Psychology and Psychiatry at UC Irvine and co-author of *The Psychology of Blacks, Black Man Emerging, Black Fathers,* and *Building Multicultural Competency: Development, Training, and Practice*

• • • • •

"Resmaa's book is an intimate and direct look at the way the Black-white dynamic is held, not only in institutions such as policing, but also in the bodies of all of those involved. Building on Dr. DeGruy's work in *Post Traumatic Slave Syndrome,* Resmaa looks at how history is held and replayed by the body's survival responses, specifically focusing on the experience of Blackness and trauma, the history and experience of whiteness and the white body, and the creation of and experience of the police force . . . .

"In addition to providing theory and analysis, this book also offers concrete practices that are part of the work of shifting the violence of the original wound."

Susan Raffo, shared owner of Integral Somatic Therapy, bodyworker, writer, and community organizer, The People's Movement Center

• • • • •

"*My Grandmother's Hands* is full of wisdom and understanding. In it, Resmaa Menakem offers a new way to understand racism and, more importantly, to heal it. This book lays out a path to freedom and peace, first for individual readers, then for our culture as a whole. A must-read for everyone who cares about our country."

Nancy Van Dyken, LP, LICSW, author of *Everyday Narcissism*

• • • • •

"At once disturbing, fascinating, and hopeful, this book provides a fresh new roadmap for personal and shared steps to eradicate racism and heal our nation. Very timely!"

Bill Eddy, lead author of *Splitting: Protecting Yourself While Divorcing Someone with Borderline or Narcissistic Personality Disorder* and co-author of *Splitting America*

MY GRANDMOTHER'S HANDS

MY GRANDMOTHER'S HANDS

Racialized Trauma and the Pathway to Mending Our Hearts and Bodies

RESMAA MENAKEM

CENTRAL RECOVERY PRESS

LAS VEGAS

Central Recovery Press (CRP) is committed to publishing exceptional materials addressing addiction treatment, recovery, and behavioral healthcare topics.

For more information, visit www.centralrecoverypress.com.

Publisher: Central Recovery Press
             3321 N. Buffalo Drive
             Las Vegas, NV 89129

25 24 23 22 21 20   3 4 5

Library of Congress Cataloging-in-Publication Data

Names: Menakem, Resmaa, author.
Title: My grandmother's hands : racialized trauma and the pathway to mending
  our hearts and bodies / Resmaa Menakem.
Description: Las Vegas, NV : Central Recovery Press, [2017]
Identifiers: LCCN 2017018669 (print) | LCCN 2017029917 (ebook) | ISBN
  9781942094487 (ebook) | ISBN 9781942094470 (pbk. : alk. paper) | ISBN
  9781942094609 (hardcover)
Subjects: LCSH: African Americans--Social conditions. | United States--Race
  relations. | Whites--Race identity--United States.
Classification: LCC E185.615 (ebook) | LCC E185.615 .M38 2017 (print) | DDC
  305.896/073--dc23
LC record available at https://lccn.loc.gov/2017018669

Author photo © by Nancy Wong. All rights reserved.

The descriptions of the anchoring practices in Chapter Twelve first appeared, in slightly different form, in the author's book *Rock the Boat*, published by Hazelden Publishing. They are copyright © 2015 by Resmaa Menakem.

Publisher's Note: This book contains general information about racialized trauma, somatic healing methods, and related matters. The information is not medical advice. This book is not an alternative to medical advice from your doctor or other professional healthcare provider.

Our books represent the experiences and opinions of their authors only. Every effort has been made to ensure that events, institutions, and statistics presented in our books as facts are accurate and up-to-date. To protect their privacy, the names of some of the people, places, and institutions in this book may have been changed.

Author's Note: This book is for informational purposes only. It is not intended as a substitute for psychotherapy from a qualified counselor. If you feel you can benefit from therapy, please consult a trained mental health professional.

Cover design by The Book Designers. Interior design by Sara Streifel, Think Creative Design.

TABLE OF CONTENTS

Part III: Mending Our Collective Body

This book is dedicated to Jodi Nowak.

Thank you for being my friend.

Love always.

If the persistence of white supremacy in twenty-first century America surprises you, this book will give you a startlingly different understanding of why. You will discover the vital force behind white supremacy is in our blood—literally—and in our nervous systems. However light or dark our skins, we Americans must all contend with these elemental forces.

If you are not surprised that widespread white supremacy continues to injure America, but have no ideas or little hope for overcoming it, keep reading. This book offers a profoundly different view of what we can do, individually and together, to grow beyond our entrenched racialized divide. This process has little to do with ideology, politics, or public policy and everything to do with neuroscience and the body.

If you see white supremacy as a belief system or ideology, in this book you will discover only a fraction of it exists in our cognitive brains. For the most part, white supremacy lives in our bodies. In fact, white supremacy would be better termed *white-body supremacy*, because every white-skinned body, no matter who inhabits it—and no matter what they think, believe, do, or say—automatically benefits from it. (Beginning with Chapter 1, *white-body supremacy* is the term I'll use.)

If you are convinced that ending white supremacy begins with social and political action, *do not read this book unless you are willing to be challenged*. We need to begin with the healing of trauma— in dark-skinned bodies, light-skinned bodies, our neighborhoods and communities, and the law enforcement profession. Social and political actions are essential, but they need to be part of a larger strategy of healing, justice, and creating room for growth in traumatized flesh- and-blood bodies.

If you believe America's racial tensions lie not in white supremacy but in its dark-skinned people and the power they wield, *do not read further*. The pages ahead will trigger your trauma reflexes and make your life more painful than it already is.

"But all our phrasing—race relations, racial chasm, racial justice, racial profiling, white privilege, even white supremacy—serves to obscure that racism is a visceral experience, that it dislodges brains, blocks airways, rips muscle, extracts organs, cracks bones, breaks teeth. . . . You must always remember that the sociology, the history, the economics, the graphs, the charts, the regressions all land, with great violence, upon the body."

TA-NEHISI COATES,
BETWEEN THE WORLD AND ME

"The reality is that we are bodies born of other bodies,

bodies feeding other bodies, bodies having sex with other

bodies, bodies seeking a shoulder to lean or cry on . . .

Bodies matter, which is why anything

related to them arouses emotions."

FRANS DE WAAL,
OUR INNER APE

WATCH YOUR BODY

As you experience this book, you'll learn to pay attention to your body.

If you have a white body, there will be times when it will reflexively constrict in order to protect you from some of the truths you'll encounter. This constriction will be followed by a thought such as "I'm not like that; I'm a good person," or "White-body supremacy has nothing to do with me," or "This isn't about me because I don't belong to a racist organization."

When this occurs, just notice what you're experiencing without doing anything about it. Don't try to undo the constriction. Don't try to hold onto it, either. Just watch your body closely and notice what sensations, impulses, and emotions arise.

Don't take the reflexive thoughts seriously, either. Don't try to support them. Don't debate them. Don't act on them at all. Just observe them as they arise, and note any images or other thoughts that may follow.

If you have a Black or other dark body, there will be times when your body will experience a sudden shock of recognition or understanding. Things you hadn't fully grasped before may suddenly become clear. This might be followed by a rush of energy in the form of joy, or anger, or outrage, or a felt sense of clarity and rightness. Let yourself experience these sensations fully, but don't hang onto them. Let them move into and through your body like a wave; then let them go.

If you're a public safety professional, you may experience *both* sets of sensations and thoughts. When one appears, allow it to flow fully into your body and mind, without doing anything about it. Then let it go, like a steadily shrinking image in your rear-view mirror.

Whatever your profession or skin color, as you read this book, at times you may sense profound hope, relief, or both. Let yourself fully experience these as they arise. Then let them go as well.

ACKNOWLEDGING
OUR ANCESTORS

Our bodies exist in the present. To your thinking brain, there is past, present, and future, but to a traumatized body there is only *now*. That *now* is the home of intense survival energy.

Most of this book is set in the present, but small parts of it will trace two bloodlines of trauma from the past to the present.

First, we'll trace trauma as it was passed from one European body to another during the Middle Ages, then imported to the New World by colonists, and then passed down by many generations of their descendants.

Second, we'll trace trauma as European colonists instilled it in the bodies of many Africans who were forcibly imported as indentured servants, and later as property, to the New World. They, in turn, passed down this trauma through many generations of their descendants.

On this same soil, trauma also followed another earlier path: one that spread from the bodies of European colonists to the bodies of Native people and then through many generations of their descendants.

An estimated eighteen million Native people were custodians of the North American continent when European colonists arrived. They and their ancestors had lived here for an estimated 14,000 years.

Today this same land contains over 204 million white Americans, over forty-six million Black Americans, and just over five million Native Americans. The story of the unique arc of trauma in the Native American body is only now beginning to be told. I don't describe this arc (except tangentially) in this book. I hope a wise and compassionate Native writer soon will.

In the meantime, I offer my respect and acknowledgment to the people who were stewards of this land long before folks from Africa and Europe made it their home.

OUR BODIES,
OUR COUNTRY

As I write these words in early 2017, America is tearing itself apart. On the surface, this war looks like the natural outcome of many recent social and political clashes. But it's not. These conflicts are anything but recent. One hundred and fifty-six years ago, they spawned the American Civil War. But even in the 1860s, these conflicts were already centuries old. They began in Europe during the Middle Ages, where they tore apart close to two million white bodies. The resulting tension came to America embedded in the bodies of Europeans, and it has remained in the bodies of many of their descendants. Over the past three centuries, that tension has been both soothed and deepened by the invention of whiteness and the resulting racialization of American culture.

At first glance, today's manifestation of this conflict appears to be a struggle for political and social power. But as we'll see, the real conflict is more visceral. It is a battle for the souls and bodies of white Americans. While we see anger and violence in the streets of our country, the real battlefield is inside our bodies. If we are to survive as a country, it is inside our bodies where this conflict will need to be resolved.

The conflict has been festering for centuries. Now it must be faced. For America, it is an unavoidable time of reckoning. Our character is being challenged, and the content of that character is being revealed.

One of two things will happen: Ideally, America will grow up and out of white-body supremacy; Americans will begin healing their long-held trauma around race; and whiteness will begin to evolve from race to culture, and then to community.

The other possibility is that white-body supremacy will continue to be reinforced as the dominant structured form of energy in American culture, in much the same way Aryan supremacy dominated German culture in the 1930s and early 1940s.

If Americans choose the latter scenario, the racialized trauma that wounds so many American bodies will continue to mutate into insanity and create even more brutality and genocide.

This book offers the necessary new insights, skills, and tools for creating the first scenario. It is written for every American—of any background or skin color—who sees this scenario as vital to our country's survival and who sees the second scenario as America's death warrant.

*

When people hear the words *white supremacy* or *white-body supremacy*, they often think of neo-Nazis and other extremists with hateful and violent agendas. That is certainly one extreme type of white-body supremacy. But mainstream American culture is infused with a more subtle and less overt variety. In her book, *What Does It Mean to Be White?*, Robin DiAngelo[1] describes white supremacy as

> . . . the all-encompassing centrality and assumed superiority of people defined and perceived as white, and the practices based on this assumption . . . . White supremacy does not refer to individual white people per se and their individual intentions, but to a political-economic social system of domination. This system is based on the historical and current accumulation of structural power that privileges, centralizes, and elevates white people as a group . . . . I do not use it to refer to extreme hate groups. I use

---

1   DiAngelo describes herself this way: "My area of research is in Whiteness Studies . . . I have been a consultant and trainer for over twenty years on issues of racial and social justice . . . I grew up poor and white."

the term to capture the pervasiveness, magnitude, and normalcy of white dominance and assumed superiority.

One aspect of this type of white-body supremacy involves seeing "whites as the norm or *standard* for human, and people of color as a *deviation* from that norm . . . an actress becomes a *black* actress, and so on." In a piece for *Salon* she adds, "Thus, we move through a wholly racialized world with an unracialized identity (e.g., white people can represent all of humanity, people of color can only represent their racial selves)." This everyday form of white-body supremacy is in the air we breathe, the water we drink, and the culture we share. We literally cannot avoid it. It is part of the operating system and organizing structure of American culture. It's always functioning in the background, often invisibly, in our institutions, our relationships, and our interactions.

The cultural operating system of white-body supremacy influences or determines many of the decisions we make, the options we select, the choices open to us, and *how* we make those decisions and choices. This operating system affects all of us, regardless of the hue of our skin.

Here's a typical example: Two economists responded to 1,300 help-wanted ads in the *Boston Globe* and the *Chicago Tribune* in the fields of customer service, clerical services, sales, and administrative support. In all, they responded with more than 5,000 made-up résumés. The names on those résumés were randomly assigned, but some (e.g., Jamal Jones and Lakisha Washington) sounded African American, while others sounded white (e.g., Emily Walsh and Greg Baker[2]). The researchers counted the number of employers who asked to set up interviews or get more information. The imaginary white candidates received interest from one in ten employers; the imaginary African American candidates received interest from one in fifteen. (Similar studies have since obtained similar results.)

---

2   As a cross-check, I had my research assistant search the names Emily Walsh and Lakisha Washington on Facebook. He found hundreds of Emily Walshes, of which zero were Black. All but two were white, and one was male. He also found many dozens of Lakisha Washingtons, all but one of whom were Black. I'd like to see a follow-up study using African names (e.g., Kojo Ofusu) instead of African American ones, to learn whether employers respond in the same way to Black job applicants who do not appear to be from America.

Here's another recent example of everyday supremacy: My wife, Maria, purchased some household items at Wal-Mart and was pushing her cart toward the exit. A Wal-Mart employee stopped her, asked to see her sales receipt, and checked the items on the receipt against the items in her cart. Maria was thirsty, so instead of leaving the store, she bought a soft drink and sat down on a bench near the exit. Over the next two to three minutes, she watched as about twenty people left the store. The employee stopped to double-check the receipts of all eight of the Black customers who walked past—and none of the non-Black ones.

Understandably, my wife was not happy about this, and she told the store manager about it. The manager, who was white, was aghast. He immediately called over the employee—who was also white—and confronted her. She was surprised, apologetic, and a bit mortified. She insisted she was not deliberately targeting Black customers, but only checking people randomly. My wife told me, "She seemed completely sincere. I believe that's what she genuinely thought she was doing." The employee was not targeting Black customers deliberately; she was targeting them unconsciously and reflexively. But the pain that such actions create for Black Americans is felt quite consciously.

Relatively few white Americans consciously recognize, let alone embrace, this subtle variety of white-body supremacy. In fact, there is often no way to measure or recognize it. Imagine a real Lakisha Washington or Emily Walsh. She would have no way of knowing why any particular employer did not respond positively to her résumé. Nor would my wife have noticed anything odd about the Wal-Mart employee's actions if she hadn't stopped to relax and have a cold drink.

For most Americans, including most of us with dark skin, white-body supremacy has become part of our bodies. How could it not? It's the equivalent of a toxic chemical we ingest on a daily basis. Eventually, it changes our brains and the chemistry of our bodies.

Which is why, in looking at white-body supremacy, we need to begin not with guilt or blame, but with our bodies.

PART I

UNARMED AND DISMEMBERED

CHAPTER 1

YOUR BODY AND BLOOD

"No one ever talks about the moment you found that you were white. Or the moment you found out you were black. That's a profound revelation. The minute you find that out, something happens. You have to renegotiate everything."

TONI MORRISON

"History is not the past, it is the present. We carry our history with us. We are our history."

JAMES BALDWIN

"There is deep wisdom within our very flesh, if we can only come to our senses and feel it."

ELIZABETH A. BEHNKE

"People don't realize what's really going on in this country. There are a lot of things that are going on that are unjust. People aren't being held accountable . . . This country stands for freedom, liberty, and justice for all. And it's not happening for all right now."

COLIN KAEPERNICK

When I was a boy I used to watch television with my grandmother. I would sit in the middle of the sofa and she would stretch out over two seats, resting her legs in my lap. She often felt pain in her hands, and she'd ask me to rub them in mine. When I did, her fingers would relax, and she'd smile. Sometimes she'd start to hum melodically, and her voice would make a vibration that reminded me of a cat's purr.

She wasn't a large woman, but her hands were surprisingly stout, with broad fingers and thick pads below each thumb. One day I asked her, "Grandma, why are your hands like that? They ain't the same as mine."

My grandmother turned from the television and looked at me. "Boy," she said slowly. "That's from picking cotton. They been that way since long before I was your age. I started working in the fields sharecroppin' when I was four."

I didn't understand. I'd helped plant things in the garden a few times, but my own hands were bony and my fingers were narrow. I held up my hands next to hers and stared at the difference.

"Umm hmm," she said. "The cotton plant has pointed burrs in it. When you reach your hand in, the burrs rip it up. When I first started picking, my hands were all torn and bloody. When I got older, they got thicker and thicker, until I could reach in and pull out the cotton without them bleeding."

My grandmother died last year. Sometimes I can still feel her warm, thick hands in mine.

*

For the past three decades, we've earnestly tried to address white-body supremacy in America with reason, principles, and ideas—using dialogue, forums, discussions, education, and mental training. But the widespread destruction of Black bodies continues. And some of the ugliest destruction originates with our police. Why is there such a chasm between our well-intentioned attempts to heal and the ever-growing number of dark-skinned bodies who are killed or injured, sometimes by police officers?

It's not that we've been lazy or insincere. But we've focused our efforts in the wrong direction. We've tried to teach our brains to think better about race. But white-body supremacy doesn't live in our thinking brains. It lives and breathes in our bodies.

Our bodies have a form of knowledge that is different from our cognitive brains. This knowledge is typically experienced as a felt sense of constriction or expansion, pain or ease, energy or numbness. Often this knowledge is stored in our bodies as wordless stories about what is safe and what is dangerous. The body is where we fear, hope, and react; where we constrict and release; and where we reflexively fight, flee, or freeze. If we are to upend the status quo of white-body supremacy, we must begin with our bodies.

New advances in psychobiology reveal that our deepest emotions—love, fear, anger, dread, grief, sorrow, disgust, and hope— involve the activation of our bodily structures. These structures—a complex system of nerves—connect the brainstem, pharynx, heart, lungs, stomach, gut, and spine. Neuroscientists call this system the *wandering nerve* or our *vagus nerve*; a more apt name might be our *soul nerve*. The soul nerve is connected directly to a part of our brain that doesn't use cognition or reasoning as its primary tool for navigating the world. Our soul nerve also helps mediate between our bodies' activating energy and resting energy.

This part of our brain is similar to the brains of lizards, birds, and lower mammals. Our lizard brain only understands survival and protection. At any given moment, it can issue one of a handful of survival commands: *rest, fight, flee,* or *freeze*.[3] These are the only commands it knows and the only choices it is able to make.

*

3   I and some other therapists also recognize a fifth command: *annihilate*. The lizard brain issues this command when it senses (accurately or inaccurately) that a threat is extreme and the body's total destruction is imminent. The *annihilate* command is a last-ditch effort to survive. It usually looks like sudden, extreme rage or like the attack of a provoked animal. Some therapists see *annihilate* as just a variant of the fight response, but I classify it separately, because *annihilation* energy looks and feels quite different from *fighting* energy. It's the difference between a punch and a decapitation. Because *fight, flee,* or *freeze* has become such a meme, I'll continue to use that phrase throughout the book. But in a therapy session, there are times when it's important for the therapist to note and work with the unique energy of an *annihilate* response. At times, I'll mention it again in this book as well. More generally, we would also be wise to recognize that much of what we call rage is actually unmetabolized annihilation energy.

White-body supremacy is always functioning in our bodies. It operates in our thinking brains, in our assumptions, expectations, and mental shortcuts. It operates in our muscles and nervous systems, where it routinely creates constriction. But it operates most powerfully in our lizard brains. Our lizard brain cannot think. It is reflexively protective, and it is strong. It loves whatever it feels will keep us safe, and it fears and hates whatever it feels will do us harm.

All our sensory input has to pass through the reptilian part of our brain before it even reaches the cortex, where we think and reason. Our lizard brain scans all of this input and responds, in a fraction of a second, by either letting something enter into the cortex or rejecting it and inciting a fight, flee, or freeze response. This mechanism allows our lizard brain to override our thinking brain whenever it senses real or imagined danger. It blocks any information from reaching our thinking brain until *after* it has sent a message to fight, flee, or freeze.

In many situations, our thinking brain is smart enough to be careful and situational. But when there appears to be danger, our lizard brain may say to the thinking brain, "Screw you. Out of my way. We're going to fight, flee, or freeze."

Many of us picture our thinking brain as a tiny CEO in our head who makes important executive decisions. But this metaphor is misguided: Our cortex doesn't get the opportunity to *have* a thought about any piece of sensory input unless our lizard brain lets it through. And in making its decision, our reptilian brain always asks the same question: *Is this dangerous or safe?*

Remember that *dangerous* can mean a threat to more than just the well being of our body. It can mean a threat to what we do, say, think, care about, believe in, or yearn for. When it comes to safety, our thinking mind is third in line after our body and our lizard brain. That's why when we put a hand on a hot frying pan, the hand jerks away instantly, while our thinking brain goes, *What the hell just happened? OW! THAT SHIT IS HOT!* It's also why you might have the impulse to throw the pan across the kitchen—even though doing so won't help you.

The body is where we live. It's where we fear, hope, and react. It's where we constrict and relax. And what the body most cares about are safety and survival. When something happens to the body that is too much, too fast, or too soon, it overwhelms the body and can create trauma.

Contrary to what many people believe, trauma is not primarily an emotional response. Trauma always happens *in the body*. It is a spontaneous protective mechanism used by the body to stop or thwart further (or future) potential damage.

Trauma is not a flaw or a weakness. It is a highly effective tool of safety and survival. Trauma is also not an event. Trauma is the body's protective response to an event—or a series of events—that it perceives as potentially dangerous. This perception may be accurate, inaccurate, or entirely imaginary. In the aftermath of highly stressful or traumatic situations, our soul nerve and lizard brain may embed a reflexive trauma response in our bodies. This happens at lightning speed.

An embedded trauma response can manifest as fight, flee, or freeze—or as some combination of constriction, pain, fear, dread, anxiety, unpleasant (and/or sometimes pleasant) thoughts, reactive behaviors, or other sensations and experiences. This trauma then gets stuck in the body—and stays stuck there until it is addressed.

We can have a trauma response to anything we perceive as a threat, not only to our physical safety, but to what we do, say, think, care about, believe in, or yearn for. This is why people get murdered for disrespecting other folks' relatives or their favorite sports teams. It's also why people get murdered when other folks *imagine* a relative or favorite team was disrespected. From the body's viewpoint, safety and danger are neither situational nor based on cognitive feelings. Rather, they are physical, visceral sensations. The body either has a sense of safety or it doesn't. If it doesn't, it will do almost anything to establish or recover that sense of safety.

Trauma responses are unique to each person. Each such response is influenced by a person's particular physical, mental, emotional, and social makeup—and, of course, by the precipitating experiences themselves. However, trauma is never a personal failing, and it is never something a person can choose. It is always something that happens *to* someone.

A traumatic response usually sets in quickly—too quickly to involve the rational brain. Indeed, a traumatic response temporarily overrides the rational brain. It's like when a computer senses a virus and responds by shutting down some or all of its functions. (This is also why, when mending trauma, we need to proceed slowly, so that we can uncover the body's functions without triggering yet another trauma response.)

As mentioned earlier, trauma is also a wordless story our body tells itself about what is safe and what is a threat. Our rational brain can't stop it from occurring, and it can't talk our body out of it. Trauma can cause us to react to present events in ways that seem wildly inappropriate, overly charged, or otherwise out of proportion. Whenever someone freaks out suddenly or reacts to a small problem as if it were a catastrophe, it's often a trauma response. Something in the here and now is rekindling old pain or discomfort, and the body tries to address it with the reflexive energy that's still stuck inside the nervous system. This is what leads to over-the-top reactions.

Such overreactions are the body's attempt to complete a protective action that got thwarted or overridden during a traumatic situation. The body wanted to fight or flee, but wasn't able to do either, so it got stuck in freeze mode. In many cases, it then develops strategies around this "stuckness," including extreme reactions, compulsions, strange likes and dislikes, seemingly irrational fears, and unusual avoidance strategies. Over time, these can become embedded in the body as standard ways of surviving and protecting itself. When these strategies are repeated and passed on over generations, they can become the standard responses in families, communities, and cultures.

One common (and often overlooked) trauma response is what I called *trauma ghosting*. This is the body's recurrent or pervasive sense that danger is just around the corner, or something terrible is going to happen any moment.

These responses tend to make little cognitive sense, and the person's own cognitive brain is often unaware of them. But for the body they make perfect sense: it is protecting itself from repeating the experience that caused or preceded the trauma.

In other cases, people do the exact opposite: they reenact (or precipitate) situations similar to the ones that caused their trauma. This may seem crazy or neurotic to the cognitive mind, but there is bodily wisdom behind it. By recreating such a situation, the person also creates an opportunity to complete whatever action got thwarted or overridden. This might help the person mend the trauma, create more room for growth in his or her body, and settle his or her nervous system.[4]

However, the attempt to reenact the event often simply repeats, re-inflicts, and deepens the trauma. When this happens repeatedly over time, the trauma response can look like part of the person's personality. As years and decades pass, reflexive traumatic responses can lose context. A person may forget that something happened to him or her—and then internalize the trauma responses. These responses are typically viewed by others, and often by the person, as a personality defect. When this same strategy gets internalized and passed down over generations within a particular group, it can start to look like culture. Therapists call this a *traumatic retention.*

Many African Americans know trauma intimately—from their own nervous systems, from the experiences of people they love, and, most often, from both. But African Americans are not alone in this. A different but equally real form of racialized trauma lives in the bodies of most white Americans. And a third, often deeply toxic type of racialized trauma lives and breathes in the bodies of many of America's law enforcement officers.

All three types of trauma are routinely passed on from person to person and from generation to generation. This intergenerational

---

4   If you'd like a more detailed understanding of human trauma, read Bessel van der Kolk's *The Body Keeps the Score: Brain, Mind, and Body in the Healing of Trauma* (New York: Viking Penguin, 2014). If you're interested in the practice of helping others heal their trauma or in addressing your own as swiftly and safely as possible, an excellent place to start is Peter Levine's Somatic Experiencing Trauma Institute (SETA), traumahealing.org. I have received training from both Dr. van der Kolk and the SETA.

transmission—which, more aptly and less clinically, I call a *soul wound*[5]—occurs in multiple ways:

- Through families in which one family member abuses or mistreats another.

- Through unsafe or abusive systems, structures, institutions, and/or cultural norms.

- Through our genes. Recent work in human genetics suggests that trauma is passed on in our DNA expression, through the biochemistry of the human egg, sperm, and womb.

This means that no matter what we look like, if we were born and raised in America, white-body supremacy and our adaptations to it are in our blood. Our very bodies house the unhealed dissonance and trauma of our ancestors.

This is why white-body supremacy continues to persist in America, and why so many African Americans continue to die from it. We will not change this situation through training, traditional education, or other appeals to the cognitive brain. We need to begin with the body and its relation to trauma.

In *Between the World and Me*, Ta-Nehisi Coates exposed the long-standing and ongoing destruction of the Black body in America. That destruction will continue until Americans of all cultures and colors learn to acknowledge the inherited trauma of white-body supremacy embedded in all our bodies. We need to metabolize this trauma; work through it with our bodies (not just our thinking brains); and grow up out of it. Only in this way will we at last mend our bodies, our families, and the collective body of our nation. The process differs slightly for Black folks, white folks, and America's police. But all of us need to heal—and, with the right guidance, all of us can. That healing is the purpose of this book.

*

---

5   I did not invent the term *soul wound*. It has been around for some time, and is most often used in relation to the intergenerational and historical trauma of Native Americans. Eduardo Duran's book on counseling with Native peoples is entitled *Healing the Soul Wound* (Teachers College Press, 2006). "Soul Wounds" was also the title of a 2015 conference on intergenerational and historical trauma at Stanford University.

This book is about the body. *Your* body.

If you're African American, in this book you'll explore the trauma that is likely internalized and embedded in it. You'll see how multiple forces—genes, history, culture, laws, and family—have created a long bloodline of trauma in African American bodies.

It doesn't mean we're defective. In fact, it means just the opposite: something happened *to* us, something we can heal from. We survived because of our resilience, which was also passed down from one generation to the next.

This book presents some profound opportunities for healing and growth. Some of these are communal healing practices our African American and African ancestors developed and adapted; others are more recent creations. All of these practices foster resilience in our bodies and plasticity in our brains. We'll use these practices to recognize the trauma in our own bodies; to touch it, heal it, and grow out of it; and to create more room for growth in our nervous systems.

White-body supremacy also harms people who do not have dark skin. If you're a white American, your body has probably inherited a different legacy of trauma that affects *white* bodies—and, at times, may rekindle old flight, flee, or freeze responses. This trauma goes back centuries—at least as far back as the Middle Ages—and has been passed down from one white body to another for dozens of generations.

White bodies traumatized each other in Europe for centuries before they encountered Black and red bodies. This carnage and trauma profoundly affected white bodies and the expressions of their DNA. As we'll see, this historical trauma is closely linked to the development of white-body supremacy in America.

If you're a white American, this book will offer you a wealth of practices for mending this trauma in your own body, growing beyond it, and creating more room in your own nervous system. I urge you to take this responsibility seriously. As you'll discover, it will help create greater freedom and serenity for all of us.

Courtesy of white-body supremacy, a deep and persistent condition of chronic stress also lives in the bodies of many members of the law enforcement profession, regardless of their skin color. If you're a policeman or policewoman, you've almost certainly either suffered or observed this third type of trauma. This book offers you a vital path of healing as well.

While I hope everyone who reads this book will fully heal his or her trauma, I know this hope isn't realistic. Many readers will learn something from this book, and perhaps practice some of the activities in it, but eventually will stop reading or turn away. If that's ultimately what you do, it doesn't mean you haven't benefited. You may still have created a little extra room in your nervous system for flow, for resilience, for coherence, for growth, and, above all, for possibility. That extra room may then get passed on to your children or to other people you encounter.

In today's America, we tend to think of healing as something binary: either we're broken or we're healed from that brokenness. But that's not how healing operates, and it's almost never how human growth works. More often, healing and growth take place on a continuum, with innumerable points between utter brokenness and total health. If this book moves you even a step or two in the direction of healing, it will make an important difference.

In fact, in this book you'll meet some people who have not fully healed their trauma, but who have nevertheless made strides in that direction and who have deepened their lives and the lives of others as a result.

*

Years as a healer and trauma therapist have taught me that trauma isn't destiny. The body, not the thinking brain, is where we experience most of our pain, pleasure, and joy, and where we process most of what happens to us. It is also where we do most of our healing, including our emotional and psychological healing. And it is where we experience resilience and a sense of flow.

Over the past decade or so, therapists have become increasingly aware of the importance of the body in this mending. Until recently, psychotherapy (commonly shortened to *therapy*) was what we now call *talk therapy* or *cognitive therapy* or *behavioral therapy.*[6] The basic strategy behind these therapies is simple: you, a lone individual, come to my office; you and I talk; you have insights, most of which are cognitive and/or behavioral; and those cognitive and/or behavioral insights help you heal. The problem is that this turns out not to be the only way healing works. Recent studies and discoveries increasingly point out that we heal primarily in and through the body, not just through the rational brain. We can all create more room, and more opportunities for growth, in our nervous systems. But we do this primarily through what our *bodies* experience and do—not through what we think or realize or cognitively figure out.

In addition, trauma and healing aren't just private experiences. Sometimes trauma is a collective experience, in which case our approaches for mending must be collective and communal as well.

People in therapy can have insights galore, but may stay stuck in habitual pain, harmful trauma patterns, and automatic reactions to real or perceived threats. This is because trauma is embedded in their bodies, not their cognitive brains. That trauma then becomes the unconscious lens through which they view all of their current experiences.

Often this trauma blocks attempts to heal it. Whenever the body senses the opportunity—and the challenge—to mend, it responds by fighting, fleeing, or freezing. (In therapy, this might involve a client getting angry, going numb and silent, or saying, "I don't want to talk about that.")

As a therapist, I've learned that when trauma is present, the first step in healing almost always involves educating people on what trauma is. Trauma is all about speed and reflexivity—which is why, in addressing trauma, each of us needs to work through it slowly, over time. We need to understand our body's process of connection and settling. We need to slow ourselves down and learn to lean into uncertainty, rather than away from it. We need to ground ourselves,

---

6   These terms describe a general approach to psychological and emotional healing. They should not be confused with Cognitive Behavioral Therapy (CBT), which is a specific model of therapy that includes six distinct, predictable phases. CBT is widely used and has a generally good track record. However, it has also been widely disparaged, and it has been the subject of some controversy within the field. In my view, CBT's primary limitation is the same limitation of talk therapy in general: it pays too little attention to the body.

touch the pain or discomfort inside our trauma, and explore it—gently. This requires building a tolerance for bodily and emotional discomfort, and learning to stay present with—rather than trying to flee—that discomfort. (Note that it does *not* necessarily mean exploring, reliving, or cognitively understanding the events that created the trauma.) With practice, over time, this enables us to be more curious, more mindful, and less reflexive. Only then can growth and change occur.

There's some genuine value to talk therapy that focuses just on cognition and behavior. But on its own, especially when trauma is in the way, it won't be enough to enable you to mend the wounds in your heart and body.

*

In America, nearly all of us, regardless of our background or skin color, carry trauma in our bodies around the myth of race. We typically think of trauma as the result of a specific and deeply painful event, such as a serious accident, an attack, or the news of someone's death. That may be the case sometimes, but trauma can also be the body's response to a long sequence of smaller wounds. It can be a response to *anything* that it experiences as too much, too soon, or too fast.

Trauma can also be the body's response to anything unfamiliar or anything it doesn't understand, even if it isn't cognitively dangerous. The body doesn't reason; it's hardwired to protect itself and react to sensation and movement. When a truck rushes by at sixty miles an hour and misses your body by an inch, your body may respond with trauma as deep and as serious as if it had actually been sideswiped. When watching a horror film, you may jump out of your seat even though you know it's just a movie. Your body acts as if the danger is real, regardless of what your cognitive brain knows. The body's imperative is to protect itself. Period.

Trauma responses are unpredictable. Two bodies may respond very differently to the same experience. If you and a friend are at a Fourth of July celebration and a firecracker explodes at your feet, your body may forget about the incident within minutes, while your friend may go on to be terrified by loud, sudden noises for years afterward.

When two siblings suffer the same childhood abuse, one may heal fully during adolescence, while the other may get stuck and live with painful trauma for decades. Some Black bodies demonstratively suffer deep traumatic wounds from white-body supremacy, while other bodies appear to be less affected.

Trauma or no trauma, many Black bodies don't feel settled around white ones, for reasons that are all too obvious: the long, brutal history of enslavement and subjugation; racial profiling (and occasionally murder) by police; stand-your-ground laws; the exoneration of folks such as George Zimmerman (who shot Trayvon Martin), Tim Loehmann (who shot Tamir Rice), and Roy Bryant and J.W. Milam (who murdered Emmett Till); outright targeted aggression; and the habitual grind of everyday disregard, discrimination, institutional disrespect, over-policing, over-sentencing, and micro-aggressions.[7]

As a result, the traumas that live in many Black bodies are deep and persistent. They contribute to a long list of common stress disorders in Black bodies, such as post-traumatic stress disorder[8] (PTSD), learning disabilities, depression and anxiety, diabetes, high blood pressure, and other physical and emotional ailments.

These conditions are not inevitable. Many Black bodies have proven very resilient, in part because, over generations, African Americans have developed a variety of body-centered responses to help settle their bodies and blunt the effects of racialized trauma. These include individual and collective humming, rocking, rhythmic clapping, drumming, singing, grounding touch, wailing circles, and call and response, to name just a few.

The traumas that live in white bodies, and the bodies of public safety professionals of all races, are also deep and persistent. However, their origins and nature are quite different. The expression of these traumas is often an immediate, seemingly out-of-the-blue fight, flee, or freeze response, a response that may be reflexively triggered by the

---

7   Micro-aggressions are the small but relentless things people do to insult or dismiss us or deny our experience or feelings. If you've ever been deliberately ignored by a sales clerk, or questioned harshly and at length by a border patrol agent, or told, "I've never seen that happen; you must have imagined it," you experienced a micro-aggression.

8   Although the formal, clinical term is *post-traumatic stress disorder,* a more accurate term would be *pervasive traumatic stress disorder.* Post means *after,* and for many Black Americans, traumatic stress is ongoing, not just something from the past.

mere presence of a Black body—or, sometimes, by the mere mention of race or the term *white supremacy* or *white-body supremacy.*

*

Many English words are loaded or slippery, especially when it comes to race. So let me define some terms.

When I say *the Black body* or *the African American body*, it's shorthand for *the bodies of people of African descent who live in America, who have largely shaped its culture, and who have adapted to it.* If you're a Kenyan citizen who has never been to the United States, or a new arrival in America from Cameroon or Haiti or Argentina, some of this book may not apply to you—at least not obviously. Aside from your (perhaps) dark skin, you may not recognize yourself in these pages. (I'm not suggesting that non-Americans without white skin aren't routinely affected by the global reach of white-body supremacy, only that some of these folks have been fortunate enough to have little or no personal experience with America's version of racialized trauma. Others have strong resiliency factors that have mitigated some of the effects of white-body supremacy in their lives.)

When I say *the white body*, it's shorthand for *the bodies of people of European descent who live in America, who have largely shaped and adapted to its culture, and who don't have dark skin.* The term *white body* lacks precision, but it's short and simple. If you're a member of this group, you'll recognize it when I talk about the white body's experience.

When I say *police bodies*, it's shorthand for *the bodies of law enforcement professionals*, regardless of their skin color. These professionals include beat cops, police detectives, mall security guards, members of SWAT teams, and the police chiefs of big cities, suburbs, and small towns.

These categories provide ways of communicating, not boxes for anyone to be forced into. It's possible that none of them fits you. Or maybe you fit into more than one. Don't try to squeeze yourself into one in particular. Instead, adapt everything you read in this book as your body instructs you to. It will tell you what matches its experience and how to work with its energy and wordless stories.

Maybe you're an African American whose body, for whatever reason, is entirely free of racialized trauma. Or maybe you're a white American or police officer whose body doesn't constrict in the presence of Black bodies, and who can stay settled and present in your own discomfort when the subject of race arises. Either way, I encourage you to try out the body-centered activities in this book. Whether or not you yourself are personally wounded by white-body supremacy, working with these exercises and letting them sink into you will help you build your self-awareness, deepen your capacity for empathy, and create more room for growth in your nervous system.

*

I'm not the first to recognize the key role of the destruction, restriction, and abuse of the Black body in American history. In *Killing the Black Body*, Dorothy Roberts wrote of centuries-long efforts by white people to control the wombs of African American women. A decade later, in *Black Bodies, White Gazes*, George Yancy explored the confiscation of Black bodies by white culture. In *Stand Your Ground*, Kelly Brown Douglas examined many social and theological issues related to the African American body. Meri Nana-Ama Danquah's *The Black Body* collected thirty writers' reflections on the role of the Black body in America. James Baldwin, Richard Wright, bell hooks, Teju Cole, and others have written eloquently on the subject of African American bodies. As I worked on this book, Ta-Nehisi Coates' *Between the World and Me*, an examination of the systematic destruction of the Black body in America, reached the number one spot on the *New York Times* bestseller list.

All these writers are wise, loving, and profoundly observant. I'm deeply grateful for their contributions, which have helped to create the foundation on which this book is built. But I come at the subject from a different direction.

Some of these writers—Yancy, Roberts, hooks, Douglas— are academics and philosophers, while others—Coates, Baldwin, Wright, Danquah, Cole—are literary authors. With piercing insight and eloquence, they reveal what white-body supremacy tries to keep hidden, and lay bare what many of us habitually overlook or cover up. In this book, I accept with gratitude the baton that these wise writers have handed to me.

My Grandmother's Hands is a book of healing. I'm a healer and trauma therapist, not a philosopher or literary stylist. My earlier book, *Rock the Boat: How to Use Conflict to Heal and Deepen Your Relationship* (Hazelden, 2015), is a practical guide for couples. In that book, as well as in this one, my focus is on mending psyches, souls, bodies, and relationships— and, whenever possible, families, neighborhoods, and communities.

In Part I, you'll see how white-body supremacy gets systematically (if often unconsciously or unwittingly) embedded in our American bodies *even before we are born*, creating ongoing trauma and a legacy of suffering for virtually all of us.

This racialized trauma appears in three different forms—one in the bodies of white Americans, another in those of African Americans, and yet another in the bodies of police officers. The trauma in white bodies has been passed down from parent to child for perhaps a thousand years, long before the creation of the United States. The trauma in African American bodies is often (and understandably) more severe but, in historical terms, also more recent. However, each individual body has its own unique trauma response, and each body needs (and deserves) to heal.

In Part II, you'll experience and absorb dozens of activities designed to help you mend your own trauma around white-body supremacy and create more room and opportunities for growth in your own nervous system. The opening chapters of Part II are for everyone, while later chapters focus on specific groups: African Americans, white Americans, and American police.

The chapters for African American readers grew, in part, out of my Soul Medic and Cultural Somatics workshops. I began offering these several years ago, along with workshops on psychological first aid. These provide body-centered experiences meant to help Black Americans experience their bodies, begin to recognize and release trauma, and bring some of that healing and room into the communal body.

The chapters for white readers draw partly from what I've learned from conducting similar workshops for white allies co-led with Margaret Baumgartner, Fen Jeffries, and Ariella Tilsen—white facilitators, conflict resolvers, and healing practitioners. The material on the community aspects of mending white bodies is supported by work I've done in collaboration with Susan Raffo of the People's Movement Center and Janice Barbee of Healing Roots, both in Minneapolis.

The chapters for law enforcement officers draw from the trainings I've led for police officers on trauma, self-care, white-body supremacy, and creating some healing infrastructure in their departments and precincts.

Part III will give you the tools to take your healing, and your newfound knowledge and awareness, into your community. It provides some simple, structured activities for helping other people you encounter release the trauma of white-body supremacy—in your family, neighborhood, workplace, and elsewhere. Because all of us, separately and together, can be healers, I begin with tools and strategies that anyone can apply, and follow them with specific chapters for African Americans, white Americans, and police.

*

As every therapist will tell you, healing involves discomfort—but so does refusing to heal. And, over time, refusing to heal is *always* more painful.

In my therapy office, I tell clients there are two kinds of pain: clean pain and dirty pain. *Clean pain* is pain that mends and can build your capacity for growth.[9] It's the pain you experience when you know, exactly, what you need to say or do; when you really, really don't want to say or do it; and when you do it anyway. It's also the pain you experience when you have no idea what to do; when you're scared or worried about what might happen; and when you step forward into the unknown anyway, with honesty and vulnerability.

---

9   The terms *clean pain* and *dirty pain* were popularized by one of my mentors, Dr. David Schnarch, and by Dr. Steven Hayer. Dr. Hayer defines and uses the terms somewhat differently than Dr. Schnarch and I do.

Experiencing clean pain enables us to engage our integrity and tap into our body's inherent resilience and coherence, in a way that dirty pain does not. Paradoxically, only by walking into our pain or discomfort—experiencing it, moving through it, and metabolizing it—can we grow. It's how the human body works.

Clean pain hurts like hell. But it enables our bodies to grow through our difficulties, develop nuanced skills, and mend our trauma. In this process, the body metabolizes clean pain. The body can then settle; more room for growth is created in its nervous system; and the self becomes freer and more capable, because it now has access to energy that was previously protected, bound, and constricted. When this happens, people's lives often improve in other ways as well.

All of this can happen both personally and collectively. In fact, if American bodies are to move beyond the pain and limitation of white-body supremacy, it *needs* to happen in both realms. Accepting clean pain will allow white Americans to confront their longtime collective disassociation and silence. It will enable African Americans to confront their internalization of defectiveness and self-hate. And it will help public safety professionals in many localities to confront the recent metamorphosis of their role from serving the community to serving as soldiers and prison guards.

Dirty pain is the pain of avoidance, blame, and denial. When people respond from their most wounded parts, become cruel or violent, or physically or emotionally run away, they experience dirty pain. They also create more of it for themselves and others.

A key factor in the perpetuation of white-body supremacy is many people's refusal to experience clean pain around the myth of race. Instead, usually out of fear, they choose the dirty pain of silence and avoidance and, invariably, prolong the pain.

In experiencing this book, you will face some pain. Neither you nor I can know how much, and it may not show up in the place or the manner you expect. Whatever your own background or skin color, as you make your way through these pages, I encourage you to let yourself experience that clean pain in order to let yourself heal. If you do, you may save yourself—and others—a great deal of future suffering.

In Chapters Ten, Eleven, and Twelve, I'll give you some practical tools to help your body become settled, anchored, and present within your clean pain, so that you can slowly metabolize your trauma and move through and beyond it. (I'll also give you parallel tools to help you quickly activate your body on demand, for times when that might be necessary.)

*

It's easy to assume the way people interact in twenty-first-century America is the way human beings have always interacted, at all times and in all places. Of course, this isn't so. It's equally easy to imagine that twenty-first-century American society is somehow fundamentally different from any other time and place in history. That isn't so, either. Here are some things to acknowledge before we go further:

- Trauma is as ancient as human beings. In fact, it's more ancient. Animals that were here eons before humans appeared also experience trauma in their bodies.

- Oppression, enslavement, and fear of *the other* are as old, and as widespread, as human civilization.

- A variety of forms of supremacy—of one group being elevated above another—have existed around the world for millennia and still exist today. Multiple forms of supremacy often intersect and compound each other, harming human beings in profoundly negative ways.

- Race is an invention—and a relatively modern one.

- *My Grandmother's Hands* looks at racialized trauma in America, how that trauma gets perpetuated through white-body supremacy, and how we can heal from it. Because of its American focus, some of its insights and activities may not be appropriate for some other countries and cultures.

- White-body supremacy in America doesn't just harm Black people. It damages everyone. Historically, it has also been especially brutal toward Native Americans, and, often, Latino Americans.

- As we'll see, while white-body supremacy benefits white Americans in some ways, it also does great harm to white bodies, hearts, and psyches.

*

So far, all you know about me is that I'm a body-centered therapist who specializes in trauma work, that I lead Soul Medic and Cultural Somatics workshops, and that I've published a book that helps couples mend and deepen their relationships. (I've also published a book of guidance for emerging justice leaders.) But for you to trust me and stick with me throughout this book, you probably want to know much more. Fair enough.

I'm a longtime therapist and licensed clinical social worker in private practice. I specialize in couples' trauma work, conflict in relationships of all kinds, and domestic violence prevention. Recently I established Cultural Somatics, an area of study and practice that applies our knowledge of trauma and resilience to history, intergenerational relationships, institutions, and the communal body. I'm also a leadership coach for emerging justice leaders. I've been a guest on both *The Oprah Winfrey Show* and *Dr. Phil*, where I discussed family dynamics, couples in conflict, and domestic violence. For ten years, I cohosted a radio show with US Congressman Keith Ellison on KMOJ-FM in Minneapolis. I also hosted my own show, "Resmaa in the Morning," on KMOJ.

I've worked as a trainer for the Minneapolis Police Department; a trauma consultant for the St. Paul Public Schools; the director of counseling services for Tubman Family Alliance, a domestic violence treatment center in Minneapolis; the behavioral health director for African American Family Services in Minneapolis; a domestic violence counselor for Wilder Foundation; a divorce and family mediator; a social worker and consultant for the Minneapolis Public Schools; a community organizer; and a consultant for the Minneapolis Park and Recreation Board.

For two years I served as a community care counselor for civilian contractors in Afghanistan, managing the wellness and counseling services on fifty-three US military bases. As a certified Military Family Life Consultant, I also worked with members of the military and their families on issues related to family living, deployment, and returning home.

But here's what may be most important: I'm just like you. I've experienced my own trauma around white-body supremacy—and around other things as well. Sometimes white people scare me. Sometimes my African American brothers and sisters scare me. Sometimes I scare myself. But when I'm scared, I know enough to let my body tap into its inherent resilience and flow, to help it settle, and to lean into my clean pain. I also have a community of healed and healing bodies that supports me and holds me accountable.

Even though I'm law abiding and my brother is a cop, police sometimes scare me. I drive a Dodge Challenger with racing stripes, so police follow me a lot, and sometimes I get pulled over.[10] I'm always friendly and polite when this happens, but I worry I'll get the wrong officer who's been struggling with his or her own trauma.

I was raised in a family that was sometimes stable, sometimes chaotic. My father struggled with chemical dependency and was violent at times. As a young adult, I was angry, frightened, and confused. It took me a long time to find my place in the world. Fortunately, I had a family, community, mentors, elders, and ancestors who all expected the best of me and encouraged me to grow up and heal.

I want you, and me, and all of us to heal, to be free of racialized trauma, to feel safe and secure in our bodies and in the world, and to pass on that safety and security to future generations. This book is my attempt to create more of that safety.

---

10   I also own a Corolla, which police follow far less often.

—BODY CENTERED PRACTICE—

Take a moment to ground yourself in your own body. Notice the outline of your skin and the slight pressure of the air around it. Experience the firmer pressure of the chair, bed, or couch beneath you—or the ground or floor beneath your feet.

Can you sense hope in your body? Where? How does your body experience that hope? Is it a release or expansion? A tightening born of eagerness or anticipation?

What specific hopes accompany these sensations? The chance to heal? To be free of the burden of racialized trauma? To live a bigger, deeper life?

Do you experience any fear in your body? If so, where? How does it manifest? As tightness? As a painful radiance? As a dead, hard spot?

What worries accompany the fear? Are you afraid your life will be different in ways you can't predict? Are you afraid of facing clean pain? Are your worried you will choose dirty pain instead? Do you feel the raw, wordless fear—and, perhaps, excitement—that heralds change? What pictures appear in your mind as you experience that fear?

If your body feels both hopeful *and* afraid, congratulations. You're just where you need to be for what comes next.

One final note: at the end of each chapter you'll find a list of *Re-memberings*, which highlight the key insights from that chapter. Re-memberings will help you easily recall these insights and use them for healing in a variety of ways: to re-member your ancestors, your history, and your body; to create more room and opportunities for growth in your nervous system; to build and rebuild community; and to discover or rediscover your full membership in the human community.

RE-MEMBERINGS

- White-body supremacy doesn't live just in our thinking brains. It lives and breathes in our bodies.

- As a result, we will never outgrow white-body supremacy just through discussion, training, or anything else that's mostly cognitive. Instead, we need to look to the body—and to the embodied experience of trauma.

- Our deepest emotions involve the activation of a single bodily structure: our *soul nerve* (or *vagus nerve*). This nerve is connected to our lizard brain, which is concerned solely with survival and protection. Our lizard brain only has four basic commands: *rest*, *fight*, *flee*, or *freeze*.

- In the aftermath of a highly stressful event, our lizard brain may embed a reflexive trauma response—a wordless story of danger—in our body. This trauma can cause us to react to present events in ways that seem out of proportion or wildly inappropriate to what's actually going on.

- Trauma is routinely passed on from person to person—and generation to generation—through genetics, culture, family structures, and the biochemistry of the egg, sperm, and womb. Trauma is literally in our blood.

- Most African Americans know trauma intimately. But different kinds of racialized trauma also live and breathe in the bodies of most white Americans, as well as most law enforcement professionals.

- All of us need to metabolize the trauma, work through it, and grow up out of it with our bodies, not just our thinking brains. Only in this way will we heal at last, both individually and collectively.

- That healing is the purpose of this book.

- This book is about the body. *Your* body.

- Whether you're a Black American, a white American, or a police officer, this book offers you profound opportunities for growth and healing.

- Trauma is not destiny. It can be healed.

- Talk therapy can help with this process, but the body is the central focus for healing trauma.

- Trauma is all about speed and reflexivity. This is why people need to work through trauma slowly, over time, and why they need to understand their own bodies' processes of connecting and settling.

- Sometimes trauma is a collective experience, in which case the healing must be collective and communal as well.

- Trauma can be the body's response to anything unfamiliar or anything it doesn't understand.

- Trauma responses are unpredictable. Two bodies may respond very differently to the same stressful or painful event.

- Healing involves discomfort, but so does refusing to heal. And, over time, refusing to heal is always more painful.

- There are two kinds of pain. *Clean pain* is pain that mends and can build your capacity for growth. It's the pain you feel when you know what to say or do; when you really, really don't want to say or do it; and when you do it anyway, responding from the best parts of yourself. *Dirty pain* is the pain of avoidance, blame, or denial—when you respond from your most wounded parts.

CHAPTER 2

BLACK, WHITE, BLUE, AND YOU

*"Once you start approaching your body with curiosity
rather than with fear, everything shifts."*

BESSEL VAN DER KOLK

As we've seen, white-body supremacy, and the trauma that causes and perpetuates it, lives primarily in the body, not the thinking brain. Now let's look at how white-body supremacy causes white, Black, and police bodies to view each other.

The white body sees itself as fragile and vulnerable, and it looks to police bodies for its protection and safety. Its view of the Black body is more complex and deeply paradoxical. It sees Black bodies as dangerously impervious to pain[11] and needing to be controlled. Yet it

---

11   Dr. David Rosenbloom, Professor of Health Policy and Management at Boston University's School of Public Health, sums it up succinctly: "Blacks have been undertreated for pain for decades." A 2016 study published in the *Proceedings of the National Academy of Sciences* (113, no. 16, 4296–4301) by psychologist Kelly M. Hoffman, et al. at the University of Virginia found that 58 percent of laypeople, 40 percent of first-year medical students, and 42 percent of second-year medical students believed that Black skin is literally thicker than white skin. (It isn't, of course. It *is* true that any human being can grow calluses—thicker skin—on an area of their body that is repeatedly irritated or abused. But this is a result of the irritation or abuse, not the person's skin color.) In addition, 20 percent of laypeople, 8 percent of first-year medical students, and 14 percent of second-year medical students believed that Black people have less sensitive nerve endings than white people. Respondents also believed that Black bodies have stronger immune systems than white bodies, and that Black people's blood coagulates more quickly. The study involved 222 white medical students and ninety-two white laypeople. For more on this, see David Love's "Study: White Medical Students Hold Outrageous Theories about Black Biology, Explaining Why Black Patients Are Under-Treated for Pain" (*Atlanta Black Star*, April 5, 2016).

also sees them as potential sources of service and comfort.

For most of our country's history, the Black body was forced to serve white bodies. It was seen as a tool, to be purchased from slave traders; stacked on shelves in the bellies of slave ships; purchased at auction; made to plant, weed, and harvest crops; pressed into service in support of white families' comfort; and used to build a massive agricultural economy.

This arrangement was systematically maintained through murder, rape, mutilation, and other forms of trauma, as well as through institutions, laws, regulations, norms, and beliefs.

It is only relatively recently that most Black Americans have had some dominion over their own bodies. The white body often feels uncomfortable with this Black self-management and self-agency.

The Black body sees the white body as privileged, controlling, and dangerous. It is deeply conflicted about the police body, which it sometimes sees as a source of protection, sometimes as a source of danger, and sometimes as both at once. When police bodies congregate in large numbers, however, the Black body is not conflicted: it sees police bodies as an occupying force.

The police body senses that all bodies need its protection. However, it sees Black bodies as often dangerous and disruptive, as well as superhumanly powerful and impervious to pain. It feels charged with controlling and subduing Black bodies by any means necessary— including extreme force.

None of this is rational, and much of it is not even conscious. A great deal of it is outright false, rooted in racialized myth. Some of it directly contradicts what we consciously believe, as well as much of our actual experience. But our bodies don't care about logic, truth, or cognitive experience. They care about safety and survival. They care about responding to a perceived threat, even when that threat is not real. As a result, our bodies scare the hell out of each other.

*

There's a way out of this mess, and it requires each of us to begin with our own body. You and your body are important parts of the solution. You will not just read this book; you will experience it in your body. Your body—all of our bodies—are where changing the status quo must begin.

*

When I begin working with new clients, one of the first things I do—before we start talking about any issues, family histories, or emotions—is help them ground themselves and orient themselves to the here and now. I work with them to slowly feel their way back into their bodies, and then to remember and reclaim them.

As you go through this book, you will remember and reclaim your own body as well. We'll start with a set of activities that will help you learn to ground yourself and feel into your body—to notice when it is open, when it is constricted, and what causes it to open or constrict, activate or settle.

A few words of guidance before we begin: When (or immediately after) you do any of the activities in this book, it's possible your body may have an unusual reaction. You might start shaking or tingling; you might laugh or cry, or burp or fart, or feel hot or cold. You may feel an impulse to move part of your body in a particular way. An image or thought might suddenly arise in your mind. An unexpected emotion might bubble up. All of these responses are normal. They don't mean you're weird or crazy. They may simply mean you have touched and released some energy that was stuck in your body. This is not only experientially healthy, but good for your body.

In the unlikely event your body reacts in some extreme way, stop the activity immediately. Take a few slow, deep breaths to help your body settle; then go on with the rest of your day. If that doesn't help, and your body has an over-the-top reaction that is too strong to handle, seek out a trauma therapist who can help you move through the stuckness. (Again, this is extremely unlikely. Most of the time, your body won't have any unusual reaction at all.)

—BODY PRACTICE—

Find a quiet, private spot. Plan to spend three to four minutes there, alone.

Sit comfortably. Take a few breaths.

Turn your head and slowly look around in all directions, especially behind you. Orient yourself in the surrounding space. If you're indoors, notice the height of the ceiling, the height and color of each wall, any doors or windows, and any other details that stand out. If you are outside, take note of any boundaries, such as a footpath, a fence, the edge of a clearing, or the shore of a pond. Notice any plant or animal life nearby. Note what sounds you hear, any smells that fill the air, any warmth or coolness, and any colors that stand out.

When you are done scanning your environment, face forward once again and return your attention to your body. Sense how your feet rest on the ground and how your butt rests on the seat.

Now notice any other sensations in your body: the bend in your knees; your spine, straight or curved; a breeze in your hair; your belly and any tension you hold there; and your chest, expanding and shrinking with each breath.

Notice what your body experiences inside your clothing. Pay attention to where your body touches your underwear, your socks or stockings, your shirt or blouse, your pants or skirt or dress.

Starting at the top of your head, bring your attention slowly down through your body. Notice each sensation as your attention passes through it: warmth, coolness, relaxation, tightness, softness, pressure, energy, numbness.

Don't skip or skim the healing and grounding exercises in this book—the ones with activities that help you remember your body or perform an action. When you reach each one, stop. Take a few slow breaths. Then, as you read that section, practice that activity in your body. If you're not in a situation where this is possible, put the book down temporarily. Pick it up again when you have the opportunity to practice the activity.

I provide these body activities throughout this book. A few involve simply stopping and noticing. Most involve doing something more—sensing, imagining, moving, or activating your body in some other way.

If you've already skipped the previous activity, *stop*. Go back and complete it before reading further. Don't keep reading and promise yourself you'll do the activity later. That's not how this book works. Before you read further, you need to experience the activity with your body.

Once you've completed that brief activity, continue with the one that follows.

—BODY PRACTICE—

Sit quietly and comfortably for a minute or two, breathing normally. Notice your breath as it enters your nose, your windpipe, your lungs. For thirty seconds, simply follow it as it goes in and out of your body.

Then bring your attention to the bottom of your feet. Sense the ground beneath them, supporting you. Stay focused here for a few breaths.

Move your attention to your back, to the sensation of it pressing lightly against the chair. Feel the chair supporting you, doing what it was designed to do.

Now think of a person or a pet or a place that makes you feel safe and secure. Imagine you're with that person or pet, or in that safe place. Let yourself experience that safety and security for a few seconds.

Now check in with your body. Start with your shoulders. How do they feel? Relaxed or constricted? Closed or open?

What about your neck? Your jaw? Your major joints—your ankles, knees, hips, wrists, elbows, and shoulders? Your back? Your sphincter? Your toes?

Stay with the experience for a couple of breaths. Notice if anything arises or changes, such as a vibration, a sensation, an image, an emotion, an impulse, or a meaning.

Now imagine the comforting person, pet, or place is gone. Instead, there's an angry stranger standing in front of you. The stranger's arms are crossed and he or she is glaring at you silently.

You look into the stranger's eyes, hoping his or her expression will soften, but it remains unchanged.

Check in with your body again. How do your shoulders feel? Your neck? Your jaw? Your back? Your sphincter? Your toes?

Gently, one by one, feel into all the places in your body where you sense constriction. Let your attention rest briefly in each one.

Now send the angry stranger away. Bring back the comforting person, place, or pet. For several breaths, relax in the safety this presence provides.

Now, gently, move your attention through your body, from your head to your toes, one more time. Feel into each spot where you sense softness. Stay with each of these for one to two seconds.

In a day or two, or as soon after that as you can, practice the following:

—BODY PRACTICE—

Find a quiet, comfortable place where you can be alone for a few minutes. Bring with you a piece of string (or rope or yarn) at least ten to twelve feet long.

Stand in an open area. Take a few deep, slow breaths.

Using the string, create a circle on the ground. Adjust its size so that when you stand in its center and you imagine someone else standing on the circle's edge, you are a comfortable distance from them.

Once the circle is the right size, take your place at its center. Breathe in and out a few more times.

Think of someone you know who is caring and supportive. This can be a friend, a relative, a neighbor, a partner, or a friendly acquaintance. Visualize this person walking slowly in your direction toward the circle.

As he or she crosses the circle's edge, pay attention to what your body experiences. Does it relax or constrict? Does it want to move forward or backward? Does it want to reach out, or protect itself, or move in some other way?

Now clear your mind. Take three or four more slow breaths.

Now visualize someone else you know, someone who is *not* particularly caring and supportive. This shouldn't be someone who is outright violent or dangerous, who has threatened you, or who is your sworn enemy. Instead, it might be a boss or coworker with whom you have some friction, or a slightly standoffish neighbor, or perhaps a relative who disagrees with you on several political or social issues.

Visualize this person walking slowly in your direction toward the circle. As he or she crosses the circle's edge, again pay attention to what your body experiences. Does it relax or constrict? Does it want to move forward or backward? Does it want to reach out, or protect itself, or move in some other way?

Notice what images, sensations, emotions, impulses, and thoughts arise in you. Don't do anything about those images—simply take note of them.

As part of your healing from the trauma of white-body supremacy, you'll learn to tell when your body is open and when it is constricted; when it is settled and when it is activated; and where and when it is in pain or discomfort. This will take some practice, and you'll have plenty of opportunities to practice in the chapters to come.

In Chapters Ten, Eleven, and Twelve, you'll learn a wide range of ways to settle your body, especially when you're under stress or duress. These skills will prove essential to healing and to creating more room for growth in your nervous system. They will also help you stay in your body, rather than fight, flee, or freeze and go numb when you experience discomfort or pain.

Being able to settle into your body is a crucial skill. But settling your body is not the best response in every situation. There will be times when you need to activate your body and act constructively. In fact, when settling is a reflexive response rather than a mindful one, it can be a form of avoiding or overriding an opportunity to serve or heal.

Some people can become extremely—almost scarily—calm and low key under stress. Instead of settling their body in order to tolerate discomfort and fully engage in the situation, they use their body-settling skills to *disengage* and *disassociate*. We've all seen some white Americans and police do this, particularly in discussions about race. (We've also all watched some African Americans do this.)

The keys to healing are staying with your body; discerning what you need to do next; and then settling or mobilizing your body, based on the situation. Of course, learning to stay with your body is just the first step. Unraveling racialized trauma takes time, practice, and attention. You may need to ask for help from one, or more, caring person—perhaps a friend, therapist, or other counselor.[12] Or you may not. As you practice the activities in Part III with others, you may discover you are naturally helping *each other* heal.

---

12   For ideas about some of the people who can help, see "Five Opportunities for Healing and Making Room for Growth" at the end of this book.

—BODY PRACTICE—

Find a quiet, private, comfortable place. Sit down. Put one hand on your knee or in your lap. Place the other on your belly.

Now hum. Not from your throat or chest, but from the bottom of your belly.

Hum strong and steady. Push the air out of your belly firmly, not gently.

Stop to breathe in, but return to the hum with each new breath.

Experience the hum in your belly. Then sense it in the rest of your body.

Continue humming for two minutes.

When you're done, reach your arms upward. Then, slowly and gently, feel your body with your hands, starting from the top of your head. Move slowly down your neck and along your chest, then below your waist, then past your knees, until your arms are fully extended downward. What do you notice?

In the chapters to come, you'll return to your body over and over. With practice, you'll get better and better at noticing its many signals—some of them strong, others subtle.

You'll also learn more about the Black body, the white body, and the police body. You'll briefly explore the history of each one and understand how each one got to be the way it is today.

In addition, in at least one of these histories, you'll likely recognize your body and the racialized trauma it holds deep inside.

RE-MEMBERINGS

- Whether or not white-body supremacy is formally and explicitly taught to us, it's in the air we breathe, the culture we share, and the bodies we inhabit.

- Because of white-body supremacy, here is how white, Black, and police bodies see each other:

  + The white body sees itself as fragile and vulnerable, and it looks to police bodies for safety and protection. It sees Black bodies as dangerous and needing to be controlled, yet also as potential sources of service and comfort.

  + The Black body sees the white body as privileged, controlling, and dangerous. It is conflicted about the police body, which it sees as sometimes a source of protection, sometimes a source of danger, and sometimes both at once.

  + The police body sees Black bodies as often dangerous and disruptive, as well as superhumanly powerful and impervious to pain.

- There is a way out of all this. It begins with your body.

- You will not just read this book. You will experience it in your body—the only place where the mending of racialized (or any) trauma can happen.

CHAPTER 3

BODY TO BODY, GENERATION TO GENERATION

*"Not to know what happened before you
were born is to remain forever a child."*

CICERO

*"No man can know where he is going unless he knows exactly where
he has been and exactly how he arrived at his present place."*

MAYA ANGELOU

Most of us think of trauma as something that occurs in an individual body, like a toothache or a broken arm. But trauma also routinely spreads *between* bodies, like a contagious disease. When someone with unhealed trauma chooses dirty pain over clean pain, the person may try to soothe his or her trauma by blowing it through another person— using violence, rage, coercion, deception, betrayal, or emotional abuse. This never heals the trauma. Instead, it increases the first person's dirty pain by reinforcing harmful and aggressive survival strategies as standard operating procedure. It creates a sense of ongoing unease in the first person's body that he or she then must override. It may also provoke a reflexively defensive or aggressive response in the second person's body.

Sometimes people inflict this pain on others deliberately, but more often it occurs spontaneously and unexpectedly. Something triggers a person's trauma; his or her lizard brain instantly launches a fight response; and the person physically or emotionally harms whomever is nearby.

Even as people in these situations inflict harm on others, their reasoning brains may think, *What the hell am I doing? I don't want to hurt this person!* More likely, though, their conscious minds make up after-the-fact self-protective rationales: *She was reaching toward her purse; there could have been a gun inside.* Or, *I told him to settle down, but he still acted upset; I felt he might attack me at any moment.*

When therapists work with couples in crisis, we often discover that at least one partner has unhealed trauma. We also commonly find that the partnership is configured so that the trauma gets repeatedly reenacted and, sometimes, passed back and forth between the two people. Healing the trauma becomes the first step in mending the relationship.

It's not hard to see how trauma can spread like a contagion within couples, families, and other close relationships. What we don't often consider is how trauma can spread from body to body in *any* relationship.

Trauma also spreads impersonally, of course, and has done so throughout human history. Whenever one group oppresses, victimizes, brutalizes, or marginalizes another, many of the victimized people may suffer trauma, and then pass on that trauma response to their children as standard operating procedure.[13] Children are highly susceptible to this because their young nervous systems are easily overwhelmed by things that older, more experienced nervous systems are able to override. As we have seen, the result is a soul wound or intergenerational trauma. When the trauma continues for generation

---

13   Over time, roles can switch and the oppressed may become the oppressors. They then pass on trauma not only to their children, but also to a new group of victims.

after generation, it is called *historical trauma*. Historical trauma has been likened to a bomb going off, over and over again.

When one *settled* body encounters another, this can create a deeper settling of both bodies. But when one *unsettled* body encounters another, the unsettledness tends to compound in both bodies. In large groups, this compounding effect can turn a peaceful crowd into an angry mob. The same thing happens in families, especially when multiple family members face painful or stressful situations together. It can also occur more subtly over time, when one person repeatedly passes on their unsettledness to another. In her book *Everyday Narcissism*, therapist Nancy Van Dyken calls this *hazy trauma*: trauma that can't be traced back to a single specific event.

Unhealed trauma acts like a rock thrown into a pond; it causes ripples that move outward, affecting many other bodies over time. After months or years, unhealed trauma can appear to become part of someone's personality. Over even longer periods of time, as it is passed on and gets compounded through other bodies in a household, it can become a family norm. And if it gets transmitted and compounded through multiple families and generations, it can start to look like culture.

But it isn't culture. It's a traumatic retention that has lost its context over time. Though without context, it has not lost its power. Traumatic retentions can have a profound effect on what we do, think, feel, believe, experience, and find meaningful. (We'll look at some examples shortly.)

What we call out as individual personality flaws, dysfunctional family dynamics, or twisted cultural norms are sometimes manifestations of historical trauma. These traumatic retentions may have served a purpose at one time—provided protection, supported resilience, inspired hope, etc.—but generations later, when adaptations continue to be acted out in situations where they are no longer necessary or helpful, they get defined as dysfunctional behavior on the individual, family, or cultural level.

The transference of trauma isn't just about how human beings treat each other. Trauma can also be inherited genetically. Recent work in genetics has revealed that trauma can change the expression of the DNA in our cells, and these changes can be passed from parent to child.[14]

And it gets weirder. We now have evidence that *memories* connected to painful events also get passed down from parent to child—and to that child's child. What's more, these experiences appear to be held, passed on, and inherited in the body, not just in the thinking brain.[15] Often people experience this as a persistent sense of imminent doom—the trauma ghosting I wrote about earlier.

We are only beginning to understand how these processes work, and there are a lot of details we don't know yet. Having said that, here is what we do know so far:

- A fetus growing inside the womb of a traumatized mother may inherit some of that trauma in its DNA expression. This results in the repeated release of stress hormones, which may affect the nervous system of the developing fetus.

- A man with unhealed trauma in his body may produce sperm with altered DNA expression. These in turn may inhibit the healthy functioning of cells in his children.

- Trauma can alter the DNA expression of a child or grandchild's brain, causing a wide range of health and mental health issues, including memory loss, chronic anxiety, muscle weakness, and depression.

- Some of these effects seem particularly prevalent among African Americans, Jews, and American Indians, three groups who have experienced an enormous amount of historical trauma.

---

14   This research has led to the creation of a new field of scientific inquiry known as *epigenetics*, the study of inheritable changes in gene expression. Epigenetics has transformed the way scientists think about genomes. The first study to clearly show that stress can cause inheritable gene defects in humans was published in 2015 by Rachel Yehuda and her colleagues, titled "Holocaust Exposure Induced Intergenerational Effects n FKBP5 Methylation" (*Biological Psychiatry* 80, no. 5, September, 2016: 372–80). (Earlier studies identified the same effect in animals.) Yehuda's study demonstrated that damaged genes in the bodies of Jewish Holocaust survivors—the result of the trauma they suffered under Nazism—were passed on to their children. Later research confirms Yehuda's conclusions.

15   A landmark study demonstrating this effect in mice was published in 2014 by Kerry Ressler and Brian Dias ("Parental Olfactory Experience Influences Behavior and Neural Structure in Subsequent Generations," *Nature Neuroscience* 17: 89–96). Ressler and Dias put male mice in a small chamber, then occasionally exposed them to the scent of acetophenone (which smells like cherries)—and, simultaneously, to small electric shocks. Eventually the mice associated the scent with pain; they would shudder whenever they were exposed to the smell, even after the shocks were discontinued. The children of those mice were born with a fear of the smell of acetophenone. So were their grandchildren. As of this writing, no one has completed a similar study on humans, both for ethical reasons and because we take a lot longer than mice to produce a new generation.

Some scientists theorize this genetic alteration may be a way to protect later generations. Essentially, genetic changes train our descendants' bodies through heredity rather than behavior. This suggests that what we call genetic defects may actually be ways to increase our descendants' odds of survival in a potentially dangerous environment, by relaying hormonal information to the fetus in the womb.

The womb is itself an environment: a watery world of sounds, movement, and human biochemicals. Recent research suggests that, during the last trimester of pregnancy, fetuses in the womb can learn and remember just as well as newborns.[16] Part of what they may learn, based on what their mothers go through during pregnancy, is whether the world outside the womb is safe and healthy or dangerous and toxic.

If the fetus's mother is relatively happy and healthy during her pregnancy, and if she has a nervous system that is settled, her body will produce few stress hormones. As a result, by the time the fetus begins journeying down the birth canal, his or her body may have learned that the world is a generally safe and settled place to be.

But if the fetus's mom experiences trauma, or if her earlier trauma causes a variety of stress hormones to regularly get released into her body, her baby may begin life outside the womb with less of a sense of safety, resilience, and coherence.

Zoë Carpenter sums this up in a simple, stark observation:

> Health experts now think that stress throughout the span of a woman's life can prompt biological changes that affect the health of her future children. Stress can disrupt immune, vascular, metabolic, and endocrine systems, and cause cells to age more quickly.[17]

---

16   A good, if very brief, overview of these studies appeared in *Science:* http://www.sciencemag.org/news/2013/08/babies-learn-recognize-words-womb.

17   This quote is from an eye-opening article in *The Nation,* "What's Killing America's Black Infants?": https://www.thenation.com/article/whats-killing-americas-black-infants. Carpenter also notes that in the United States, Black infants die at a rate that's over twice as high as for white infants. In some cities, the disparity is much worse: in Washington, DC, the infant mortality rate in Ward 8, which is over 93 percent Black, is *ten times* the rate in Ward 3, which is well-to-do and mostly white.

All of this suggests that one of the best things each of us can do—not only for ourselves, but also for our children and grandchildren—is to metabolize our pain and heal our trauma. When we heal and make more room for growth in our nervous systems, we have a better chance of spreading our emotional health to our descendants, via healthy DNA expression. In contrast, when we don't address our trauma, we may pass it on to future generations, along with some of our fear, constriction, and dirty pain.

*

Trauma hurts. It can fill us with reflexive fear, anxiety, depression, and shame. It can cause us to fly off the handle; to reflexively retreat and disappear; to do things that don't make sense, even to ourselves; or, sometimes, to harm others or ourselves.

One of my mentors, Dr. Noel Larson, used to say, "If something is hysterical, then it is usually historical." If your (or anyone's) reaction to a current situation has more (or far less) energy than it normally would, then it likely involves energy from ancient historical trauma that has lost its context. In the present, your body is experiencing unmetabolized trauma from the past.

The same may be true if you respond with an uncharacteristically *low* amount of energy—for example, if you react to the news of a good friend's death with a brief, flat "That's too bad." In this case, the ancient historical trauma has triggered a freeze response—what therapists call *dissociation*—rather than a fight or flight reaction.[18] In either case, this trauma may have been passed down to you through your parents' or other ancestors' actions, through their DNA, or through both.

Sometimes the body couples and compounds this trauma with the energy of other traumatic events. This can cause people to suddenly and completely (though usually temporarily) lose their cool without having any idea why. Remember, to the traumatized body, all threats—current or ancient, individual or collective, real or imagined—are

---

18   There are other possible causes, of course. Similar low-energy responses are common among people with depression, dysthymia, bipolar disorder, narcissistic personality disorder, or antisocial personality disorder (i.e., sociopaths).

exactly the same. The lizard brain senses danger and commands the body to fight, flee, or freeze.

Trauma is unique to each body. What one person experiences as trauma, another may experience as nothing more than a big challenge. I've had clients who were beaten, raped, or deeply betrayed, yet who metabolized their pain and healed. I've had others who were traumatized by loud noises or the affection of unfamiliar, overeager dogs.

That said, most people experience trauma if an experience they have:

- Is unexpected (for example, the 2007 collapse of the 35W highway bridge in Minneapolis).

- Involves the death of many people, especially children (for example, the Tulsa race riot of 1921).

- Lasts a long time or repeats itself multiple times (such as Hurricane Katrina and its aftermath).

- Has unknown causes (for instance, when your partner suddenly and mysteriously disappears).

- Is deeply poignant or meaningful (such as the killing of twenty-seven people—twenty of whom were children between the ages of six and seven—at Sandy Hook Elementary School).

- Impacts a large area and/or many people (for example, an earthquake, a plague, a terrorist attack, persecution, or enslavement).

These are the effects of trauma involving specific incidents. But what about the effects of repetitive trauma: unhealed traumas that accumulate over time? The research is now in: the effects on the body from trauma that is persistent (or pervasive, repetitive, or long-held) are significantly negative, sometimes profoundly so. While many studies support this conclusion,[19] the largest and best known is the Adverse Childhood Experiences Study (ACES), a large study of 17,000 people[20] conducted over three decades by the Centers for Disease Control and Prevention (CDC) and the healthcare conglomerate Kaiser Permanente. Published in 2014, ACES clearly links childhood trauma (and other "adverse childhood events" involving abuse or neglect[21]) to a wide range of long-term health and social consequences, including illness, disability, social problems, and early death—all of which can get passed down through the generations. The ACE study also demonstrates a strong link between the number of "adverse childhood events" and increased rates of heart disease, cancer, stroke, diabetes, chronic lung disease, alcoholism, depression, liver disease, and sexually transmitted diseases, as well as illicit drug use, financial stress, poor academic and work performance, pregnancy in adolescence, and attempted suicide. People who have experienced four or more "adverse events" as children are twice as likely to develop heart disease than people who have experienced none. They are also twice as likely to develop autoimmune diseases, four and a half times as likely to be depressed, ten times as likely to be intravenous drug users, and twelve times as likely to be suicidal. As children, they are *thirty-three times* as likely to have learning and behavior problems in school.

Pediatrician Nadine Burke-Harris offers the following apt comparison: "If a child is exposed to lead while their brain is developing, it affects the long-term development of their brain . . . It's the same way when a child is exposed to high doses of stress and trauma while their brain is developing . . . Exposure to trauma is particularly toxic for children." In other words, there is a biochemical component behind all this.

---

19   See, for example: "Early Trauma and Inflammation" (*Psychosomatic Medicine* 74, no. 2, February/March 2012: 146–52); "Chronic Stress, Glucocorticoid Receptor Resistance, Inflammation, and Disease Risk" (*Proceedings of the National Academy of Sciences* 109, no. 16, April 17, 2012: 5995–99); and "Adverse Childhood Experiences and Adult Risk Factors for Age-Related Disease: Depression, Inflammation, and Clustering of Metabolic Risk Markers" (*Archives of Pediatrics and Adolescent Medicine* 163, no. 12, December 2009: 1135–43).

20   Of the people studied, 74.8 percent were white; 4.5 percent were African American; 54 percent were female; and 46 percent were male.

21   The ten "adverse childhood events" are divorced or separated parents; physical abuse; physical neglect; emotional abuse; emotional neglect; sexual abuse; domestic violence that the child witnessed; substance abuse in the household; mental illness in the household; and a family member in prison.

When people experience repeated trauma, abuse, or high levels of stress for long stretches of time, a variety of stress hormones get secreted into their bloodstreams. In the short term, the purpose of these chemicals is to protect their bodies. But when the levels of these chemicals[22] remain high over time, they can have toxic effects, making a person less healthy, less resilient, and more prone to illness. High levels of one or more of these chemicals can also crowd out other, healthier chemicals—those that encourage trust, intimacy, motivation, and meaning.

All of this suggests that trauma is a major contributor to many of our bodily, mental, and social ills, and that mending our trauma may be one of the most effective ways to address those ills.

The results of the ACE study are dramatic. Yet it covered only fifteen years. How much more dramatic might the results be for people who have experienced (or whose ancestors experienced) centuries of enslavement or genocide?[23]

Historical trauma, intergenerational trauma, institutionalized trauma (such as white-body supremacy, gender discrimination, sexual orientation discrimination, etc.), and personal trauma (including any trauma we inherit from our families genetically, or through the way they treat us, or both) often interact. As these traumas compound each other, or as each new or recent traumatic experience triggers the energy of older experiences, they can create ever-increasing damage to human lives and human bodies.

---

22   These chemicals are cortisol, adrenaline, and norepinephrine. They are secreted by the adrenal gland.

23   Please don't imagine that we African Americans claim to have cornered the market on adverse childhood experiences. In fact, in his brilliant book *Hillbilly Elegy: A Memoir of a Family and Culture in Crisis* (New York: HarperCollins, 2016), white Appalachian J. D. Vance cites the ACE study in reference to himself, his sister Lindsay, and "my corner of the demographic world": working-class Americans. As Vance notes, "Four in every ten working-class people had faced multiple instances of childhood trauma." If you want to deeply understand the hearts, psyches, and bodies of many Americans today, you can do no better than to read both *Hillbilly Elegy* and Ta-Nehisi Coates's *Between the World and Me* (New York: Spiegel & Grau, 2015).

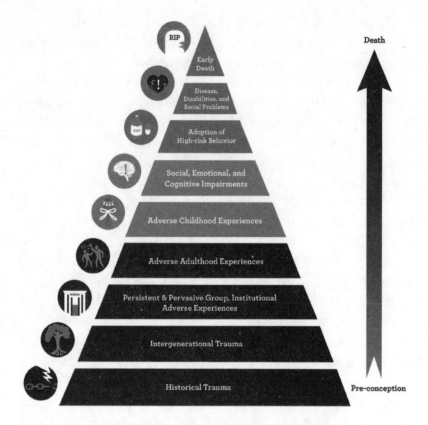

Figure 1. How Trauma Compounds

(Based partly on a figure used in the
Adverse Childhood Experiences Study.)

So far, we've looked at trauma that happens *to* us. But there are other kinds of trauma that are even more common: trauma from watching or experiencing *someone else* get traumatized. Witnesses to murder, rape, torture, and other acts of physical violence often have their own trauma responses. They may help the victim, or fight the perpetrator, or flee the scene, or freeze in place. Someone who witnesses a flood, a fire, a terrorist attack, an armed robbery, or someone's public humiliation may respond similarly. These types of trauma are called *secondary trauma* or *vicarious trauma*. Almost every human being holds some of this trauma in his or her body.

A particularly poisonous form of secondary trauma involves not only witnessing the harming of another human being, but *inflicting* that harm. Often, the perpetrator tries to avoid this trauma by dissociating (a form of flight) during the event, and then, immediately afterward, overriding any impulse to process the trauma or discharge its energy from his or her body. Such attempts to flee from trauma only deepen it—and create an extreme form of dirty pain. Because the perpetrator knows he or she has committed a moral transgression, his or her actions also create profound shame. Therapists call this a *moral injury*.

In their work, many police officers experience moral injury or have witnessed it in their coworkers. Unfortunately, very few manage to metabolize this shame and trauma; few are even aware of it, let alone of what they need to do to metabolize it; and still fewer receive encouragement or support from their coworkers, superiors, or organizational structures.

What do you think happens when a police officer who recently experienced a moral injury returns to duty with the unhealed trauma still stuck in his or her body? How might this affect his or her job performance? His or her family? His or her health? The people in the community or neighborhood he or she serves?

*

It's easy to see how white-body supremacy has created soul wounds for many millions of African American bodies over the past three centuries. It's less obvious what the *inflicting* of that trauma has done to white bodies.

When I lead workshops on trauma for people in service professions, I often show them a clip from *12 Years a Slave*, the film based on the memoir of Solomon Northrup, a free African American from upstate New York who was kidnapped and sold into enslavement in 1853. In the clip, we see slave trader Theophilus Freeman (played by Paul Giamatti) coldly check the health, strength, and muscle tone of his human merchandise. As buyers come by to make purchases, Freeman orders one young African man to run and jump in place for a potential customer. Freeman tells the customer, "You see how fit the boy is. Like ripe fruit. He will grow into a fine beast."

In the same scene, Eliza, a young Black mother, pleads with Freeman to have mercy and not separate her from her daughter. William Ford, a white customer and plantation owner, is moved by her pleas. He asks Freeman, "For God's sake, are you not sentimental in the least?" Freeman ignores them both, breaks up the family, and says to Ford, "My sentimentality stretches the length of a coin."

Also in that scene, Freeman commands Northrup (played by Chiwetel Ejiofor) to stand and approach him. When Northrup doesn't respond, Freeman slaps him hard—and loudly—across the face. The clip ends here.

At that point I turn to my audience and say, "Now I want to ask you a few questions." I pause, letting the participants imagine what I am about to ask. Then I say, "What do you think is going on inside the slave trader's body? Do you think he experiences settling, relaxation, and resilience? Or do you think he experiences constriction and discomfort?"

I continue, "And what do you think is happening in the bodies of the other white folks in the room? Do you think they're relaxed and settled? What do you imagine a white body has to do in order to be settled in that situation? What got passed down to those white bodies for them to tolerate that level of cultural brutality? What happened to those bodies in the past that causes them to not react when they watch other people being traumatized? Where in their bodies do you think some of these white people might be experiencing constriction?"

After another pause, "Why is William Ford the only person who speaks up on behalf of any of the Black bodies? What do you think is stopping the white bodies from doing something to help?"

Finally, "What are you experiencing right now in *your* body?"

Now ask yourself this same question. Notice what your own body wants to do. Take notice of whatever sensations and thoughts arise. Notice if you want to fight, or run, or freeze in place. Just notice.

*

Now I'd like you to explore how intergenerational trauma may have affected your life and body. You can do this by reflecting briefly on four events in the lives of your ancestors.

Find a quiet, comfortable place where you can be alone and undistracted for at least fifteen minutes. Now consider these questions.

1. *When did your ancestors settle in America?*[24] Did they come here voluntarily, or were they refugees, servants, or enslaved people? Were they fleeing brutality, oppression, plague, war, or poverty? Did they come here in search of a better life? How old were they? How healthy were they? Was there a community or a group of relatives here to welcome and assist them?

   Did your ancestors speak English when they got here? What other language or languages did they speak? What possessions and skills did they bring with them? To the best of your knowledge, were they hopeful or desperate? Prosperous or poor?

   As far as you know, did any of your ancestors ever talk about the Native people who arrived on this continent many centuries earlier? If so, what did they say?

   If you are an immigrant to America yourself, please respond to this question by reflecting on your own experience.

2. *What traumatic events directly affected your mother? Your father?* How did each event affect them at the time? How did it affect the choices they made later? How did it affect the way they raised you?

3. *What traumatic events directly affected your grandparents?* How did each event affect them at the time? How did it affect the choices they made later? How did it affect the way they raised your father or mother?

---

24   If you are Native American and have no immigrant ancestors, please skip reflection #1.

4. When your mother was pregnant with you, was the pregnancy easy or difficult for her? Was she generally healthy or ill? Happy or unhappy? Hopeful or unhopeful? What challenges did she face during her pregnancy? What else was going on for her and the family?

*

Besides trauma, there is something else human beings routinely pass on from person to person and from generation to generation: resilience.[25] Resilience is built into the very cells of our bodies. It is as much a part of us as our ability to heal. Like trauma, resilience can ripple outward, changing the lives of people, families, neighborhoods, and communities in positive ways.

However, resilience is often misunderstood. It is typically viewed as the ability to bounce back from adversity, often in a heroic, individualized act. Furthermore, that ability is often seen as something learned or acquired in childhood—the result of supportive parenting, the presence of other caring adults, and so on. But the full picture of resilience is much broader and much more organic.

First, resilience is both intrinsic *and* learned, a combination of nature (what you're born with) *and* nurture (the circumstances you encounter, especially as you grow up). Second, resilience manifests both individually *and* collectively. Sometimes it does take the form of a personal, individual act. Often, however, resilience is expressed communally by a group, a family, an organization, or a culture.

Suppose you're running a marathon. Halfway through, exhausted, you trip and fall. Your legs ache and you're bleeding from both knees. You pull yourself to your feet and decide it's time to quit the race. Then five of your friends and family members show up beside you. "You can do it!" they shout. "You finished last year; you can finish this time. Go for it!" Next thing you know, you're off and running again.

Clearly this required resilience. But the resilience wasn't just inside of you. It also came from the words and actions of people who care for

---

25   Human resilience has been widely studied for decades. Many professionals have done excellent research on the topic; I especially recommend the work of Ann S. Masten, particularly her book *Ordinary Magic: Resilience in Development* (New York: The Guilford Press, 2014).

you, and from your relationship with them. Ann Masten, one of the leading researchers on resilience in children, expresses it this way: "I like to say that the resilience of a child is distributed. It's not just in the child. It's distributed in their relationships with the many other people who make up their world."[26]

Third, resilience isn't just about responding to—or getting through—a difficult experience. Resilience also manifests in a form that's more about being than doing. This aspect of resilience helps us stay grounded and settled, no matter what happens to us. It enables us to sustain and protect ourselves—and each other—over time. It's a way for our body to access possibility and coherence, regardless of the circumstances. It's not so much a response as it is a way of showing up, a way of tapping into the energies that surround and move through everything in our world.

Resilience *can* be built and strengthened, both individually and collectively. We African Americans took pains to build resilience in ourselves and our children for many generations; if we didn't, we wouldn't have survived. For 400 years, with many successes and many failures, we have sought to counter new and old trauma with both the resilience we were born with and the resilience we grew and taught each other to grow.

I often tell people that resilience is not a thing or an attribute, but a flow. It moves *through* the body, and between multiple bodies when they are harmonized. It is neither built nor developed; it is taken in and expressed as part of a larger relationship with a family, a group, a community, or the world at large.

Notice how this takes place not just in the cognitive mind, but in the body, and in the minds and bodies of others, and in the collective body of people who care about us.

Here are some especially good pieces of news about resilience: recent findings in neuroscience reveal that the human brain always has the capacity to learn, change, and grow. It is genetically designed to mend itself. While trauma can inhibit or block this capacity, that effect is not permanent; once the trauma has ceased and been

---

26   Andy Steiner, "Ann Masten: Children's Natural Resilience Is Nurtured Through 'Ordinary Magic,'" *MinnPost*, September 17, 2014.

addressed, growth and positive change become possible once again.[27] Later chapters will offer a variety of activities to help your brain and body heal.

*

One morning, as my mother and I were taking a long walk together, she said to me, "Resmaa, you've written about my mother's hands, but you haven't said a word about her feet." My grandmother had feet that were small and thick, like hobbit feet, but I'd never thought much about them. She liked to take her shoes off and put her feet up, but that had seemed completely normal to me, especially for an older person.

"What's special about her feet?" I asked.

My mother paused, then looked at me. "You don't know, do you?" I shook my head.

"You know those hands of hers—her thick fingers covered with calluses? Her feet were the same way. What, you think she had shoes to wear when she was little? When she was four years old, she was out in the fields, barefoot, picking cotton. The fields were full of thorns, and they cut her feet up, day after day, until she grew calluses all over them, just like on her hands."

*

Over generations, many of us African Americans have developed thick emotional skins in a variety of ways.[28] This has served us well, protecting us from a great deal of damage and pain in a dangerous world. This is how resilience works. It doesn't always create full healing, but it may build protection and prevent (or blunt) future wounding. It can create in the body a little more room for growth and development. This, in turn, can create an opportunity for passing on caring, context, and growth to other bodies—especially the bodies of the next generation.

---

27   An immense amount of research supports this. A useful overview can be found in K. Ganguly and M. M. Poo's "Activity-Dependent Neural Plasticity from Bench to Bedside," *Neuron* 80, no. 3, October 2013: 729–41.

28   There's an irony here. Recall Kelly Hoffman's study, which found that many white Americans imagine African Americans to have thicker *physical* skin than white Americans? Although that belief is demonstrably incorrect, a case can be made that, over the generations, the *emotional* skins of many African Americans may have thickened.

—BODY AND BREATH PRACTICE—

Go to a quiet, comfortable place where you can be alone for about ten minutes. Sit down and take a few deep, slow breaths. Feel free to either close your eyes or leave them open.

You are about to invite the presence of an ancestor. You don't know who this will be. You also don't know how he or she will appear—as an image, a memory, a sensation in your body, an emotion, or a flow of energy. All you know is that this person lived at least three generations before you and died before you were born. They might be a great-grandparent or an ancestor from the distant past. You do not get to choose who this person will be; he or she will choose you.

Just sit quietly, following your breathing, and invite this unknown person into your presence.

Don't plan to converse or interact with this ancestor. Don't try to identify or figure out anything about him or her. Simply observe this person's presence and notice how your body responds.

If your ancestor doesn't appear quickly, that's fine. Just continue sitting and breathing. Give the person up to five minutes to make an appearance.

If he or she appears as an image, what does he or she look like? Is the person female or male? How old does he or she appear to be? What is he or she wearing? What expression is on his or her face?

Does your ancestor seem safe and settled? Happy? Fearful? Distressed? If your ancestor is moving, what is he or she doing? Is the person alone, or with a companion?

Whether your ancestor appears in an image or in some other form, how does your body experience his or her presence? Does it feel comforted? Welcomed? Loved? Relaxed? Wary? Afraid? Constricted? Does it want to move toward or away from your ancestor? Does your body want to touch or hold the person, or push him or her away?

When you are ready, thank your ancestor for visiting you. Then get up and continue with your day.

If, at any time, your ancestor's presence feels threatening, gently but firmly send him or her away. Then take a few slow, deep breaths to return yourself to the here and now. Orient yourself to the room by slowly looking around, especially behind you. If you still feel an uncomfortable presence, leave the room.

RE-MEMBERINGS

- Trauma can spread from one body to another, like a contagious disease—through families and from generation to generation.

- When someone with unhealed trauma chooses dirty pain over clean pain, he or she may try to push his or her trauma through another human being, by using violence, rage, coercion, betrayal, or emotional abuse. This only increases the dirty pain, while often creating trauma in the other person as well.

- When one settled body encounters another, there can be a deeper settling of both bodies. But when one unsettled body encounters another, the unsettledness tends to compound in both bodies. In families and large groups, this effect can multiply exponentially.

- Over months or years, unhealed trauma can become part of someone's personality. As it is passed on and compounded through other bodies, it often becomes the family norm. If it gets transmitted and compounded through multiple families and generations, it can turn into culture.

- Trauma can damage the genes in our cells. That damage can be passed on from parent to child, and from the child to his or her own child.

- One of the best things each of us can do for ourselves, and for our descendants, is metabolize our pain and heal our trauma. When we heal, we may spread our emotional health and healthy genes to later generations.

- Trauma and other adverse childhood events are associated with a wide range of illnesses, disabilities, social problems, and early death. All of these can also get passed down through the generations.

- *Secondary trauma* or *vicarious trauma* involves watching *someone else* be traumatized (and, sometimes, giving aid to them). An especially poisonous form of secondary trauma can occur when a person not only witnesses another person being harmed, but also inflicts that harm.

- Resilience is built into the cells of our bodies. Like trauma, resilience can ripple outward, changing the lives of people, families, neighborhoods, and communities in positive ways. Also like trauma, resilience can be passed down from generation to generation.

- The human brain always retains the capacity to learn, change, and grow. While trauma can inhibit or block this capacity, once the trauma has been addressed, growth and positive change become possible again.

CHAPTER 4

EUROPEAN TRAUMA AND THE INVENTION OF WHITENESS

"What white bodies did to Black bodies
they did to other white bodies first."

JANICE BARBEE

"There is no such thing as race. None. . . . Scientifically,
anthropologically, racism is a construct—a social construct. And
it has benefits. Money can be made off of it, and people who don't
like themselves can feel better because of it. It can describe certain
kinds of behavior that are wrong or misleading."

TONI MORRISON

"It is entirely up to the American people whether or not
they are going to try to find out in their own hearts why it
was necessary to have a nigger in the first place . . . and the
future of the country depends on that."

JAMES BALDWIN

"A really bad idea, embraced by millions of people,
is still a really bad idea."

TONY BLAUER

"I'm a get medieval on your ass."

MARCELLUS WALLACE, IN QUENTIN TARANTINO'S *PULP FICTION*

This book owes a great deal to Dr. Joy DeGruy, author of *Post Traumatic Slave Syndrome.*[29] In her groundbreaking work, DeGruy traces the history of Black trauma in America. She looks in detail at the violence and abuse inflicted on enslaved African people in America; at the continued trauma inflicted on their descendants; and at how this trauma has been passed down—and continues to be passed down—through generation upon generation of African Americans. *Post Traumatic Slave Syndrome* explains how and why so many African Americans today continue to live in the shadow of this trauma. It also offers some useful initial steps toward healing.

DeGruy's book was published in 2005, when we knew considerably less than we do now about trauma as a bodily phenomenon. Back then, trauma was widely considered to be mostly mental and emotional. As a result, DeGruy focuses primarily on the emotional and historical aspects of trauma.[30]

As we now know, however, without a clear and present focus on the body, trauma cannot be fully addressed. One of the purposes of *My Grandmother's Hands* is to build on DeGruy's important work. Another purpose of it is to look a little further backward in time than DeGruy did. *Post Traumatic Slave Syndrome* begins its investigations in the year 1619, when the first Africans arrived in America. These human beings were kidnapped, placed in chains, forcibly relocated, and sold into enslavement to immigrants from Europe and their descendants.

---

29   Joy DeGruy, *Post Traumatic Slave Syndrome: America's Legacy of Enduring Injury and Healing* (Portland, OR: Joy DeGruy Publications, 2005).

30   While the title of DeGruy's book clearly telegraphs the essence of her work, it's worth noting that *post* means *after*—and today, many African Americans continue to experience new or ongoing racialized trauma. Enslavement ended in 1865, but racialized trauma continues.

However, trauma of this kind did not begin in 1619. For thousands of years before that, human beings murdered, butchered, tortured, oppressed, abused, conquered, enslaved, and colonized one another.

While people from England, Spain, Portugal, France, Scotland, Sweden, and Holland had all colonized parts of America by the late 1600s, it was the English who controlled nearly all the colonized territories in what would become the United States in 1776.[31]

The 1500s and 1600s in England were anything but gentle times. People were routinely burned at the stake for heresy, a practice that began in the twelfth century and continued through 1612. Torture was an official instrument of the English government until 1640. The famous Tower of London was, in part, a huge torture chamber. One of many torture devices in the Tower, the rack, was used to stretch human bodies and pull them apart. Here is a description of the apparatus at work:

> This caused terrible pain for the victim as well as increasing physical damage as the torture continued. Tendons were ripped, joints separated and bones fractured. The sounds of muscles and tendons tearing and snapping provided audible signs of the damage being done.[32]

During much of the Middle Ages in England, torture wasn't just wildly popular; it was a spectator sport. In his essay "Violence and the Law in Medieval England," historian Sean McGlynn puts it this way:

> Throughout the whole medieval period there was popular demand for malefactors to receive punishment that was both harsh and purposefully terrifying. This reflected people's enthusiasm and the desire to see justice being done. There was even an executions transfer market: bids were made to stage the executions of condemned men in front of home crowds. . . . Mutilations sent

---

31   Spain held on to Florida until 1763, when it traded the territory to Great Britain. In the 1783 Treaty of Paris, which ended the American Revolutionary War, Florida was returned to Spain. In 1821, Spain ceded Florida to the United States.

32   Andrew Walsh, "Torture: Rack and Manacles," on the blog *Tudor Stuff: Tudor History from the Heart of England,* May 5, 2009, https://tudorstuff.wordpress.com/2009/05/05/torture-rack-and-manacles.

out a message of warning and deterrence; executions offered the ultimate guarantee against repeat offenders . . . with few prisons and no police force, severe punishment was deemed invaluable as a deterrent to crime.[33]

In her book *A Distant Mirror*, Barbara Tuchman offers this parallel description of everyday life in medieval England:

The tortures and punishments of civil justice customarily cut off hands and ears, racked, burned, flayed, and pulled apart people's bodies. In everyday life, passers-by saw some criminal flogged with a knotted rope or chained upright in an iron collar. They passed corpses hanging on the gibbet and decapitated heads and quartered bodies impaled on stakes on the city walls.[34]

It is not hard to understand why so many people from England fled to the American colonies. (Fleeing is, of course, a survival response.) Many of the English who colonized America had been brutalized, or had witnessed great brutality first-hand. Others were the children and grandchildren of people who had experienced such savagery in England.

Barbarism was not the only reason to flee England. The Great Plague raged through much of the country in 1665 and 1666, killing an estimated 100,000 people in London alone—almost a quarter of the city's population. In the village of Eyam, the Plague killed four out of five residents over fourteen months. Many English immigrants were desperately trying to get away from poverty, starvation, and overcrowding.

For all their talk of the new Jerusalem, the Pilgrims and Puritans were not explorers. They were refugees fleeing imprisonment, torture, and mutilation. In England, one Puritan writer, William Prynne, had his ears cut off and his forehead branded (burned with a red-hot iron) with the letters *SL*, which stood for *seditious libeler*. Another Puritan,

---

33   Sean McGlynn, "Violence and the Law in Medieval England," *History Today* 58, no. 4, April 2008, www. historytoday.com/print/10927.

34   Barbara W. Tuchman, *A Distant Mirror: The Calamitous 14th Century* (New York: Random House, 1978), p. 135.

John Lilburne, was flogged with a whip, dragged by an oxcart through London, and forced into a pillory. Others had their noses split or their tongues bored with hot irons.

In *Post Traumatic Slave Syndrome*, DeGruy asks, "Isn't it likely that many slaves were severely traumatized? Furthermore, did the trauma and the effects of such horrific abuse end with the abolition of slavery?" We need to ask these same questions about the English colonists who made their way to America. Isn't it likely that many of them were traumatized by the time they arrived here? Did over ten centuries of medieval brutality, which was inflicted on white bodies by other white bodies, begin to look like culture? Did this intergenerational trauma and its effects end with European immigrants' arrival in the New World?

The trauma that now lives in the bodies of so many African Americans did not begin when those bodies first encountered white ones. This trauma can be traced back much further, through generation upon generation of white bodies, to medieval Europe.

For America to outgrow the bondage of white-body supremacy, white Americans need to imagine themselves in Black bodies and experience what those bodies had to endure. They also need to do the same with the bodies of their own white ancestors. And they need to ask themselves this question: "If we don't address our ancient historical trauma, what will we pass down to our children, and to their children and grandchildren?"

When the English came to America, they brought much of their resilience, much of their brutality, and, I believe, a great deal of their trauma with them. Common punishments in the New World English colonies were similar to the punishments meted out in England, which included whipping, branding, and cutting off ears. People were routinely placed in stocks or pillories, or in the gallows with a rope around their neck. While they were thus immobilized, passersby would spit or throw garbage at them.

In America, the Puritans also regularly murdered other Puritans who were disobedient or found guilty of witchery. Powerful white bodies routinely punished less powerful white bodies. In 1692, during the Salem witch trials, eighty-year-old Giles Corey was stripped naked and, over a period of two days, slowly crushed to death under a pile of rocks.

I'll spare you further details of the ways in which the English in America, and their descendants, dislodged brains, blocked airways, ripped muscle, extracted organs, cracked bones, and broke teeth—those of Blacks, Native Americans, and other white colonists. However, here is what we need to recognize about this New World murder, cruelty, oppression, and torture: until the second half of the seventeenth century, these traumas were inflicted primarily on white bodies by other white bodies—all on what would become US soil. (There were some exceptions, most notably the war with the Pequot tribe in the 1630s.)

Throughout the United States's history as a nation, white bodies have colonized, oppressed, brutalized, and murdered Black and Native ones. But well before the United States began, powerful white bodies colonized, oppressed, brutalized, and murdered other, less powerful white ones. The carnage perpetrated on Blacks and Native Americans in the New World began, on the same soil, as an adaptation of longstanding white-on-white practices.[35] This brutalization created trauma that has yet to be healed among white bodies today.

*

As I observed earlier, trauma was not invented in the seventeenth century. It is as old as our species. But our concepts of whiteness, Blackness, and race *were* invented in the seventeenth century. While they seem self-evident to Americans today, these concepts would have appeared foreign and bizarre—even outright addled—to an American colonist in the early 1600s. Back then, no one used the term *white people*, other than perhaps as a descriptor (as in *white paint, white gloves, white hat*, etc.). Instead, there were English, Dutch, French, Spanish, and Portuguese colonists, and members of Indian tribes, such as the Pequot, Narragansett, Wampanoag, and Mohawk.

---

35   It is also notable that many colonists and their descendants felt entitled to push aside the millions of human beings who had already lived in the so-called New World for many centuries. This required a numbness to the deep suffering of a vast number of other people. Was this numbness, this dissociation, a traumatic freeze response?

Beginning in 1619, when people from Africa first set foot on American soil, there were also African indentured servants. Although the antecedents of what would eventually become white-body supremacy were already established, European colonists and their children did not think of themselves as belonging to the white race—or to any race.

Today we have a great bounty of written materials—books, pamphlets, diaries, letters, public records, etc.—penned by Americans in the 1600s. In all of these, we do not find the descriptive racialized phrases *white person, white woman,* or *white man* until the 1680s. It was only in the late seventeenth century that white Americans began in earnest to formalize a culture of white-body supremacy in order to soothe the dissonance that existed between more powerful and less powerful white bodies; to blow centuries of white-on-white trauma through millions of Black and red bodies; and to attempt to colonize the minds of people of all colors. The concept of "the Negro" was created to help white Americans deal with the hatred and brutality that they and their ancestors had themselves experienced for many generations at the hands of more powerful white bodies. The phantasm of race was conjured to help white people manage their fear and hatred of other white people. In the next chapter, we'll look more closely at how these efforts were strategically and systematically carried out.

—BODY PRACTICE—

For now, find a quiet, comfortable place where you can be alone for ten to fifteen minutes. Once you're settled, take a deep breath. Then consider the following questions:

When were your ancestors first declared Black or white (or Asian, or American Indian, or something else)? Who determined this? How was that determination communicated to your ancestors?

Where did this happen? What were the surrounding circumstances?

How did this categorization change your ancestors' immediate situation? How did it change their future?

How is your body responding to these questions? Where do you experience resistance or constriction? Where do you sense a recognition or affirmation?

Do these questions seem insightful and important, or stupid and pointless? Do you want to laugh, or cry, or cuss, or run away?

RE-MEMBERINGS

- Trauma was not invented in 1619. For thousands of years before that, human beings murdered, butchered, tortured, oppressed, abused, conquered, enslaved, and colonized one another.

- By the late 1600s the English controlled nearly all the colonized territory in what would become the United States. In England, the 1500s and 1600s were not gentle times. People were routinely burned at the stake, tortured, hung, and otherwise brutalized.

- Many of the English who fled to America were victims or first-hand observers of this brutality. Others were desperately trying to get away from poverty, starvation, overcrowding, and the Great Plague.

- It seems likely that many of the English colonists who made their way to America were deeply traumatized—and brought their trauma with them.

- Throughout America's history, white bodies have colonized, oppressed, and murdered Black ones. But well before the United States was founded, powerful white bodies colonized, oppressed, and murdered other white ones.

- Our concepts of whiteness, blackness, and race were invented in the seventeenth century. The terms *white person*, *white woman*, or *white man* did not appear until the 1680s.

- It was only in the late seventeenth century that white Americans began in earnest to formalize a culture of white-body supremacy.

- This culture was designed to blow centuries of trauma through millions of Black bodies and to attempt to colonize the minds of people of all colors.

- For America to outgrow the bondage of white-body supremacy, white Americans need to imagine themselves in Black, red, and brown bodies and *experience* what those bodies had to endure. They also need to do the same with the bodies of their own white ancestors.

CHAPTER 5

ASSAULTING THE BLACK HEART

*"I imagine one of the reasons people cling to their
hates so stubbornly is because they sense, once hate is gone,
they will be forced to deal with pain."*
JAMES BALDWIN

*"One doesn't have to operate with great malice to do great harm.
The absence of empathy and understanding are sufficient."*
CHARLES M. BLOW

"We ain't free. We just loose."
PAVIELLE

Race is a myth—something made up in the seventeenth century that
has been carried forward, day by day and century after century, into
the present. As Quinn Norton observes, "Whiteness is one of the
biggest and most long-running scams ever perpetrated." It's a classic

example of what therapists call *gaslighting*:[36] getting people to override their own experience and perceptions by repeating a lie over and over, and then "proving" it with still more lies, denials, and misdirection. Eventually, if the gaslighting is successful, the lies are widely accepted as truth—or even as essential facts of life, like birth, death, and gravity.

For all its fraudulence, however, race is a myth with teeth and claws, one that continues to tear bodies apart. Institutions, structures, beliefs, practices, and narratives have been created around it and have helped to perpetuate it. Until we recognize it for the collective delusion it is, it might as well be real.

Here is one of the many paradoxes of race: On the one hand, whiteness—and blackness, redness, and yellowness—are thought of as unchangeable attributes people are born with. Yet the definition of whiteness has changed many times over the past 300-plus years. At various periods in America's history, immigrants from Germany, Ireland, and Italy, as well as Jews from Eastern Europe, were considered non-white.[37] I don't just mean they were looked down on and mistreated, though they surely were. They were also formally and officially designated non-white by American laws, regulations, and policies, as well as in the American press. Phrases like "the Irish race" and "the Jewish race" were widely used and accepted. Multiple disciplines of science were regularly invoked to validate the ostensible truth, usefulness, and importance of racialized distinctions.

In short, the invention of race required much more than just the domination of Black (and red) bodies. It also required the creation of a deep conceptual divide—what my colleague Ariella Tilsen calls The Great Othering. As we have seen, this divide was not created until well after enslavement became a familiar part of colonial America.

---

36   The term *gaslighting* comes from a 1938 play, and films released in 1940 and 1944, called *Gas Light*. In them, a man attempts to convince his wife (and other people) that she is insane by manipulating small elements of her environment and insisting that she imagines things and remembers events incorrectly. One version of the film was released under the title *Angel Street*.

37   In March of 2017, I heard a listener who called in to a National Public Radio talk show explain that she wanted to support Muslims, but that she herself was white, not Muslim. As if, somehow, Christianity equaled whiteness and Islam equaled non-whiteness. Such is the endurance, ubiquity, and perniciousness of white-body supremacy. (For the record, in the United States, 79 percent of African Americans identify as Christian, while only 70 percent of white Americans do. Thirty percent of American Muslims report their race as white; 23 percent report it as Black.) See the Pew Research Center's study on US demographic groups and religious affiliations, at www.pewforum.org/2015/05/12/chapter-4-the-shifting-religious-identity-of-demographic-groups/ and www.people-press.org/2011/08/30/section-1-a-demographic-portrait-of-muslim-americans.

Enslavement itself changed greatly from the seventeenth century to the eighteenth. Originally, laborers were imported not only from Africa, but also from Scotland, Ireland, and England. These laborers, known as *bondsmen* or *indentured servants*, were employed for a specified number of years by wealthy landowners. After each laborer had fulfilled his or her contract of servitude, he or she would be given freedom, as well as a chunk of money or, sometimes, a small parcel of land.

Some laborers entered into these arrangements willfully. Some were tricked or forced into them, much like Solomon Northrup was two centuries later. Some bondsmen from the British Isles were convicts who were "pardoned" by being sold into servitude. When these bondsmen and women completed their contracts as servants, they became free peasants in the New World. This created a growing class of free peasants whose skin colors ranged from very pale to very dark.

In the late 1600s and early 1700s, these white and Black immigrants worked and lived together on plantations that were owned by powerful white male bodies. In fact, in several early worker revolts, Black and white people rose up together against plantation owners. These revolts posed serious threats to the power and supremacy of wealthy white landowners.

In response, these landowners (and other powerful white people) came up with a divide-and-conquer strategy. They gave white workers small parcels of land to work, thus essentially creating a peasant class in the New World. The land owners taught these white people, "You're just like us: you're white and you have land to work." They also gave some poor white people quasi-leadership positions as plantation overseers, providing them with some authority over Black bodies and lives. At the same time, they forbade Blacks from owning land, and told them, "You're Black, and you're completely unlike us." Powerful white people also created formal structures and institutions to reinforce these notions. Black bodies were deliberately presented as straw men for white bodies to blow their ancient historical trauma through. What had been white-on-white (or, usually, powerful-white-on-less-powerful-white) trauma was transformed, in carefully calculated fashion, into white-on-Black trauma, which was then institutionally enforced.

This was not an informal shift that resulted from slowly changing attitudes. *It was a deliberate strategy devised to create such changes.* Political leaders in Virginia legislated whiteness into existence in America, and thereafter quickly institutionalized it. The first such law appears to have been enacted in 1691.

Over the years, all of this proved effective in shifting the power divide from landowners versus workers to white people versus Black people. Today we would describe it as a work of evil genius. It undermined poor white folks' sense of identity and convinced them to fight against their own interests. It created a false settling in the bodies of many poor, white Americans. And it soothed some of the antipathy poor white people felt toward far more powerful and wealthy white landowners. To this day, many white Americans continue to live under the thumb of these delusions.

What made this strategy so profoundly effective and, ultimately, so enduring is that it simultaneously colonized and recolonized the minds, hearts, and bodies of everyone except prosperous landowners. Poor white Americans had no voting rights because they did not own land.[38] Nevertheless, they took pride in their status as white people, and routinely lorded this status over Black bodies. To maintain this status, many pledged their allegiance and subservience to plantation owners. (They were also well aware of the implied—and sometimes explicit— threat that they, too, could be enslaved, or have their meager privileges taken away, if wealthy white landowners so decreed.) Meanwhile, Black people were no longer permitted to own land and no longer able to work their way out of bondage after a specified number of years.[39]

---

[38] White men who did not own land were not granted the right to vote until much later—as early as 1792 in Kentucky and as late as 1856 in North Carolina. Women could not vote until 1920; Natives Americans not until 1924; and Chinese immigrants not until 1943. Residents of Washington, DC, could not vote in presidential elections until 1961. Voting rights for Black Americans and other non-white citizens were not guaranteed by law throughout the United States until 1965, after the passage of the Voting Rights Act. (As I write this in early 2017, strenuous efforts are under way in several states—most notably North Carolina, Texas, and Wisconsin—to *de facto* rescind this right for many non-white Americans through gerrymandering.)

[39] This is, of course, an extremely compressed sketch of a long string of events. For an eye-opening overview in under 3,000 words, I highly recommend Quinn Norton's article "How White People Got Made" (*The Message*, October 17, 2014, https://medium.com/message/how-white-people-got-made-6eeb076ade42#.7v5uq14ut). For a more detailed history of how whiteness was created, taught, and turned into a cultural norm, consider any one of these insightful books: Nell Irwin Painter's *The History of White People* (New York: W. W. Norton & Company, 2010), Noel Ignatiev's *How the Irish Became White* (Oxon, UK: Routledge, 1995), David R. Roedinger's *Working Toward Whiteness: How America's Immigrants Became White* (New York: Basic Books, 2005), and Matthew Frye Jacobson's *Whiteness of a Different Color: European Immigrants and the Alchemy of Race* (Cambridge, MA: Harvard University Press, 1998). Also interesting is Karen Brodkin's *How Jews Became White Folks and What That Says About Race in America* (New Brunswick, NJ: Rutgers University Press, 1998).

This strategy was not new. In many cases, white immigrants were doing what had been done to them (or their ancestors) in other countries before they came to America. If you look at what the English did to the Irish, for example, you will find many parallels, including Irishmen depicted as gorillas and the phrase "no Irish need apply" in many help-wanted ads. What do you think got passed down in the bodies of Irish Americans from one generation to the next, all without words or context?

This re-colonization soothed some of the long-held pain passed down from generation to generation in white bodies. It created a system that told poor white people, "You have been born into a club of privilege, and your descendants will be born into it as well." As a result, these white Americans were able to believe they had a claim to power and privilege that had eluded their ancestors. The irony, of course, was they were still second-class Americans, but now they had third-class Americans to beat down, look down upon, and collectively blow their own trauma through.

Dividing working-class Black and white people from each other was repeated with later waves of immigration: Italians, Irish, eastern European Jews, and other European immigrant groups were initially regarded as stupid, barbaric, and dangerous. Within a generation or two, however, each of these new white immigrant groups was socialized, colonized, and accepted by other Americans by being inducted into the false community of whiteness. One group (and one generation) of poor white people after another began to see their interests aligned with those of the ruling class.

It's not hard to see how this dynamic—the victimized becoming the victimizers—continues today. Nor is it difficult to recognize how many systems and institutions that reinforce this dynamic remain in place today.

As part of the re-colonization, white folks were told, "Whether we're rich or poor, we're all white, so there is no need for us to fight each other. Instead, we need to band together to fight the villains among us: Black bodies." Now there was an easily identifiable group that white

Americans, whether poor or rich, could blow their unmetabolized trauma through.

But trying to soothe trauma by blowing it through other human beings provides no healing. It offers only temporary relief from dirty pain. Meanwhile, in the process, it both increases the pain and passes it on to others. The essential nagging dissonance in and between white bodies doesn't disappear. Over time, the efforts to manage this dirty pain in white bodies, both individually and collectively, led to the ever-greater institutionalization of white-body supremacy—in science, history, economics, governance, courts, policing, education, employment, housing, medicine, psychology,[40] and just about everything else. (Today, many Americans are working hard at dismantling institutionalized white-body supremacy, while many other Americans are struggling to maintain it.)

We've been trained to think of the past in terms of a written historical record. But events don't just get written down; they get recorded and passed on in human bodies. Let's look at these events from the viewpoint of the body, through a somatic (body-centered) timeline. The past 1,500-plus years in North America can be broken into five somatic eras:

The Middle/Dark Ages (roughly 500 through 1500) For many generations prior to colonists' arrival in the New World, powerful English people routinely inflicted terrible punishments on other English bodies. Similar atrocities occurred in other countries in Europe. It was standard operating procedure for centuries.

The Native American Decimation and European Colony Era (roughly 1500 through 1610) European explorers made initial contact with Native Americans. Soon afterward, immigrants from England, Holland, Spain, Portugal, and France followed to establish colonies. Relations between some

---

40   One typical example: in 1851, white American physician Samuel Cartwright presented a paper before the Medical Association of Louisiana in which he described a mental illness he called *drapetomania*. This ostensible disorder—which, accordingly to Cartwright, only infected Black people—caused slaves to flee captivity rather than accept their subjugation. Cartwright proposed the preventive measure of "whipping the devil out of them." Other physicians suggested curing drapetomania by cutting off enslaved people's big toes.

colonists and some Native American tribes were cordial; between others they were tense or deadly. However, the main threat to Native people came from European diseases, against which Native Americans had little or no resistance. Illness swept through Native settlements in much the same way that plagues had swept through Europe. In 1618–1619, for example, smallpox killed 90 percent of the Native Americans living on or near Massachusetts Bay.

The Enslavement Era (1619 through 1865) The English became the dominant colonizers of the New World. English colonists forcibly imported Africans to North America and asserted dominion over them.[41] Colonists created whiteness, which enabled them to soothe the dissonance among white bodies; to delegitimize, dehumanize, and totemize Black ones; to create a culture of white-body supremacy; and to build institutions, processes, and relationships that maintained this culture. The white body became the standardized, normal body; other bodies, especially Black bodies, were defined as aberrant or substandard.

The Jim Crow Era (1877 through 1965) When the Thirteenth Amendment was ratified and enslavement became illegal in 1865, there was a brief period in which some racial barriers fell, and white bodies began to struggle with accepting Black bodies as normal and human. This trend reversed sharply in the south in 1877, when the first Jim Crow laws were enacted. These laws created and enforced the segregation of Black and white bodies, thus renewing and legitimizing the war on Black bodies. The laws also bolstered white-body supremacy through a variety of old and new institutions—most notably the lynching of nearly 3,500 Black bodies. Other less violent practices also directly affected Black

---

41   The trading of enslaved Africans was not only a New World industry, however. Businesses from many European countries, including England, France, Holland, Spain, Portugal, and Sweden sold and shipped enslaved Africans. Other businesses built ships, sold insurance, and created other industries around the trade of enslaved people from Africa.

bodies. For example, Black people were not allowed to kiss or show affection in public, and Black men were not permitted to offer to shake the hand of any white person.

The Neo-Crow Era (1966 through the present) In 1965, segregation became illegal throughout the United States, and for the next two decades the Civil Rights movement lessened some of the overt dissonance between white and Black bodies. It did not, however, soothe the centuries-old dissonance that still existed between poor white bodies and powerful white ones.

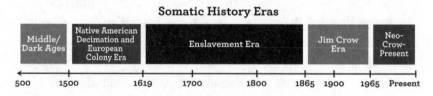

Figure 2. Somatic History Eras

In the early 1980s, another reversal started. As part of a major escalation of the War on Drugs, Black bodies began to be arrested, tried, and jailed in unprecedented numbers, even though Black people used illegal drugs at rates similar to white people. The US prison population exploded, from 300,000 to over two million, mostly through drug convictions. Today, almost 40 percent of people incarcerated for drug law violations are Black, even though Black Americans make up about 13 percent of the country's population.

The Great Othering around the imaginary concept of race continues today in many other forms. It is routinely practiced in *de facto* segregation in neighborhoods and schools, in discrimination in the workplace, through the practices discussed in previous chapters, and in a variety of less obvious ways. In Chapter 6, we'll look at how white-body supremacy continues to routinely violate Black bodies. But for now, let's focus on how white-body supremacy persistently assaults the psyches, souls, and hearts of African Americans—often in trauma-inducing ways.

I've already noted some of the obvious discriminatory assaults, such as employers' distrust of African American names; drivers being regularly pulled over by police, often for no offense at all (a.k.a. Driving While Black); and repeated efforts by one of the largest American television networks to blame, chastise, belittle, and shame many African Americans. (This is in addition to the endeavors of more overtly white supremacist groups, movements, and media.) This institutionalized white-body supremacy doesn't just affect the psyches of Black folks. It has a corrosive effect on their bodies as well.

Subtler forms of violation also remain integral to American culture. Three of the most common and pervasive are everyday stressors, micro-aggressions, and a lack of regard.

Everyday stressors are the extra difficulties African Americans have to handle, address, or work around on an ongoing basis. When my completely normal and law-abiding teenage son leaves for school in the morning, I watch him until he gets on the bus, to be sure the police don't confront and harass him. When I get on a crowded elevator and white people immediately move their phones and handbags out of my reach, I have to let go of my disgust and override my impulse to cuss them out. When I shop and get followed or eyed suspiciously by a store clerk, I have to nod politely, ignore the surveillance, override the gripping sensation in my neck and the heat in my face, and squelch the impulse to scream, "Leave me the hell alone!"

Micro-aggressions are the small but persistent and pervasive ways in which white people deliberately (though often unconsciously) express their disdain for Black bodies. When a cashier places change into a white shopper's hand but drops it into mine from an inch above, that's a micro-aggression. When a sales clerk assists a white customer before me, even though I walked in first, that's another. When I try to hail a taxi and an available one sails past me, then stops to pick up a white man or woman a block away, that's another one.

Perhaps the most damaging, yet least visible, assault on Black hearts is an ongoing lack of human regard. Here are some ways in which white Americans routinely fail to show regard to Black human beings:

- Not listening or paying attention to someone, or outright ignoring them, as if Black bodies were invisible.

- Interrupting or talking over Black people.

- Not taking someone seriously (for example, saying, "You don't really mean that," or "You don't really think that," or "You don't really feel that way," or "It's wrong to feel that way").

- Giving a brief, perfunctory, minimalist, or noncommittal response (such as "Fine—whatever you say" or "Yes, I care. I need to go now").

- Refusing to acknowledge someone's lived experience, either by denying that it happened or by fleeing into statistics or legalisms.

- Acting visibly frustrated and impatient with someone, as if his or her presence is burdensome, or as if what he or she is saying is childish or ludicrous.

- Saying, "Be reasonable," then demanding something unreasonable or impossible.

- Speaking words of care or concern, but without empathy or sincerity. This is especially common among police and elected officials when dealing with racialized issues and with crimes committed against African Americans. For instance, a police chief may say, "We've got to do a better job at training our officers so they avoid racial profiling," but in such a way that the actual, unspoken message becomes, "I'm saying the words I'm required to say, but they're just for show. I intend to continue with business as usual."

The main messages behind all of these are the same: first, *You're not important*; and, second, *This bullshit I'm doing right now—I and others like me are going to keep doing it indefinitely*. People experience these vibratory messages in their bodies. For many African Americans, they are achingly familiar.

Everyone, no matter what their skin color, experiences such minor violations occasionally. When they occur only now and then, they are easy enough to shrug off as tolerable, then heal from and forget. But when these violations happen repeatedly (whether over months for an individual or centuries for a group), in many different situations and with many different people, over time they create the toxic hazy trauma described in Chapter 3.

—BODY PRACTICE—

As before, find a quiet, comfortable place where you can be alone.

Allow five to ten minutes for each of the following four activities. Feel free to do them on separate occasions, all at once, or in any combination.

1. ***Think back to an incident in which you felt you were the target of a micro-aggression.*** The incident does not need to involve race (or people of more than one race). Any mild, passive-aggressive move qualifies as a micro-aggression.

   Replay this incident in your mind from beginning to end. When and how did the event turn ugly (if it did)? When and how did you recognize it as a micro-aggression?

   Now replay the event again. This time, focus on your body and its reactions. At what point does it tell you that something is wrong? How does it let you know this? When, where, and how does it experience pain or discomfort? Where, when, and how does it feel good? Constrict? Move or activate? Release?

2. ***Recall an incident in which you*** committed ***a micro-aggression against someone else, either deliberately or unconsciously.*** Again, it does not need to involve race. Any mild passive-aggressiveness counts as a micro-aggression.

Replay the incident in your mind from beginning to end. What did you say, do, and observe? What did the other person (or people) say and do?

At what point did you plan the micro-aggression, or realize that you had already committed one?

Now relive the entire incident again, paying close attention to your body. When, where, and how does it experience pain or discomfort? When, where, and how does it feel good? Constrict? Move or activate? Release?

3. *Think back to an interaction in which you experienced a lack of regard from someone else.* In your mind's eye, relive that interaction from beginning to end. Then replay it, paying close attention to your body. What sensations did you experience when you first recognized the other person's lack of regard? Where, when, and how does it experience pain or discomfort? Where, when, and how does it feel good? Constrict? Move or activate? Release?

4. *Recall an interaction in which you expressed a lack of regard for another human being in his or her presence.* Review the incident in your mind from beginning to end. At what point could you experience that lack of regard in your body? How and where did you experience it?

Replay the event once more. This time, focus on what your body experiences from moment to moment. Where, when, and how does it experience pain or discomfort? Where, when, and how does it feel good? Constrict? Move or activate? Release?

The hearts, psyches, and souls of African Americans have also been routinely attacked by another group: ourselves. Many African

Americans berate themselves—and each other—for being Black, for being too Black, for not being Black enough, for being less than perfect, or simply for existing. We compare our bodies against the ostensibly superior qualities of white ones, using the brown paper bag test, the blue vein test, the fine-tooth comb test, the lip size test, and so on.

Oppressed people often internalize the trauma-based values and strategies of their oppressors. These values and strategies need to be consciously noticed, called out as traumatic retentions, and challenged. Black Americans need to do this with other Black Americans; Native Americans need to do it with other Native Americans; American Jews need to do it with other American Jews; and so on. These values and strategies then need to be unlearned, not just by the thinking brain, but by the body, through its ongoing relationships with other healing bodies.

White-body supremacy lives in the bodies of most Americans, including many African Americans. Many of our bodies hold the patently false images, concepts, and felt sense discussed earlier. They create Black self-hate and self-repulsion, which are both trauma responses: attempts to manage the underlying discomfort and confusion, rather than to metabolize it in the body and move through it.

African American self-hate plays out in multiple ways. The first involves us disrespecting and distrusting each other in everyday interactions—deeming each other worthless, inflicting violence on other Black bodies in the same neighborhood, calling each other by the n-word, comparing ourselves to monkeys, and so on. The second involves prominent African Americans trying to renounce their Blackness (for example, Clarence Thomas and Ben Carson), or publicly denouncing supportive or benign aspects of African American culture (like Stacey Dash). In many of us, this self-hate lives so deep in our bodies that our thinking brains are unaware of it. Because white-body supremacy has been standardized, it operates unquestioned—and often invisibly.

A sobering example of this effect involves Malcolm Gladwell, usually one of our clearest, most levelheaded thinkers. Gladwell's mother is Black; his father is white. When writing *Blink: The Power of Thinking without Thinking*, Gladwell took the Implicit Association Test, which measures a person's unconscious assumptions and associations. Gladwell discovered, to his dismay, that *he* had unconscious negative associations with Black skin.[42]

Another fairly common traumatic retention is a reticence to own a home or a business, or even to be part of a startup food coop. It's not hard to see how people whose ancestors were considered property would not be delighted by the concept of ownership. This attitude has more recent origins as well. As Repa Mekha, CEO of the community-building organization Nexus Community Partners, told me, "During the late nineteenth and early twentieth centuries, Black business owners in the South were routinely threatened, beaten, and sometimes lynched when they dared to compete against white-owned businesses." More recently, an unusually large number of African Americans lost their homes in the Great Recession, because in the run-up to the financial collapse, Black Americans were twice as likely as white Americans to be given subprime loans.

Arguably, African Americans' most pernicious traumatic retention involves successful African Americans who look down on—and sometimes mistreat—their less well-off brothers and sisters. This is yet another holdover from plantation life. Typically, plantation owners and their families treated Black servants who worked (and sometimes lived) in the plantation family's home marginally better than they treated Black field workers. House servants were still considered property and were routinely bought, sold, beaten, raped, and sometimes murdered; but their white owners saw them as inherently superior to field hands. Some Black house servants internalized this false superiority and lorded it over men and women who worked the fields. This attitude lives on in some African American psyches today, though few who hold it realize its origins.

*

---

42   Malcolm Gladwell, *Blink: The Power of Thinking without Thinking* (New York: Little, Brown and Company, 2005), pp. 82–84.

My grandmother was a kind and gracious woman—most of the time. Despite her painful upbringing, she was not quick to anger. When other people were happy or received good news, she was happy for them and never jealous. If there was somebody she didn't like, it was usually for a good reason. Either the person had done something that would make any reasonable human being angry, or that person was generally unpleasant to be around.

But there was one group of people my grandmother spoke of with disdain: dark-skinned brothers and sisters. She would shake her head and say of a neighbor, "She looks like *such* an African." Once I overheard her say to my mom about one of my friends, "That boy is *blaaaaaack*. Straight outta Africa."

When I heard her say such things, I'd get angry and bewildered. How could she diss our friends and neighbors for their skin color or other physical features? Surely she knew better. This was years before I understood that my grandmother was acting out a traumatic retention known as *colorism*—a form of internalized Black self-hate that reflects white-body supremacy's elevation of lighter skin over darker skin.[43]

My mother would have none of it. "Mama," she would say, "You can think what you like, but don't do that around the kids. That is hateful, Mama, and we have enough of it already from white folks. We don't need to do it to each other."

"I'm just sayin," my grandmother would start.

"*Mama*," my mother would say with great emphasis, and the discussion would be over.

That pushback from my mother—and her steadfast refusal to pass on any of her mother's Black self-hatred to me and my brothers—was hugely healing. It created a little bit of extra room for me to grow up resilient, healthy, and able to feel regard for the Black body. Instead of self-hate, my mother taught me to see Blackness as an asset. Her

---

43   The elevation of light skin over dark skin occurs as both an opposition and a continuum. There is of course the basic, obvious duality of white as good, pure, and true, and dark as bad, impure, and corrupt. But there is also a continuum, with whiteness (and purity and goodness) at one end and darkness (and dirtiness and evil) at the other. The continuum begins with the blonde-haired, blue-eyed WASP and ends with the jet-black African. In between are all other gradations of skin color. Somewhere in the middle, near "swarthy" Greeks and Egyptians, are most Jews and Muslims—even those with blonde hair and blue eyes. If a Jew or Muslim has dark skin, however, his or her skin color, rather than religion, determines his or her place on this continuum. You may recognize colorism as an inherited form of *Stockholm Syndrome* or *capture bonding*, in which a captive develops a psychological alliance with his or her captors as a survival strategy.

resilience helped me mitigate the white-body supremacy and Black self-hate that were all around me. Today, when I look in the mirror, I see an African face and body, and I feel good about them. I do my best to reinforce these positive feelings in my children, my nieces and nephews, and my other kinfolk.

Because of that small amount of room for growth my mother helped create in my life and in my nervous system, I was able to become a therapist, a trainer, a speaker, and (I hope) a good husband and father. It has also enabled me to pass down some of my own resilience to my children. With my now-grown daughter Brittney and my teenage son Tezara, I do my best to create still more room for growth in their nervous systems, so each of them can live a life that's even bigger and fuller than mine.

I loved my grandmother every moment of my life. I still do. I know she did not invent the racialized trauma that both white and Black people blew threw her. None of those people, or their parents, or their grandparents, or many generations of their ancestors, invented this trauma. It was passed down and passed down and passed down. It is now up to us—to you and to me and to everyone else who cares about human beings—to put a stop to this cycle of trauma. This means metabolizing the trauma in *our* bodies. It means accepting and moving through clean pain, individually and communally.

—BODY PRACTICE—

Find a comfortable, quiet spot where you can be alone for about ten minutes.

Think back to a recent time when you overheard a Black man or woman denigrating another Black person for their Blackness, or for their ostensibly Black behavior. Think of a monologue, discussion, or argument, not just the offhand use of a derogatory term.

Recall where you were when this event took place. Then imagine yourself back in that place and replay the incident from beginning to end, paying close attention to your body.

At each moment, what does your body experience? When, where, and how does it experience pain or discomfort? Where, when, and how does it feel good? Constrict? Relax? Want to move or activate?

At any point, do you have the urge to speak up, interrupt, or step in? How does your body experience this urge? How do you respond to it? Do you do something, or do you override the urge?

What does your body experience when the incident is over?

Trauma is not destiny. It can look like destiny when people choose to blow their trauma through others. But when you make a deliberate choice not to pass on your trauma to others, that choice begins to mend some of the trauma. It changes what looks like a destiny of dirty pain into an experience of clean pain. Clean pain has a healing and transformative capacity that dirty pain does not.

By protecting others—especially our young children—from our trauma, we offer them safety and the opportunity to build resilience. They can then pass these down to the next generation. We create more room for growth in their nervous systems by first creating more room in our own.

When we heal our own trauma, individually and collectively, we don't just heal our bodies. By refusing to pass on the trauma we inherited, we help heal the world.

My grandmother never mended all of her own trauma. But, with the exception of the way she would disrespect very dark-skinned people, she also took care to never pass on any of it to us. She was often nervous and fearful, but she never tried to get others to share her anxiety and fear. Instead, she did her best to make other family members happy. She usually succeeded, too.

She spent many hours cooking for us. She offered us comfort, caring, love, and appreciation. For many years, her entire extended family spent Christmas Day at her home. Each year she created an experience that was generous, joyful, and healing. And she had a knack for doing small things that made a difference.

When my son Tezara was little, we visited my grandmother often. Tezara spent a lot of time running around my grandmother's yard—and, when it was cold outside, from room to room in her house. During most visits, there was a moment when Tezara would suddenly stop, turn, and look across the room at his great-grandmother. For an instant, their eyes would meet, and my grandmother would smile. Time stopped. I would see the love pass between them—an aging, caramel-skinned queen and a prince in sneakers and a sweatshirt. Then the world would resume, and Tezara would be off on his next adventure.

In that shared, intimate glance, love traveled across many generations. It traveled into the past, through all the ancestors who had helped my grandmother become who she was. It traveled forward, through my mother, then through me and my wife, and into Brittney and Tezara who, I hope, will someday pass on that simple act of healing to their own children.

RE-MEMBERINGS

- Race is a myth, but a myth with teeth and claws. Institutions, structures, beliefs, and narratives have been created around it. Until we recognize it for the collective delusion it is, it might as well be real.

- The definition of whiteness has changed many times over the past three centuries. At various periods in America's history, immigrants from Germany, Ireland, and Italy, as well as Jews from Eastern Europe, were considered non-white.

- In the late 1600s and early 1700s, white and Black immigrants worked and lived together on plantations and repeatedly rose up together against plantation owners. In response, landowners gave white workers small parcels of land and said, "You're like us; you're white and you own land." In other cases, they appointed poor white people to quasi-leadership positions that gave them authority over Black bodies and lives.

- Over the years, the power divide shifted from landowners versus workers to white folks versus Black folks.

- The colonization of minds and bodies soothed some of the long-held pain that had been passed down from generation to generation in white bodies. Poor white Americans were increasingly able to believe they had a claim to power and privilege that had eluded their ancestors.

- There was now an easily identifiable group that white people—whether poor or rich—could blow their unmetabolized trauma through.

- This dirty pain became institutionalized as white-body supremacy—in governance, courts, policing, education, employment, housing, and so on.

- Dividing working-class Black and white people from each other was repeated with later waves of immigrants. Italians, Irish, Eastern European Jews, and other European immigrant groups were initially regarded as stupid, barbaric, dangerous, and, most of all, non-white. Within a generation or two, however, each group was colonized, socialized, and absorbed into the false community of whiteness.

- The Black heart, soul, and psyche continue to be violated in many ways today, including through everyday stressors, micro-aggressions, and a lack of regard.

- Many African Americans berate themselves—and each other—for being Black, for being too Black, for not being Black enough, for being less than perfect, or simply for existing. This self-hate lives so deep in many of our bodies that our thinking brains are completely unaware of it.

- Trauma is not destiny. It can look like destiny when people choose to blow their trauma through others. But when you make a deliberate choice not to pass on your trauma to others, that choice begins to heal some of the trauma.

- By protecting others from our trauma, we offer them safety and the opportunity to build resilience, both of which can then be passed down to the next generation.

CHAPTER 6

VIOLATING THE BLACK BODY

"When the color of your skin is seen as a weapon,
you will never be seen as unarmed."

SIGN CARRIED BY A BLACK LIVES MATTER ACTIVIST

"I'm terrified at the moral apathy—the death of the heart which
is happening in my country. These people have deluded themselves
for so long, that they really don't think I'm human.
I base this on their conduct, not on what they say."[44]

JAMES BALDWIN

"Indeed, in America there is a strange and powerful belief that
if you stab a black person ten times, the bleeding stops and the
healing begins the moment the assailant drops the knife."

TA-NEHISI COATES

"This country does not like Black people very much."

BOMANI JONES

---

44   James Baldwin, *I Am Not Your Negro* (New York: Vintage Books, 2017), p. 39.

One night my wife and I sat on the sofa, cuddling and watching television. It had been a long, stressful day, and it felt good to relax together. Our thirteen-year-old son Tezara was upstairs in his room, playing a video game. The national news came on. The lead story, from Cleveland, was about the shooting of a young Black boy, Tamir Rice, who had been playing alone in a park with a toy gun, and the manhandling of his sister, Tajai.

Maria's hand closed tightly around mine.

The newscaster explained that the shooting was not random. The shots were fired by an on-duty policeman. The patrolmen drove up in a police car and stopped a few feet from Rice; one immediately leaped out and wordlessly shot Rice dead.

I felt my throat constrict. I looked at Maria, who let go of my hand and pulled her forearm across her belly. Her eyes were tearing up.

We both shared the same thought. While we live in a different Midwestern city from the Rice family, this boy could have easily been our son.

I heard myself shout, "*God damn.* Those dirty motherfuckas. Watch. They're going to get away with shooting that baby. Fuck them."

A wave of helplessness washed over me. I thought, *I can't protect my son from this. I can't protect my wife or my grown daughter from it. I can't even protect myself from it.*

My jaws clenched, and a sharp pain shot from my gut across the left part of my heart. Tears welled up in my eyes.

I had to see my son. I went upstairs and knocked on his door.

"Come in," he said.

I opened the door. Tezara was focused on his Xbox, playing Minecraft. I stood in the doorway and watched him play. He was happy, absorbed, unaware.

Finally, I said, "Wassup?"

He didn't look up. "Nothin. Whatcha want?"

I thought, *I want you to be safe. I want to not have to watch you every weekday morning, to make sure you're okay, until you climb onto the school bus. I want to trust our police instead of fear them. I want you to be able to play in a public park and not have someone put a bullet in your body. I want you to live to be a man, not end up like Trayvon Martin, Tamir Rice, and Emmett Till.*

*

The man who shot and killed Tamir Rice, white police officer Timothy Loehmann, was never charged with a crime. Since that shooting, many have argued for and against Loehmann's innocence. But putting Loehmann in jail—or letting him go free—won't help us understand what actually happened. Nor will it help us move beyond our own collective dirty pain surrounding the murder. Instead, let's look at Rice's murder from the wordless, thoughtless viewpoint of the body:

> A white body with centuries of traumatic dissonance in its DNA encountered a Black body. The white body experienced reflexive fear. In a fraction of a second, this fear activated the white body's unmetabolized historical trauma, which in turn reflexively triggered a fight, flee, or freeze response. The white body destroyed the Black body—a body that it feared was dangerous and imagined was impervious to pain. This was exactly what the body was conditioned and trained to do.

Dark-skinned immigrants to the US sometimes ask, "Why are so many of us doing well after being here only a few years, while so many African Americans are doing badly, even though their ancestors were here for centuries?" When asked out of genuine curiosity and concern, rather than hatred or dismissiveness, it's a valid question—and an important one.

The answer to why so many of us have difficulties is because our ancestors spent centuries here under unrelentingly brutal conditions. Generation after generation, our bodies stored trauma and intense survival energy, and passed these on to our children and grandchildren. Most of us also passed down resilience and love, of course. But, as we saw with my grandmother—and as we see with so many other human beings—resilience and love aren't sufficient to completely heal all trauma. Often, at least some of the trauma continues.

For well over 300 years, the Black body in America has been systematically brutalized, mutilated, murdered, abused, controlled, raped, objectified, and demonized by guns, whips, chains, and manacles; by shootings, lynchings, and rape; by laws, policies, social norms, and codes of behavior; and by images and concepts. For centuries, trauma upon trauma compounded.

A second answer is that the great majority of immigrants—even many of those fleeing persecution, tyranny, or war—made the choice to come to America. They were allowed to keep their languages, their religions, their origin stories, and their symbols. Up to a point, they were permitted to keep their cultures. Although not all were allowed to keep their own names, they all maintained the right to name their children.

In contrast, our African American ancestors were kidnapped, sold as property, transplanted here as cargo against their will, given new names and identities, and often not permitted to name or raise their own children. They were severed from their families, their communities, and their own bodies.

*

Here are some of the most pervasive images and concepts created by white-body supremacy surrounding the Black body:

- The Black body is dangerous and threatening.

- The Black body is impervious to pain.

- The Black body is incredibly strong and resilient—almost invulnerable.

- The Black body is hypersexual.

- The Black body is dirty.

- The Black body is unattractive, especially in comparison with the white body.

- Therefore, the Black body needs to be managed and controlled—by any means necessary.

Except among members of white supremacist groups such as the KKK and the Aryan Nations, these concepts are not attitudes, cognitive beliefs, ideas, or philosophies. They are far simpler and far more primitive. They are nonverbal sensations felt by white bodies, along with fear, hate, and constriction. Or, to put it another way, they are nonverbal stories white bodies tell each other. Even to call them concepts isn't accurate. *Sensations* or *impressions* come closer.

These sensations or impressions are demonstrably untrue, irrational, and, in some cases, literally impossible. But bodies—white, Black, and otherwise—don't care about what's rational, possible, or true. They just want to experience safety. And they don't distinguish between genuine threats, possible threats, and imaginary threats; they have been conditioned to fight or flee.

When such sensations are embedded in a white body, that body experiences discomfort and a lack of safety in the presence of a Black body, especially an unfamiliar one. As a result, when many white American bodies encounter Black bodies, the white bodies automatically constrict, and their lizard brains go on high alert. Most forms of dialogue, diversity training, and other cognitive interventions are going to have little effect on this reflexive fear response, because the white body has been trained to respond in this noncognitive way.

Today, these sensations and impressions continue to drive the behavior of many white Americans—even many good-hearted ones—as well as many American institutions. They explain, at least in part:

- The high arrest, conviction, and incarceration rates of African Americans, especially for nonviolent crimes.

- The high rate of killings of African Americans by police (who often shoot unarmed or unresisting people, then later say, "I feared for my life").

- Widespread racial profiling.

- The disproportionate—and often violent—police responses to dark-skinned people (including children) who get change at a bus station, play in the park, bring a homemade clock to school, don't put away their cell phones, drive with a broken tail light, or simply walk down a sidewalk.

• White bodies that see a Black body in distress, but do little or nothing to help—and may not even notice (or care about) their distress.

• The creation of institutions, media outlets, and social norms that encourage the reflexive constriction of white bodies in discussions of race, or in the presence of Black bodies.

• White bodies that lock their car doors, cover their purses with their arms, or hurry away when a Black body approaches.

• Police who, when called to an incident, reflexively tackle, shoot, or arrest African Americans, but merely take white people aside and ask them questions.

• The transformation of police departments in many African American neighborhoods into occupying forces.

• The enormous growth of the prison-industrial complex over the past twenty-five years.

*

When two or more unfamiliar bodies first encounter one another, each body tends to either relax in recognition or constrict in self-protection. This happens quickly, automatically, and often unconsciously. Typically, each body goes briefly on alert while its lizard brain discerns, ASAP, whether the other body is safe or dangerous. In an instant, it scans hundreds of clues to make that determination: the other body's size, posture, clothing, speed of approach; what the body is saying or doing; the vibrations it seems to be giving out; the expression on the person's face; and so on.

One shortcut the lizard brain uses to make this determination is by asking, *How closely does this body match mine?* It's no surprise, then, that many white bodies relax when they encounter other unfamiliar white bodies, but constrict when they encounter unknown Black ones. This results in the following common situations:

- When a Black body violates a rule, one white body reflexively deputizes another to bring the Black body under control.

- After police have cornered or tackled an African American, they often back off when a white person steps in and says, "It's okay, officers. Thanks, but you're not needed here. Everything's fine."

- When a white person enters a room and suddenly realizes that everyone else in the room is Black, they may reflexively pause, look around, and carefully evaluate whether the situation is safe.

- When a large number of Black bodies move into a traditionally white neighborhood, many white bodies move out, in a collective response called (appropriately) *white flight*.

The same thing often happens in Black bodies, of course; they may relax in the presence of other unfamiliar Black bodies, and constrict in the presence of unknown white (or non-Black) ones. It's the same self-protective response. But, unlike white Americans, African Americans don't have widespread, formalized institutions to soothe this constriction and discomfort.

—BODY PRACTICES—

The following activities are designed for white (and other non-Black) readers: Imagine yourself in each of the following situations, one situation at a time. Pay close attention to what you experience in your body in each moment. In particular, notice any constriction or relaxation.

1. You are invited to an African American coworker's wedding reception. When you arrive—a bit late—you discover that you are one of over 300 other guests. As you stand in the doorway, you scan the room. You are the only non-Black person in the hall. Even the servers are all Black.

Stop. What are you experiencing in your body? What thoughts are going through your head?

You feel a hand touch your shoulder. You turn and see an unfamiliar face: a smiling, middle-aged Black man. He says, laughing a bit, "Go on in. We don't bite."

Pause for a moment. What do you notice in your body right now? What urges do you experience?

2. Your son (or brother, father, or other male family member) has been telling you about Clarissa, his new fiancée, for the past few weeks. Several times he has told you how loving, smart, beautiful, and funny she is. He has said that she is several years older than him, but he has not told you her exact age, or shown you her picture.

One day he invites you to dinner with him and Clarissa at a nearby restaurant. You accept. When you arrive and spot him at a table, he is looking with great admiration at the woman next to him. She seems equally enamored with him.

She is Black—and very dark-skinned. She has long dreadlocks and wears a dashiki. As you near the table, you also realize that she is seated in a wheelchair.

Stop and notice what you experience in your body right now.

3. As you drive home from work, the car in front of you hits a large pothole and veers to the right. You slow down, expecting the car to return to the center of the road, but it doesn't. It continues onto the sidewalk, crosses a lawn and a driveway, and smacks hard into a tree with a resounding *thunk*.

You pull over, get out, and hurry to the damaged car. As you reach it, the driver's door opens and a man stumbles out. He is scowling—and he is very tall, very buff, very tattooed, and Black.

Pause and notice what you sense in your body right now.

4. The following activity requires doing something in real life.

Visit a physically safe place you know will be populated with a lot of Black bodies. Have dinner at an African restaurant. Attend a worship service at an African American church or mosque. Go to a performance of a hip hop artist, or a Black theater troupe, or an African musical group on an American tour. Throughout the experience, periodically pause and pay attention to your body. What is it experiencing? What urges and thoughts arise?

A week or two later, go to a different physically safe place filled with Black bodies. Once again pay attention to your body, moment by moment. Does it feel or react differently this time?

This is not a cultural immersion exercise. It's about noticing what you experience in your body in real time.

RE-MEMBERINGS

- Some of the most pervasive images, sensations, and impressions of the Black body include:
    - The Black body is dangerous and threatening.
    - The Black body is impervious to pain.
    - The Black body is incredibly strong and resilient—almost invulnerable.
    - The Black body is hypersexual.
    - The Black body is dirty.
    - The Black body is unattractive, especially in comparison with the white body.
    - Therefore, the Black body needs to be managed and controlled—by any means necessary.
- When these images, sensations, and impressions are embedded in a white body, that body feels unsafe and

uncomfortable in the presence of a Black body, especially an unfamiliar one. As a result, when many white American bodies encounter Black bodies, the white bodies automatically constrict, and their lizard brains go on high alert.

- When two or more unfamiliar bodies first encounter one another, each body goes on alert while its lizard brain discerns, ASAP, whether the other body is safe or dangerous. One shortcut the lizard brain uses to make this determination is by asking, *How closely does this body match mine?* The lizard brain then tells the body to either relax in recognition or constrict in self-protection. Both white and Black bodies often do this.

CHAPTER 7

THE FALSE FRAGILITY
OF THE WHITE BODY

"The ultimate measure of a man is not where he stands in moments of comfort and convenience, but where he stands at times of challenge and controversy."

MARTIN LUTHER KING, JR.

"The power of the white world is threatened whenever a black man refuses to accept the white world's definitions."

JAMES BALDWIN

"Why do so many of you reflexively defend, identify with, and antagonize on behalf of whiteness whenever blackness is involved?"

JESSE WILLIAMS

The notion of Black fearsomeness and invulnerability requires its mirror image: the fantasy of white fragility.[45] For centuries, white

---

45   The term was coined by Robin DiAngelo in her article "White Fragility," *International Journal of Critical Pedagogy* 3, no. 3 (2011): 54–70.

Americans have lived under a strange and contradictory delusion: *Black bodies are incredibly strong and frightening and impervious to pain. They can handle anything short of total destruction. But white bodies are extremely weak and vulnerable, especially to Black bodies. So it's the job of Black bodies to care for white bodies, soothe them, and protect them—particularly from other Black bodies.* White bodies have lived by this myth, and allowed it to guide their behavior, for many generations.

Cognitively, the myth makes no sense; it boils down to *I need you to protect me from you.* But our bodies don't give a damn about sense. They accept whatever they feel will help them survive and stay safe. For hundreds of years, the myth has been reinforced by a second fantasy, which became the rationale for oppression and carnage: *Because white bodies are so vulnerable to Black ones, when a Black body is not subservient to a white one, it must be brutalized or destroyed. There can be no mercy, no second thoughts, and no halfway measures. Because Black bodies are nearly invulnerable, that brutality and destruction must be swift, and it must be ruthless.*

Two centuries ago, there was a deliberate strategy behind these fantasies: It helped destroy solidarity between Black and white farmhands; created bonds between rich land owners and poor white workers; and enabled everyone to tell at a glance who was to be feared, who was to be served, and who was to do the serving. This strategy created a set of standards for how people were to interact and be with each other. Thus, over time, white-body supremacy became the standard order of things.

Historically, the myth was most visible on (but was not limited to) plantations where enslaved Africans served as cooks, wet nurses, nannies, and victims of sexual exploitation by white plantation owners and their families. We continue to see it just as systemically today—in hospitals, nursing homes, assisted living facilities, and childcare centers, where a high percentage of caregivers are Black. It is also no accident that, in the twenty-first century, large numbers of African Americans work as cooks, private-care nurses and aides, and prostitutes.

The myth of white fragility thus provided white bodies with the necessary justification to act on their strongly felt need to dominate, control, and brutalize Black ones. White bodies *felt* that maintaining these power dynamics was essential to their survival. The myth of white fragility emboldened many generations of white bodies to harm Black ones, and to excuse and legitimize that harm, under the guise of providing safety for white bodies.

Today we've partly dismantled some of the older, most overt structures of institutionalized white-body supremacy, but many have reappeared in a subtler, legitimized, widespread way. The myth of the fragility of white bodies and the corresponding fear of Black ones live on.

The deadliest manifestation of white fragility is its reflexive confusion of fear with danger and comfort with safety. When a white body feels frightened by the presence of a Black one—whether or not an actual threat exists—it may lash out at the Black body in what it senses as necessary self-protection. Often this is a fight, flee, or freeze response triggered by the activation of the ancient trauma that began as white-on-white violence in Europe centuries ago.

In some cases, when a white body simply experiences discomfort, its lizard brain may interpret this as a lack of safety and react with violence. Thus white fragility grants permission to white and police bodies to regularly kill Black ones—even unarmed, unresistant ones— in ostensible self-defense ("I feared for my life," "I thought his wallet was a gun," and so on).

Another form of white fragility involves the strong and immediate defensive response whenever a white body is challenged on the subject of race and equity, or whenever the topic of race is raised, implied, or even hinted at. Robin DiAngelo describes this reaction well:

> White Fragility is a state in which even a minimum amount of racial stress becomes intolerable, triggering a range of defensive moves. These moves include the outward display of emotions such as anger, fear, and guilt, and behaviors such as argumentation, silence, and leaving the stress-inducing situation. . . . This insulated environment of racial privilege builds white expectations for racial comfort while at the same time lowering the ability to tolerate racial stress.[46]

---

46   Robin DiAngelo, "White Fragility," *International Journal of Critical Pedagogy* 3, no. 3 (2011): 54.

These defensive moves include forms of fighting, fleeing, or freezing and, occasionally, verbally annihilating. Collectively, these—along with the emotions DiAngelo describes—can bypass the thinking parts of the brain. Here are some common ways in which white Americans use white fragility to avoid facing their unhealed trauma:

- **False compatriotism:** "I'm Jewish, or Muslim, or lesbian, or trans, or someone who grew up in poverty, etc., so I face the same oppression and issues that African Americans do."

- **Fleeing into statistics:** "Eighty-five percent of the city's residents say they haven't experienced racism, so you must be imagining things; on a per capita basis, Black people commit more crimes than white people, so racial profiling is an obvious, sensible, and fair police response."

- **Fleeing into legalism:** "I know it looks like that cop shot your child, but we need to wait until all the facts are in."

- **Blaming the victim:** "If Tamir Rice had had the common sense not to play with a toy gun in a public park, he'd be alive today."

- **Blaming the victim's caregivers:** "You should have taught your son not to litter; then he wouldn't have gotten grabbed by the throat."

- **Blaming the Black body:** "If Eric Garner had taken better care of himself, he'd still be alive."

- **Distraction and misdirection:** "You're actually talking about class, not race."

- **Exceptionalism:** "Everything you say is true for most white people. But I'm different. I'm not like those other, racist white people. I get a free pass."

- **Taking offense:** "You were rude to challenge my wife in front of everyone; now you've ruined the party."

- **Pre-emptive verbal strikes:** "Oh, let me guess. You're going to play the race card now."

- **Pre-emptive physical strikes:** "She was reaching for something; it could have been a gun; I was afraid she would shoot me. How could I know she was just getting her phone to call 911?"

- **Crying:** This sends the message "I'm so fragile and in so much pain! Now soothe me!"

- **Proclaiming one's white guilt:** This sends the message "I'm so bad! Now soothe me!"

- **Defensiveness through association:** "Listen. My boss is Black, and my mom marched with Dr. King."

- **Incredulity:** "Reparations? That's crazy talk! It's not like Germany paid reparations after World War II!"[47]

Over time, these strategies have become part of our standard cultural language. Today, a variety of institutions—from Fox News to the NRA to MSNBC—ardently support many of them, making them appear rational and even noble, rather than trauma responses in the form of avoidance, fear, and gaslighting.

*

As I discussed earlier, when a body observes the willful harming of another—especially if it inflicts that harm—it may experience its own *secondary* or *vicarious trauma*. For the past three centuries, many white Americans have experienced this trauma in multiple ways. They controlled, brutalized, and murdered Black bodies. They watched others harm and kill Black bodies. They failed to prevent, stop, or challenge such attacks—or they tried to step in and were brutalized for their attempted interventions.

In addition, for centuries before that, many Europeans experienced similar trauma as they watched other white bodies be controlled, brutalized, and murdered, or as they were subjected to that oppression themselves by other white bodies. But they were unable to metabolize

---

47   Germany did pay thirty-three billion dollars in reparations to Allied governments and about 800 million dollars to Israel.

the horror of what they witnessed or experienced, so that horror was stored as trauma in their bodies. This trauma—as well as a variety of self-protective strategies that got built around it—have been passed down and compounded over many generations. They were likely passed down epigenetically as expressions of people's DNA. They were also passed down as habits, actions, sensations, urges, images, narratives, beliefs, and ideas. Over generations, the original context was forgotten,[48] and the trauma became cultural traits or norms (for example, the Ku Klux Klan or certain white churches), or the traits of individual personalities (such as Jesse Helms or Strom Thurmond).

White fragility is thus a reflexive, protective response—a way for the white body to avoid experiencing the pain and discomfort of its trauma. It is a classic form of dirty pain.

What has this meant for African Americans?

For starters, many of us—for our own real or perceived safety—routinely collude in protecting and soothing white bodies. We do this in an endless number of ways. In the presence of white bodies, many of us dress, speak, and act in deliberately "non-threatening" ways[49] (I call this *de-Blackening*). We avoid wearing natural hairstyles or African clothing or jewelry. We strip our speech of African American (and African) idioms, cadences, and expressions. We modulate our voices with white American cadences and tonalities.

When talking with white people, we may carefully avoid topics we think might trigger their defenses, such as inequality, oppression, social issues, and, especially, race. Some of us never veer from small talk. We try to protect ourselves by protecting white people from their own fears about us.

For many African Americans, this collusion becomes second nature—a protective, reflexive response. Just as many white bodies go on alert when they sense a Black body nearby, many Black bodies also go on alert when they sense a white one in the vicinity. But there is a

---

48   But not by everyone. In *Hillbilly Elegy*, J. D. Vance acknowledges (though not with the kind of language a therapist would use) the intergenerational trauma in his long bloodline of Scotch-Irish ancestors.

49   Like many African Americans, I have both a Black voice and a "generic" (more white-sounding) voice. Which voice I use depends on whom I engage with. If I sense that using my African American voice will encourage constriction in someone else's body, I use my generic voice. This use of multiple voices is quite common and not necessarily racialized. For example, Southerners routinely adopt a generic (a white, Midwest-sounding) voice when addressing Northerners.

crucial difference here: The white body tends to shift into immediate self-protection; but the Black body is habituated to shift into *soothing the white body* as a self-protective strategy.

Brent Staples wrote a brilliant essay on this topic called "Just Walk On By: Black Men and Public Space."[50] For years, as Staples walked down city sidewalks and white bodies approached and noticed him, he watched those bodies stiffen, constrict, reposition purses, cross the street, and sometimes run away to avoid him. Eventually Staples developed a strategy of whistling Vivaldi's "Four Seasons" as white people walked near him. This quickly and effectively soothed white bodies. On hearing a Vivaldi melody, they would routinely relax; some people would even start whistling the melody with him.

As Staples explains in "Just Walk On By," this was only one of his many strategies for soothing nearby white bodies:

> I now take precautions to make myself less threatening. I move about with care, particularly late in the evening. I give a wide berth to nervous people on subway platforms during the wee hours, particularly when I have exchanged business clothes for jeans. If I happen to be entering a building behind some people who appear skittish, I may walk by, letting them clear the lobby before I return, so as not to seem to be following them.

For decades, I reflexively honored white fragility myself. I did many of the things Staples describes, all while thinking I was being thoughtful and compassionate. Time after time, I stood back or aside, or smiled, or otherwise deliberately demonstrated to white bodies they needn't fear me. At age thirty, though, I grew out of this, with the help of my beautiful wife, who first called it to my attention twenty-one years ago. I recognized that I was enabling and colluding with white fragility and white-body supremacy. Today I afford white bodies exactly the same respect and space that I allow other bodies.

I am aware there is some risk to doing this. When we fail to soothe and protect white bodies, or fail to accept white fragility and white-

---

50   First published in *Ms. Magazine* in 1986, the essay has since been republished in many textbooks.

body supremacy, some of us with dark skin get pulled over, tackled, searched, often arrested, and sometimes killed. This creates an ongoing dilemma. Many white Americans need to be confronted—firmly and compassionately—on their white fragility. Yet much of that fragility is a trauma-driven, lizard-brain defensiveness that quickly fights, flees from, or freezes out all such caring confrontation.

There is only one way through this stalemate. White Americans must accept, explore, and mend their centuries-old trauma around the oppression and victimization of white bodies by other, more powerful white bodies.

Constricted bodies, frozen attitudes, and closed minds are common side effects of racialized trauma (and trauma in general). Until this racialized trauma is addressed, changing attitudes or opening minds is largely impossible, especially on a large scale. However, once white Americans begin this all-important healing process, minds, nervous systems, attitudes, relationships, and culture can all have a little more room to grow and transform.

At the heart of white fragility, deeply embedded in the white body, lies the following conviction: *We white people are incapable of feeling safe in the presence of Black bodies. We are also incapable of soothing our own historical dissonance with each other. We are not just physically vulnerable; we are also emotionally helpless when we are around Black bodies.*

This collective story of martyrdom has been held tightly in many generations of white bodies. It is of course patently untrue. Americans of European descent have histories that demonstrate great courage, ingenuity, ability, achievement, and resilience in virtually all aspects of life but one: their relationship with African American bodies. In this one realm many feel frightened, vulnerable, and small—emotions that are nothing more than a trauma-driven, racialized phobia.

White Americans, like Americans of all skin colors, have successfully grown thick emotional skins when they needed to. Americans rebelled against and defeated the British in the American Revolution. We defeated our foes in two World Wars. We won the Cold War with the Soviet Union. We Americans, including most white Americans, can be extremely strong and resilient when we want to be.

White Americans would do well to ask themselves these questions: "Why do I believe that I'm feeble and helpless in the presence of a Black body? What evidence do I have that this is actually true? How does that belief serve me? How does it serve anyone?" They would also do well to pay close attention to what arises in their bodies as they ask these questions.

It's time for all of us to drop the façade of white fragility. It's absurd; it's patently untrue; and it harms everyone who encounters it.

*

On the surface, white-body supremacy looks like a highly favorable arrangement for white people. They get to reap a wide range of benefits, while forcing other, darker bodies to bear all the costs. This does not tell the whole story, however, which is that white-body supremacy comes at a great cost to white people.

There is the moral injury, which creates shame, and ever more trauma, in white bodies. But white-body supremacy also greatly diminishes white Americans' awareness of their own strength and abilities. As a result, while the most overt and vocal white supremacists trumpet the superiority of European blood, many white Americans cower in fear and trembling—or beg for help and comfort—in the presence of people with dark skin.

There is a real head-banging quality to all this. Which is why any attempts to address it through the head—the thinking, reasoning brain—are doomed. And it is why every answer needs to begin with the body.

Whiteness does not equal fragility. That's a dodge created by white fragility itself—a way for white Americans to avoid the responsibility of soothing themselves, metabolizing their own ancient historical and secondary trauma, accepting and moving through clean pain, and growing up. I urge white readers to recognize this myth for what it is, to hold it up to the light, and to call bullshit on it.

Most of us with dark skin will strongly support this courageous action. We have been calling bullshit on white fragility for centuries.

—BODY PRACTICES—

Find a quiet place where you can be alone and undisturbed for ten to fifteen minutes. Get comfortable and relax.

Think back to an incident when you were especially strong, resilient, and resourceful. The event may have lasted as little as half a minute (for example, when you spoke up forcefully and eloquently on someone's behalf), or as long as a week, or months, or years (for example, when you put yourself through college while raising two kids on your own).

Now, moment by moment (for brief events), or milestone by milestone (for longer ones), mentally relive that process. At each moment or milestone, pay attention to what you experience in your body: strength or weakness, energy or drowsiness, activation or settledness, constriction or relaxation, hope or despair, purpose or uncertainty. What impulses, images, or meanings arise?

Take ten slow, deep breaths. What is your body experiencing right now?

FOR WHITE READERS:

Recall an incident—if possible a recent one—when you asked a Black body to comfort or protect you in some way. Mentally relive that incident from beginning to end. Pay close attention to what you experience in your body at each of these points:

- When you first felt a need to make the request.

- When you made the request.

- When the person said yes or no to your request.

- When he or she did (or didn't do) what you asked.

Take ten deep, slow breaths. Then ask yourself: In retrospect, was the comfort or protection you asked for genuinely necessary? Could you have soothed or protected yourself? If you had, how might the outcome have been different?

Now come back to the present and orient yourself. Look around slowly, including behind you.

FOR NON-WHITE READERS:

Recall a time when you deliberately and willingly altered your behavior to comfort or protect a white body. This should *not* be a situation where you were asked, told, or paid to help. It should be one in which you decided to help *on your own*. Mentally relive that incident from beginning to end. Pay close attention to what you experience in your body, and to the thoughts that go through your mind, at these points:

- When you first thought a white body might want comfort or protection from you.

- When you considered whether to provide that comfort or protection.

- The moment when you decided you would provide it.

- When you provided it.

- When the white body responded to your actions.

- Immediately after the encounter was over.

Take ten deep, slow breaths. Then ask yourself: In retrospect, did your soothing or protection work? Was it genuinely necessary? Could the person have provided his or her own soothing or protection? If you had not stepped in to comfort or protect the person, how might the outcome have been different for you? For the other person?

Are you glad you did what you did? Why or why not? If you were to find yourself in a similar situation now, what, if anything, would you do differently?

Now come back to the present and orient yourself. Look around slowly, including behind you.

RE-MEMBERINGS

- For centuries, Americans have lived with a strange, contradictory myth: *Black bodies are incredibly strong and frightening and can handle anything short of total destruction, while white bodies are weak and vulnerable, especially to Black bodies. So it's the job of Black bodies to care for white bodies, soothe them, and protect them—particularly from other Black bodies.*

- This myth has been reinforced by a secondary fantasy: *Because white bodies are so vulnerable to Black ones, when a Black body is not subservient to a white one, it must be destroyed. And because Black bodies are nearly invulnerable, that destruction must be swift and ruthless.*

- A common form of white fragility involves a strong and immediate defensive response whenever a white body is challenged on the subject of race and equity, or whenever the topic of race emerges.

- This has inspired a contorted form of white self-talk: *We white people are incapable of soothing ourselves and feeling safe in the presence of Black bodies. We are not just physically vulnerable; we are also emotionally helpless when we are around Black bodies.*

- White fragility is a reflexive, protective response—a way for the white body to avoid experiencing the pain of its historical trauma inflicted by other white bodies.

- Many white Americans need to be confronted—firmly and compassionately—on their white fragility. Much of that fragility is a trauma-driven, lizard-brain defensiveness that quickly fights, flees from, or freezes out all such caring confrontation.

- There is only one way through this stalemate. White Americans must accept, explore, and mend their centuries-old trauma around oppression and victimization.

- Whiteness does not equal fragility. That's a dodge created by white fragility itself; it's a way for white Americans to avoid the responsibility of soothing themselves, metabolizing their own historical and secondary trauma, accepting and moving through clean pain, and growing up.

CHAPTER 8

WHITE-BODY SUPREMACY AND THE POLICE BODY

"There is very little relationship between who is locked up and the concept of justice. Americans don't understand that people in prison are often there because of where the policing was. What's more: White people need to start telling the truth about the way this justice system works. Because every white person—particular middle- and upper-class white people—knows that they are not as worried about their children becoming trapped in the system unjustly."

HEATHER ANN THOMPSON

"Be careful what you practice; you may get really good at the wrong thing."

TONY BLAUER

"I can't believe what you say, because I see what you do."

JAMES BALDWIN

Soon after I started working on this book, my friend Bryan called me from Florida. Bryan is a white combat vet and anything but a wimp. He was deeply shaken. He said, "Resmaa, I'm beginning to understand some of the things you've been telling me. Today I was driving along, doing the speed limit, when a cop comes up behind me and turns on his flashing lights. I pull over, roll down my window, and put my hands on the steering wheel, just like you're supposed to.

"The cop walks up, looks in, sees my registered handgun on the seat beside me, and loses his mind. Before I can say anything, he shouts to his partner, 'GUN! GUN! HE'S ARMED!'

"I'm not even touching the gun. It's lying there in full view on the seat, while my hands are on the steering wheel. And this is Florida, where it's completely legal to have a gun in your car.

"The first cop whips out his own gun, jams it hard against my temple, and shouts at me from a foot away, 'DON'T YOU FUCKING MOVE YOUR HANDS! GET OUT OF THE CAR, NICE AND SLOW, OR I'LL BLOW YOUR FUCKING HEAD OFF!'

"So I get out like he told me to, and I start to say, 'It's registered. The permit is in the glove—' He doesn't let me finish. He's still shouting. 'SHUT THE FUCK UP. DO WHAT I TELL YOU.' He grabs my hands, yanks them behind my back in a hold, and slams me up against the car. And he won't stop shouting. 'YOU MAKE ONE MOVE AND YOU'RE FUCKING DEAD.'

"By now I'm scared he's going to blow my head off no matter what I do, so I start shouting back. 'I DIDN'T DO ANYTHING. WHY ARE YOU DOING THIS TO ME? WHY DID YOU PULL ME OVER? THIS IS AMERICA! YOU CAN'T JUST THREATEN ME FOR NO REASON!'

"He doesn't like this at all, and he slams my face hard against the car. We spend the next minute or so shouting at each other while his partner checks out my driver's license and my gun permit.

"Everything checks out fine, so eventually he puts his gun away and lets me go. He doesn't say a single goddamn word. He and his partner just walk back to their car and drive off.

"Resmaa, that was half a day ago, and I still have no idea why he pulled me over in the first place."

I started saying, "I can't begin to tell you how sorry I am you had to go through that, Bryan. Because——"

"I know, Resmaa," he said. "Because I'm white, I'm still alive. I have no doubt at all that if I were Black, my body would be in the morgue right now. I've never seen or experienced anything like this before. It was crazy. It made no sense at all."

"I'm glad you're still alive."

"Resmaa, *you* have a conceal-and-carry permit. What would you have done in that situation?"

"I never keep my gun in view. When I get pulled over, I take out the keys, toss them on top of the dashboard, and put both hands on top of the steering wheel, like you did. When the cop walks up, I put a big smile on my face and say, 'Good morning, officer. Is there a problem?' When I'm carrying, I always have my permit and my driver's license in my visor, not in my wallet. I turn on the dome light, even if it's noon and sunny. I immediately hand the cop my permit and my license. If I'm asked to step out of the car and I have the gun on me, I say, 'I'm happy to step out. Would you like to remove my legally registered handgun first? It's on my right hip.'

"I know my Black body could be triggering all kinds of reflexive survival strategies in the cop's body. So I do my best to de-Blacken. My goals are to not die and get safely home to my family."

For a moment, Brian was silent. Then he said, "I'm starting to see all this Driving While Black shit differently."

*

My brother Christopher and his wife Laura have a fifteen-year-old son, Xavier. Laura is white; Xavier's skin tone is similar to that of former President Obama's, perhaps a bit lighter. One afternoon, as Xavier started walking home from school, he got a call from his mom. "Hey, Xavier. Grandma and I are headed home from the mall. Want us to pick you up?"

"Yeah," Xavier said. "Cool. I just left school."

"We're about five minutes away. Keep walking and we'll pick you up at the corner where the Dairy Queen is."

My mother and sister-in-law got to the intersection half a minute before Xavier did. As they parked, they saw him walking down the block in their direction.

A moment later, a police cruiser drove up and pulled over. Two white officers leaped out. Wordlessly, they descended on my nephew, who was doing nothing other than walking down the sidewalk, and tackled him to the ground.

My mom threw open her door and started to climb out, but my sister-in-law stopped her. She said, "Mama, let me get this." She didn't need to add, "I'm white. The police will listen to me."

Laura hurried up to the police. They had Xavier pinned to the ground. She said firmly, "This young man is my son. Has he done something wrong? Has he committed a crime?"

The police took their hands off Xavier, stood up, and literally backed away a few steps. There was a moment of tense silence. Finally one of them said, "We thought he matched the description of someone who committed a robbery earlier today. Up close, we can see that he doesn't."

My sister-in-law said firmly, "Good. Are my son and I free to go?"

"Yes, ma'am."

Laura hustled Xavier into her car and drove off.

On the verge of tears, Xavier said, "Thanks, Mom. What did I *do*? I was just *walking*."

My sister-in-law's hands shook. "Mama," she said, "I think he needs to hear the answer from you."

*

American police are not an alien race. The great majority of them come from the same traumatized groups I described in earlier chapters. But they don't just live with the typical intergenerational trauma. They also work in a field that regularly requires them to witness other people's trauma and tragedy—and, as a result, to experience their own *secondary trauma* or *vicarious trauma*.

Unfortunately, most law enforcement professionals are not trained in how to discharge the excess energy that remains in their bodies after a traumatic event.[51] Nor, typically, is there organizational infrastructure in place to support their self-care and healing. As a result, many police live with the biochemicals of chronic stress in their bloodstreams.

Some police officers try to manage this energy—or soothe their bodies—through drinking, drugs, disassociation, sexual misconduct, isolation, or some combination of these. Some suffer from burnout, compassion fatigue, chronic anger, and a variety of physical health issues. One result is that when police patrol some Black neighborhoods, it is often a case of repeatedly traumatized bodies confronting other repeatedly traumatized bodies. On top of all this, police culture in some locales is built around *us-versus-them* thinking. And when intergenerational trauma lives and breathes in the bodies of both us and them, almost any encounter can lead to tragedy.

The culture of policing includes both men and women, and it extends well beyond police and county sheriffs. It includes security guards, mall cops, truancy officers, members of the National Guard, and anyone else whose job it is to enforce the law.

In many American communities today, police officers are charged with managing and, when necessary, subduing or harming Black bodies, particularly in situations that ordinary white citizens feel they can't handle. This is why, when called to a situation involving both Black and white bodies, police often subdue and cuff the Black ones, but take the white ones off to the side for questioning. (Aside from the obvious injustice, this is also bad police work, because it can result in a white body blowing the head off a police officer.) It's also why a Black teenage girl who doesn't put away her cell phone gets tackled and thrown across the floor by a school police officer, while a group of white bikers who have a shootout in a restaurant parking lot are allowed to stand around uncuffed, have their rights read to them, and be led away, untouched. It is why a police officer may go ballistic and shoot an unarmed Black man who is lying motionless in the street with

---

51   This is starting to change. Police departments in some cities now provide such training for their officers. I personally led a series of trainings for the Minneapolis Police Department on handling personal and secondary trauma.

his hands up, but may try to talk down a white man they have cornered who is brandishing a knife.

We can condemn all of this as racist—and it surely is. But, in many cases, it is not cognitive. It's reflexive and reptilian. To many police bodies, even many Black ones, African Americans are foreign bodies that need to be corralled, controlled, damaged, or destroyed.[52]

Often this "foreign body" designation is literal. A high percentage of cops who work in large American cities live in the suburbs and have little off-duty contact with the residents of the neighborhoods where they work. To their bodies, *everyone* in that neighborhood is a foreign body—and they are the protective antibodies. This is the quintessential us-vs.-them stance. Meanwhile, from the viewpoint of neighborhood residents, the police are the foreign bodies, brought in from the outside as an occupying force. This arrangement does not build trust. Instead, it tends to create mutual fear and suspicion.

This situation is partly the result of police culture, which in many American cities has become a dysfunctional blend of politics, statistical demands, anger, frustration, broken (and inappropriately upheld) loyalties, and fear. Often police feel unsupported by their chiefs, and by the mayors those chiefs report to. Often they have arrest quotas to fulfill because their effectiveness is measured by the number of people they haul in and, sometimes, by the number of tickets they issue in order to generate revenue. In some neighborhoods—almost always those with lots of dark-skinned folks—hauling people in is virtually their sole job.

Over the past two decades, the nature of policing in many American communities has changed from *protect, serve, and keep the peace* to *control, arrest, and shoot.* Cops who used to walk beats now cruise them in police cars. Police departments have become increasingly militarized; today, some American cities literally own tanks. Tactics that were formerly used only by SWAT teams have become standard operating procedure. Policing has become more and more like soldiering. In some communities, police forces have transformed from community servants into occupying forces.

---

52   There is a good deal of history behind this. As you'll learn later on, American policing has many of its roots in the pursuit of runaway slaves.

This isn't just happening with public safety officers. The same move toward militarization is now taking place with private security teams in malls and airports—and even in our schools. While it is largely happening in African American communities, to a lesser degree it is happening throughout our country.

In many towns and neighborhoods—parts of Baltimore, for example, or Ferguson, Missouri—police are no longer expected to act like police. They must instead act like soldiers. It is not a role many police have been trained to fulfill. Neither is it a role that offers much job satisfaction. It rarely reflects officers' reasons for becoming public safety professionals in the first place.

All of this creates enormous chronic stress and confusion for police bodies, because the body of a police officer and the body of a soldier need to live by completely different rules. A police officer's body needs to be calm and settled 90 percent of the time and activated 10 percent of the time—when he or she is responding to a call or making an arrest. But when a soldier is in combat or some other potentially dangerous situation, his or her body needs to be activated and alert at least 90 percent of the time.

These changing (and often contradictory) demands, as well as the chaos and confusion that make up contemporary police culture, are wreaking havoc on police bodies and psyches. It's no wonder our police have high rates of domestic violence and alcohol abuse.[53] Police bodies are visibly suffering from their own form of trauma and, in turn, inflicting unnecessary harm on the less powerful, including some of the people they have pledged to protect.

*

In early 2016, a few miles from my home in Minneapolis, Matthew Hovland-Knase drove his motorcycle at high speed past officer Lonnie Soppeland, who was in his patrol car. After clocking Hovland-Knase

---

53   Elizabeth Willman's article, "Alcohol Abuse among Law Enforcement," (http://www.jghcs.info/index.php/l/article/viewFile/150/147), provides a good overview of many of the studies on the subject. An article by Conor Friedersdorf in *The Atlantic*, "Police Have a Much Bigger Domestic-Abuse Problem Than the NFL Does" (https://www.theatlantic.com/national/archive/2014/09/police-officers-who-hit-their-wives-or-girlfriends/380329/), highlights two studies showing that at least 40 percent of police officer families experience domestic violence—four times the rate as in the general population.

at 110 miles per hour, Soppeland turned on his siren and went after the motorcyclist. A high-speed chase followed. Eventually, Hovland-Knase pulled over and stopped. He sat on his motorcycle, quiet and still; he did not reach for a weapon or attempt to run.

Soppeland got out of his patrol car with his gun drawn. He shouted, "Get your hands where I—" Then he fired a shot into Hovland-Knase's body.

Hovland-Knase moaned and said, "Please help me! I'm bleeding... Oh, you actually shot me, didn't you?"

Soppeland removed medical supplies from his car. As he began administering first aid, he said to the wounded man, "It was not intentional, I can tell you that."

The shooting was quickly investigated by the county sheriff's office. Soppeland told a detective, "The firearm discharged once unintentionally. It was not my conscious choice . . . I could feel the effect of the adrenaline."

Soppeland, who had received firearm training about three weeks earlier, explained, "I feel the muscle memory from that recent training of squeezing the trigger contributed to the unintentional discharge during a high stress situation."

Or, in simpler terms: "My thinking brain didn't shoot the guy on the motorcycle. My body did."

Officer Soppeland was white. He shot an unarmed, unresisting man—who was also white—because he had just experienced "a high-stress situation" (in this case, a high-speed chase). Yet law enforcement professionals routinely face high-stress situations. That is the nature of their job.

What would have happened if Soppeland had also been as well trained in settling his body, and in self-care, as he was in the use of his firearm?

And what happens when a police officer's body interprets the mere presence of a Black body—or the presence of a Black body and an object that could possibly be a gun—as a high-stress situation?

*

The killing of Tamir Rice suggests an answer. So does the killing of Philando Castile, which, like the shooting described above, also occurred only a few miles from my home in 2016. Police officer Jeronimo Yanez pulled over driver Castile, who was with his girlfriend and her daughter. Castile was polite and cooperative. Officer Yanez asked for Castile's ID and insurance. Castile gave him his insurance. Castile then calmly explained that he had a permit to carry a handgun and that the gun was in the car. Then he slowly reached for his ID. Yanez responded abruptly by shooting Castile seven times in quick succession, killing him.

By some accounts, Yanez was an exemplary patrolman who had graduated at the top of his class. Until he shot Castile, he had a spotless record. Officer Yanez was charged with second-degree manslaughter.

John Choi, the Ramsey County Attorney whose office charged Yanez, has said publicly that "no reasonable officer—knowing, seeing, and hearing what officer Yanez did at the time—would have used deadly force under these circumstances."

True. Trauma responses are never reasonable. They are protective and reflexive. They don't involve the reasoning mind.

At his trial, Yanez said of the encounter, "I thought I was going to die." But were his actions really the result of what he thought? Or did a non-thinking part of his brain, infected with the ancient trauma of white-body supremacy, reflexively react?

Yanez, a trained police officer, was terrified of Castile, a calm, compliant young man whom he'd pulled over for a broken taillight. Castile was in a car with an equally compliant young woman and her small child. Castile politely explained[54]—presumably in an effort to attempt to settle Yanez's nervous system—that he had a gun, which was legally registered in his name. Yanez then shot him dead.

What if, some time before his encounter with Castile, Officer Yanez had addressed any racialized trauma that was stored and stuck in his body? Or, what if his employer had recognized the need to provide some healing infrastructure to help its officers address this ancient trauma? Might either one have prevented Castile's death? How many

---

54   His words were: "Sir, I have to tell you . . ."

other killings might be prevented in the future if our law enforcement professionals were to heal the trauma in their bodies?

Some other questions to consider: if Castile had been white, would Yanez have shot him dead? And another: Can you recall an incident in which a police officer pulled over a white driver who was calm and compliant and had a child in the car—and then shot that driver dead because the officer "thought I was going to die"? And another question: if such a thing were to actually happen, do you think a jury would agree that the officer's fear justified the killing of the white driver?

As we have seen, thinking that "I am going to die" when encountering a Black body is baked into the bodies—and the lizard brains—of many Americans. This includes many police officers, who are typically trained to react quickly and use their guns when they (or their lizard brains) sense a threat.

In July of 2016, police in North Miami Beach, Florida responded to a 911 call. When they arrived, they saw an autistic man who had wandered away from his group home sitting in the street. Mental health worker Charles Kinsey, who is Black, had come to retrieve him. When police arrived, Kinsey lay in the street and held his hands up to show that he was unarmed and unthreatening.[55] He told officer Jonathan Aledda that he was unarmed, and said of his patient, "All he has is a toy truck. A toy truck. I am a behavior therapist at a group home." Aledda fired three shots at Kinsey anyway, wounding him in the leg. Kinsey asked Aledda, "Sir, why did you shoot me?" Aledda replied, "I don't know."

Can there be a clearer example of a trauma response? Or of how non-cognitive and reflexive such a response is? Or of how the mere presence of a Black body—no matter how passive, submissive, motionless, and unthreatening—can trigger such a response in a police body? You can observe the interaction for yourself; a video of the incident is easy to find online.

Aledda was charged with attempted manslaughter and culpable

---

55   Can you imagine a white therapist doing this, either reflexively or deliberately? Can you imagine a white therapist even *considering* that such a response might be necessary for his safety and survival? (For Kinsey, of course, even this response failed to keep him from being shot by a police officer.)

negligence. Aledda pled not guilty.[56] As I write this paragraph in June 2017, Aledda is awaiting trial.

Or consider this possible trauma response, which resulted in yet another unarmed African American man shot and killed by a white police officer. In September of 2016, in Tulsa, Oklahoma, Officer Betty Shelby shot and killed Terence Crutcher. When Officer Shelby saw Crutcher walking down a road, she pulled over in her squad car, got out, and asked Crutcher if a nearby SUV was his. Crutcher answered and put his hands in his pockets. Shelby could not make out his response, so she ordered Crutcher to take his hands out of his pockets. He complied, put his hands up, and began walking away. Shelby drew her gun and ordered Crutcher to stop and get on his knees. Crutcher kept his hands up but did not stop walking. Shelby fired multiple shots, killing Crutcher.

At her trial, Officer Shelby said of the incident, "I've never been so scared . . . I thought he was going to kill me." Recalling the incident later in a CBS news interview,[57] she said, "I'm feeling that his intent is to do me harm . . ." She said of Crutcher, ". . . he caused the situation to occur. So in the end, he caused his own [death]."

In the same CBS news report, Crutcher's sister Tiffany explained, "What we saw on that video is what my dad always taught us to do if we were pulled over by a police officer. Put your hands in the air and put your hands on the car. And my brother did what my father taught us . . . My brother's dead because she didn't pause." The lizard brain does not pause. Trauma responses are all about speed.

The shootings of Castile, Rice, Kinsey, and Crutcher, like the killings of many other African Americans by police, suggest that what gets passed down as standard police training may include ancient traumatic retentions.[58] Thus, although a police officer takes an oath to

---

56   If this astonishes you, that astonishment is itself a reflection of white-skin privilege. From a self-preservation viewpoint, Aledda's plea may have been wise, since no Florida police officer has been convicted in state court for an on-duty shooting since 1989—and that sole conviction was overturned on appeal, and the police officer acquitted by a higher court.

57   http://www.cbsnews.com/news/terence-crutcher-unarmed-black-man-shooting-60-minutes-2/.

58   Of course, other aspects of standard police training may be overtly and deliberately racist. For instance, in target practice, police usually shoot at standard outlines of human faces and bodies. Instead, North Miami officers were trained to shoot at actual mug shots of African American men. A year and a half before North Miami officer Aledda shot Kinsey, this practice was reported by a sergeant of the Florida National Guard, who arrived at the shooting range to discover the bullet-riddled image of her brother's face being used as a target. Another example: a Baltimore Police Department's shift commander created a template for making trespassing arrests with the suspect description "black male" already filled in.

protect and serve, he or she may unwittingly become an apparatus for the destruction of Black bodies.

Here is another pernicious twist of white-body supremacy: When a police body unnecessarily harms a Black one, all attention is typically deflected away from police culture—and from any widespread pattern of behavior—and onto the particular officer and the particular incident under scrutiny. The incident is treated by police culture as an anomaly, even when—as in Ferguson, Missouri—the widespread pattern is painfully evident. As part of this same pattern, people in the community, including those who witnessed the incident, are told to wait "for all the facts to come out," to be patient, to let the investigation take its course. Ultimately, as part of that same pattern, the officer is often not held accountable because, as they tell the investigator or the grand jury, "I feared for my life," or "I was scared to death," or "I've never been so scared in my life," or "I thought I was going to die." (That last sentence, verbatim, is what Jeronimo Yanez said at his trial, a few days before I finished writing this paragraph. The sentence before that, verbatim, is what Officer Betty Shelby said in her trial for shooting Terence Crutcher.)

Both Yanez and Shelby were found not guilty.

We need to take these phrases very seriously. In some instances they are not a dodge, but an honest description of a trauma-inspired fight, flee, or freeze—or, in many such cases, annihilate—response. A lizard brain has sensed a threat, overridden the thinking brain, and sent out an order to destroy. When seen in this way, many apparently senseless murders become more understandable.

This does not, however, make lizard-brain panic a valid defense for murder.

But that is precisely how those words are often used, accepted, and validated—as a "reasonable" excuse for destroying yet another Black body. Variations of the phrase "I feared for my life" get repeated over and over by law enforcement professionals who fired their weapons when they shouldn't have:

> "My thinking brain didn't shoot the guy; my body did because
> I feared for my life."

"My thinking brain didn't shoot the guy; my body did because I was in a high-stress situation and feared for my life."

"My thinking brain didn't shoot the guy; my body did because the guy had dark skin, so I feared for my life."[59]

The fear these police officers speak of is surely real. But claiming that this fear gives them the unrestricted right to shoot bullets into bodies is a form of gaslighting.

The trauma of white-body supremacy is also real. It lives in many police bodies of all colors, just as it lives in many other American bodies of all colors. But a grown-up response to trauma is to heal it, not to blow it through other bodies—or blow holes in other bodies.

What will happen if "I was scared to death" results in the acquittal of enough police officers who have shot dark-skinned human beings? Will that phrase become the standard, default defense—the magic words—of almost *any* law enforcement professional who pumps bullets into a person of color? (Note, by the way, how "I feared my life" perfectly combines white fragility, imagined Black imperviousness and invincibility, and the lizard-brain annihilation response.)

Have we crossed that line already? Are American police officers now sanctioned to shoot dark bodies at will, with a tacit understanding that saying "I was scared to death" in court will exonerate them?

If so, then should Black men routinely be frightened of being shot by police, especially when they are pulled over for little or no reason? What if one of those Black drivers, scared to death, were to shoot

---

59   In 2012, George Zimmerman left his home to follow and accost his neighbor, Trayvon Martin, who was walking through their gated community in Sanford, Florida. Zimmerman, who brought a gun to the encounter, shot and killed Martin because, as he said in his trial, he feared for his life. Zimmerman was found not guilty by a jury. In 2015, less than a mile from my home, four white men wearing ski masks appeared at a peaceful event protesting the recent killing of Jamar Clark by a white policeman. At least one of the four men, Allen Scarsella, carried a gun, which he allegedly described in a text message as "specially designed by Browning to kill brown people." Protestors, most of whom were African American, noticed the four men in masks, surrounded them, and asked why they were there. They also demanded that the men remove their masks. Scarsella then drew his gun and shot five protestors. At his trial, Scarsella's public defender explained that Scarsella fired the shots because he was "scared out of his mind." These and other similar incidents raise some questions. First, under what circumstances is it legitimate to deliberately precipitate a conflict, shoot one or more people, and be considered guiltless because you were scared? Second, if "I feared for my life" or "I was scared out of my mind" becomes a legitimate defense, then can anyone who fears dark skin guiltlessly shoot any Black body that comes near? What about any Black body he or she seeks out, accosts, and shoots? Does your reflexive, lizard-brain fear of my dark body trump my right to exist? A Minnesota jury provided one answer to these questions in February of 2017: It found Scarsella guilty on all counts. He was given a fifteen-year prison sentence. A different Minnesota jury provided the opposite answer four months later: it found Jeronimo Yanez not guilty.

the police officer who pulled him over? Does "I feared for my life" constitute a valid defense for that dark-skinned man? If it does, then we are in deep trouble. If it does not—but it becomes one for police—then we are also in deep trouble.

The day after I wrote the above paragraph—which was also the day after Jeronimo Yanez was found not guilty of killing Philando Castile—the *New York Times* published this quote from Philip M. Stinson, who teaches criminal justice at Bowling Green State University: "As soon as the officer gets on the stand and subjectively says, 'I was fearing for my life,' many juries are not going to convict at that point . . . We've seen it over and over again."[60]

Another aspect of this gun violence that needs to be called out is some police officers' and departments' lack of concern for the wounded or dying Black bodies they have just shot. When Officer Soppeland shot Matthew Hovland-Knase, he did exactly the right thing: he immediately went to his patrol car, retrieved his first aid kit, and gave medical attention to the white man he had just shot. In contrast, after Jonathan Aledda shot Charles Kinsey, Aledda handcuffed Kinsey and left him bleeding in the street for the next twenty minutes. In Ferguson, Missouri, after Michael Brown was fatally shot by officer Darren Wilson, his body was left in the street for four hours. After Officer Timothy Loehmann shot Tamir Rice, he and his partner Frank Garmback offered Rice no medical assistance; they simply left him on the ground to bleed to death. When Rice's sister arrived and tried to help him, she was tackled and handcuffed.

The list of such incidents is long. As we'll see, this contempt for the wounded or dead Black body can be traced through many centuries. But it began in medieval Europe with a disdain for white bodies, not Black ones. It was in the New World where this disdain shifted, from mutilated and murdered white bodies to mutilated and murdered dark ones.

*

---

60   https://www.nytimes.com/2017/06/17/us/police-shootings-philando-castile.html?hp&action=click&pgtype=Ho mepage&clickSource=story-heading&module=second-column-region&region=top-news&WT.nav=top-news

The widespread failure to address the trauma in police officers' bodies only deepens it. In fact, because of their role in our culture, law enforcement professionals often compound it and pass it on to African Americans in the very neighborhoods they are charged to protect.

There was a time when police were called *peace officers*, because their job was to keep the peace, at least in some communities. But it's hard to keep the peace when your own body is constricted, unsettled, stressed, and traumatized.

In some ways, police culture has got things exactly backward. White-body supremacy and fragility have charged our law enforcement professionals with managing Black bodies, when what many public safety professionals need most is to learn to manage *their own* bodies.

Trauma is anything the body perceives as too much, too fast, or too soon. Whenever trauma is involved, the first step in mending any relationship—or any emotional dysregulation—involves working through that trauma. And in order for someone to do that trauma work, he or she must first learn to slow down, observe his or her body, and allow it to settle.

A settled body helps the other bodies it encounters to settle as well. This is why a calm, settled presence matters so much whenever we're around other bodies—in a partnership, a family, a brotherhood, or a community.

—BODY AND BREATH PRACTICES—

Find a quiet, comfortable place where you can reflect privately for ten to fifteen minutes. Bring pen and paper—or a laptop or tablet—with you.

Think back to a time when you personally witnessed the apprehension or arrest of a Black body. This should not be something from television, film, YouTube, or the Internet; it should be a real-life incident in which your body was present.

As best you can, recollect and re-experience that incident as completely as you can from beginning to end. Pay attention—moment by moment—to what you felt in your body and what thoughts and emotions you experienced.

Write down each of those physical, emotional, and mental responses in as much detail as you can, including where in your body you felt it, whether it was pleasant or unpleasant, and whether it involved constriction or opening.

Clear your mind and take ten deep, slow breaths.

Return to the here and now. Reorient yourself by looking around, including behind you.

Now, as best you can, recollect and re-experience the last time you witnessed, in person, the apprehension or arrest of a white body. As before, pay close attention to what you felt in your body in each moment, and to what thoughts and emotions you experienced.

Once again, write these down in as much detail as you can.

Clear your mind with ten more long, slow breaths.

Now compare the two written accounts. Are they quite similar, or do they differ? If they differ, write down how they differ. How might you account for those differences?

FOR LAW ENFORCEMENT PROFESSIONALS:

Pick a workday some time in the next ten days. Circle it on your calendar or otherwise note it down in some way.

When the end of that workday arrives, spend three to four minutes sitting alone in a quiet place, with paper and pen (or a laptop or tablet) nearby. For those few minutes, simply inventory all the sensations, both physical and emotional, you experience in your body.

You can start with the strongest sensation, then proceed to the next strongest, and the next, and so on. Write them down. Also note any strong images or compelling thoughts that arise.

If you prefer, you can instead start at the top of your head and, slowly, scan down your body—to your forehead, your eyes and ears, your nose, your mouth, your neck and chin, and so on until you reach the soles of your feet. Again, write down what you experience in your body, as well as any strong images or compelling thoughts that come up.

Clear your mind and take ten long, slow, deep breaths.

Return to the here and now. Reorient yourself by looking around, including behind you.

Then ask yourself: "If I had the ability to quickly settle my body whenever I wanted to—including at work—how might this change what I'm experiencing right now?"

While working on this book, I led a series of training sessions for the Minneapolis Police Department. My task was to help members learn to take better care of their bodies; to reduce and avoid unnecessary stress, both on and off the job; and to deliberately settle their bodies under a wide range of circumstances. When we began our work together, I was not surprised to discover that, for many officers, I was the first professional to ever guide them in these ways.

RE-MEMBERINGS

- The policing profession has its own culture, customs, norms, rituals, expectations, and codes of behavior.

- In many American communities, part of the police officer's ethic is to manage and, when necessary, subdue or harm Black bodies, especially when ordinary white citizens feel they can't.

- Chronic stress, and routinely dealing with traumatized people, can be traumatizing to the police body.

- To many police bodies, African Americans are foreign bodies that need to be corralled, controlled, damaged, or destroyed.

- From the viewpoint of the people being corralled, controlled, and damaged, the *police* are the foreign bodies, brought in from the outside as an occupying force.

- Over the past two decades, the policing imperative in many American communities has morphed from *protect, serve, and keep the peace* to *control, arrest, and shoot.*

- The movement toward militarization is now also taking place with private security teams in malls and airports— and even in our schools.

- As a result, in many towns and neighborhoods, police are expected to act like soldiers.

- But police and soldiers live by completely different rules. A police officer's body needs to be calm and settled 90 percent of the time, and activated 10 percent of the time. In contrast, a soldier's body needs to be activated and alert 90 percent of the time.

- White-body supremacy thus takes a huge toll on the bodies of our law enforcement professionals, regardless of their race.

- When a police body unnecessarily harms a Black one, the officer is often not held accountable because, as he or she explains, "I feared for my life." In some cases, this is an honest description of a trauma-inspired fight, flee, or freeze response. Yet it is never a valid defense of murder.

- White-body supremacy has charged our law enforcement professionals with managing Black bodies. Instead, we need to help our police learn to manage their *own* bodies.

CHAPTER 9

CHANGING THE WORLD
BEGINS WITH YOUR BODY

"If you don't understand yourself, you don't know anybody else."
NIKKI GIOVANNI

*"Health is not simply the absence of illness. Real health is
the will to overcome every form of adversity and use even the
worst of circumstances as a springboard for new growth and
development. Simply put, the essence of health is the constant
renewal and rejuvenation of life."*
DAISAKU IKEDA

As many researchers now believe, the ongoing violations of the Black
body and heart have resulted in widespread trauma. This racialized
trauma shows up as an array of adaptive but dysfunctional behaviors,
including hypervigilance, heightened anxiety and suspicion, ADD/
ADHD, Obsessive-Compulsive Disorder, and addiction. It can also
appear as dysfunctional and non-adaptive behavior such as disordered
thinking, difficulty concentrating, panic attacks, learned helplessness,

self-hatred, hopelessness, depression, and a survival reflex that tends to involve violence. As Joy DeGruy and others have noted, all of these are common symptoms of a pervasive and persistent stress disorder.

In many African American bodies, this trauma has led to a variety of physical problems, the most common of which are high blood pressure, diabetes, obesity, compromised immune systems, heart problems, digestive disorders, chronic inflammation, and musculoskeletal disorders. When we measure the health and lifespans of African Americans, the aggregate results are routinely poorer than for white Americans. For the past several decades, we've tried to address this one body at a time, primarily through medication, exercise programs, lifestyle changes, stress management, and other such strategies. These have had only limited success.

As any experienced trauma therapist will tell you, however, for anyone to genuinely address these health issues, the person needs to address the trauma that fuels them. Without that foundational healing, all other healing becomes difficult or impossible, because the body is still stuck in the trauma. This is not just the case for African Americans. White Americans and police officers need to mend their own trauma as well.

Each of these groups has serious health issues of its own (though, overall, the ones that afflict Black Americans are the most severe). For example, white women in America suffer from high rates of cancer.[61] Law enforcement professionals have unusually high rates of alcohol abuse, high blood pressure, anxiety, depression, divorce, and domestic violence. Many suffer from burnout; many take medical retirement. It seems likely that some of these health and social problems are related to underlying trauma that needs to be addressed if any real change is to occur.

Most of all, however, white Americans and police officers need to retrain their bodies to feel safe in the presence of African American bodies.

White-body supremacy—in all its forms—twists the meaning of a simple, self-evident reality: *There is something wrong with African Americans.*

---

61   See https://www.cdc.gov/cancer/dcpc/data/race.htm.

Of course something is wrong with many African Americans, in the same sense that you'd say, "Something is wrong with me" if you became sick or injured. What's wrong with many of us is that racialized trauma is deeply embedded in our bodies, constricting us and limiting our ability to live full lives. What's wrong is that white-body supremacy continues to violate the Black body and assault the Black psyche and soul. We Black Americans need to heal this trauma and grow out of it, both individually and collectively.

There is also something wrong with most white Americans and law enforcement professionals, most of whom live with racialized trauma of their own. A key difference, however, is that white Americans also benefit from the system of white-body supremacy. They need to heal and grow out of their own trauma as well.

But there is another way to interpret the statement: "There is something wrong with African Americans." It can be read as "There is something inherently shameful, impure, and second-rate about being African American." This is, of course, patently untrue. But it is nevertheless deeply embedded in many American bodies—white, Black, and otherwise. Part of mending our racialized trauma will involve growing out of this intensely toxic idea. There is nothing second-rate or impure about African Americans. Something happened *to* us—and continues to happen to us. That "something" is white-body supremacy.

This brings us to the almost invisible way in which many white progressives discourage Black bodies, psyches, and hearts from healing. White progressives are deeply committed to the idea that there is nothing wrong with African Americans; that white and Black (and red and yellow) bodies are born with exactly the same potential; and that any differences in academic achievement, social skills, language acquisition, and so on must be entirely the result of social, cultural, familial, and educational influences.

Of course all of these play important roles in any young person's development. But many white progressives have reflexively resisted the evidence that many African Americans are impacted by racialized historical trauma created by white-body supremacy. White progressives have similarly resisted the evidence that a different—and also damaging—form of historical trauma is passed down through white American bodies. Until each of these manifestations of trauma is mended, it will continue to constrict people's bodies and lives and limit their efforts to grow and heal.

But as of this writing, many white progressives remain committed to interventions that ignore or dismiss the crucial role historical trauma plays in people's lives. Thus, paradoxically, they sabotage healing for many Americans of all skin colors, and unwittingly perpetuate the trauma. I hope they will receive these words as a loud wake-up call.

The place to begin the all-important healing of trauma is with the body. *Your* body. Each of our bodies. In Part II, we'll look at how each of us—white, Black, or otherwise—can better settle and manage our body. We'll also learn how to deliberately and mindfully activate it in situations that require it.

Healing does not occur in a vacuum. We also need to begin mending our collective body. This mending takes place in connections with other bodies—in groups, neighborhoods, and communities. In Part III of this book, we'll look at how healing can ripple outward from one body to another, and from groups of bodies into our systems and structures. This communal healing can help us steadily build respect, recognition, community, and, eventually, culture.

RE-MEMBERINGS

- The trauma held in Black bodies shows up as a wide array of physical problems and dysfunctional behaviors—all of which are common symptoms of persistent and pervasive stress.

- White Americans and police officers have their own common health issues, which are also related to underlying historical, intergenerational, and personal trauma.

- To date we have tried to address these issues one body at a time, and we have achieved only limited success.

- This is because we have not first focused on healing the underlying trauma. That healing is an essential first step.

- The place to begin that healing is in each of our bodies—starting with yours.

PART II

REMEMBERING OURSELVES

CHAPTER 10

YOUR SOUL NERVE

"Take responsibility for yourself, because no one's going to take responsibility for you."

TYRA BANKS

My grandmother was a strong and loving woman. But her body was frequently nervous. She often had a sense that something terrible was about to happen. It was an ancient, inherited sensation that rarely left her—a traumatic retention.

She would soothe that sense of impending disaster in a variety of ways. When she was in the kitchen, she would hum—not a steady tone, but entire melodies. Her humming was never soft and intimate, but loud and firm, as if she were humming for an audience. As a small child, if I knew the song she was humming, sometimes I would hum along with her, and my body would experience safety and settledness.

She also frequently comforted herself by rocking, both forward and backward and from side to side. When I would watch her rock, it never looked nervous or neurotic. Instead, it felt like a sacred ritual, imbued with meaning and purpose. Sometimes she would hum as she rocked.

She had a well-used rocking chair, but she could also rock comfortably on any sofa, chair, or bed—or standing up. Once, when we were visiting a sick relative in the hospital, I watched her rock on an uncomfortable chair beneath a heart monitor.

Sometimes she let us grandkids sit on her lap as she rocked. When I close my eyes, I can still feel my body settling into her soft, thick arm holding me steady and safe across my chest, and the wavelike motion of being rocked, of becoming part of a flow.

*

As I briefly noted earlier, most human behavior involves a part of the body that many people don't know about—the soul nerve. The soul nerve is the unifying organ of the entire nervous system. Health and mental health professionals call it the *vagus nerve* or *wandering nerve*, but I call it the *soul nerve*—a much stickier and more descriptive term.[62]

The soul nerve is not a nerve in the way we typically think of one. It is a highly complex and extraordinarily sensitive organ that communicates through vibes and sensations. This communication occurs not only between different parts of the body, but also from one person to another. Your soul nerve reaches into most of your body, including your throat, lungs, heart, stomach, liver, spleen, pancreas, kidney, and gut (both your large and small intestine). It is the largest organ in your body's autonomic nervous system, which regulates all of your body's basic functions.

The largest part of your soul nerve goes through your gut, which has about 100 million neurons, more than your spinal cord. This is why we sense so many things in our belly—and why some biologists call the gut our "second brain." This second brain is where our body senses flow, coherence, and the rightness or wrongness of things.

One of the organs your soul nerve does *not* connect to, however, is your thinking brain. It connects directly to your brainstem—your lizard brain.

---

62   Psychiatrist Stephen Porges has done much of the pioneering work on the vagus nerve. To learn more about this all-important organ and how it makes us human, check out the many articles and YouTube videos for non-professionals online. My discussion of the soul nerve in this book is, of necessity, greatly simplified.

We are only now beginning to understand how the soul nerve works. The organ itself was not identified until 1921, and much of what we know today was discovered only in the past two decades. There are a great many things about it we still don't understand.

We do know that the soul nerve is where we experience a felt sense of love, compassion, fear, grief, dread, sadness, loneliness, hope, empathy, anxiety, caring, disgust, despair, and many other things that make us human. When your body has an emotional response, such as when your stomach clenches, your voice catches, your pulse races, your shoulders tighten, your breathing quickens, your body braces for impact, or you have a sense that danger is lurking, that's your soul nerve at work. When you feel your heart opening or closing down; when you feel anxious in the pit of your stomach; when you sense that something wonderful or terrible is about to happen; when something feels right or wrong in your gut; when your heart sinks; when your spirit soars; or when your stomach turns in nausea—all of these involve your soul nerve.

When your body feels relaxed, open, settled, and in sync with other bodies, that's your soul nerve functioning. When it feels energized, vibrant, and full of life, that's also your soul nerve. When it feels tight, constricted, and self-protective, that's your soul nerve, too. And whenever you have a fight, flee, or freeze response, that involves your soul nerve as well. In fact, one of the main purposes of your soul nerve is to receive fight, flee, or freeze messages from your lizard brain and spread them to the rest of your body. Another purpose is precisely the opposite: to receive and spread the message of *it's okay; you're safe right now; you can relax.*

Your soul nerve is vital to your health and well being. It regulates your breathing, heart rate, and blood pressure. It helps prevent inflammation. And it can reduce pain, improve your mood, and help you manage fear.[63] We also know that your soul nerve is intimately involved with how your body interacts with other bodies, and with how your body makes memories. Without your soul nerve, you literally

---

63   I won't go into all the physiology behind the health benefits. Simply know that it involves a variety of electrical signals sent to and from the vagus nerve, increased oxygenation of the blood, a drop in blood pressure and heart rate, increased airflow in and out of the sinuses, and other measurable body responses.

would not be human. But your soul nerve, like your lizard brain, has zero capacity to think.

Your soul nerve tells most of the muscles in your body when to constrict, when to release, when to move, and when to relax and settle. Much of this is outside of your deliberate, conscious control. However, as you will discover, with some attention and patience, you *can* learn to work with your soul nerve. With practice, you can begin to consciously and deliberately relax your muscles, settle your body, and soothe yourself during difficult or high-stress situations. This will help you avoid reflexively sliding into a fight, flee, or freeze response in situations where such a response is unnecessary.

The following pages provide simple practices in *soul nerve training*. They are foundational practices in noticing your body, helping it settle, and working with your soul nerve. They require no special skills or equipment, and they can be done almost anywhere.

Please don't just read through these practices. Actually *do* some of them, day by day, even if only for a minute or two at a time. You may be surprised at how beneficial they can be. For maximum benefit, do them with your eyes open, either standing up or seated comfortably, but with your back straight. You can also lie down for most of them, but you'll discover you may easily fall asleep.

Do these practices by yourself at first. Once your body becomes familiar with them, do them with other people as well.

To your thinking mind, these activities may seem simple, even primitive. But to your body, soul nerve, and lizard brain, they will be powerfully soothing and grounding. Eventually they can become second nature, feeling to your body much like comfortable clothing.

Most of these practices are ancient; some are thousands of years old. While our ancestors were largely unaware of the biomechanics of the soul nerve, they understood their own bodies. They learned— and taught their families and neighbors—what worked to help their bodies settle. They often did many of these practices together, and these communal practices helped to heal not just individual bodies, but families and other groups as well.

You'll recognize some of these practices as things I've described my grandmother doing; as things many small children do intuitively; as things parents often do with their babies; as things enslaved people did as they worked together on plantations; and as practices from many religions. Almost all of them have also been proven to work in controlled lab experiments.[64]

Your body, of course, does not give a damn whether a practice is ancient or modern, secular or religious, proven or unproven. It just wants to experience safety and security. At first, it's best if you practice the activities in a quiet, comfortable spot where you can be alone. As your body becomes more familiar with them, try to practice them in times of stress or difficulty as well. Eventually, those will be the times when you will *most* engage in these practices. You will use them to help settle your body, stay present, and remain connected with other people—even in the midst of pain or confusion.

If any of these activities triggers extreme panic or a fight, flight, or freeze response in your body, stop doing it. Before doing that activity again, I encourage you to find a safe, knowledgeable person to guide you through it—preferably a well-trained somatic therapist who works with trauma.

—BODY AND BREATH PRACTICES—

HUMMING

Focus your attention on the center of your belly, behind your navel.

Breathe in and out, deeply and slowly, a few times. Feel your belly pull the air all the way down into it.

On the fourth or fifth exhalation, hum a low, even tone.

Inhale naturally and repeat this a few times, varying your pitch with each new exhalation.

---

64   For example, the benefits to the body of chanting "OM" were studied, confirmed, and reported in Bangalore G. Kalyani, Ganesan Venkatasubramanian, Rashmi Arasappa, et al., "Neurohemodynamic Correlates of 'OM' Chanting: A Pilot Functional Magnetic Resonance Imaging Study," *International Journal of Yoga* 4, no. 1 (2011): 3–6.

Do this for two or three minutes.

Then stop and notice what your body experiences afterward. What has changed from before you started humming? What has stayed the same? What sensations, thoughts, and images are arising?

What does your body want to do now? Does it want to move? Hum some more? Run and hide? Fight?

Without doing anything else, just notice whatever your body is experiencing right now.

Alternative: pick a song with a simple melody that feels comforting to your body. It can be anything—a hymn, a gospel tune, a lullaby, a military march, a punk rock song. Hum it all the way through from beginning to end from your belly. When you're done, stop and pay attention to your body.

Feel free to experiment with a variety of tunes.

BELLY BREATHING

Focus your attention on the center of your belly, behind your navel.

Breathe in and out, deeply and slowly, a few times. Pull the air all the way down into your belly.

Keep breathing, deeply and slowly. Follow your breath as it flows in through your nose, down your throat, into and through your lungs, and into your belly. Keep following it as it flows back out again. (You won't actually pull air into your belly, of course, but it will feel that way.)

Continue breathing this way for four to five minutes.

Stop and notice what you experience in your body.

BUZZING

Get comfortable. Take a few deep, slow breaths. Focus your attention behind your navel.

Relax your shoulders. Rest your tongue gently behind the top row of your teeth. Relax your jaw and let your mouth hang open.

Breathe out slowly and firmly. As you exhale, make a buzzing sound, like a bee. Extend the buzz and the exhalation as long as you can without strain or discomfort.

Repeat for two to three minutes. Then stop and notice what you experience in your body.

Experiment with different tones, volumes, and vibrations until you find some that feel the most comfortable.

SLOW ROCKING

Get comfortable and take a few slow, deep breaths. Then, slowly rock your upper body from side to side, or forward and back.

If you like, play or hum a slow, soothing tune and rock to its beat.

Feel free to experiment with standing versus sitting; with rocking side to side versus forward and back; with a range of different (but always slow) speeds; and with sitting in a variety of seats and positions. Discover what feels best to your body.

When you are done, stop and notice what your body is experiencing.

Alternative: Keep your body still, but let your head and neck rock slowly from side to side.

RUBBING YOUR BELLY

Get comfortable and take a few deep breaths. Let your shoulders relax.

Place your palm on the center of your belly, just above your navel. Press in gently. Hold your hand in place for a moment or two.

Then, slowly rub your belly for three to four minutes, in whatever way feels good to your body.

When you're done, pay attention to all the sensations in your body.

You can do this with or without clothes, but remove any heavy outerwear.

Alternative 1: Rub the center of your breastbone.

Alternative 2: Rub your solar plexus—your center of gravity, halfway between your breastbone and your navel.

20's

Get comfortable. Slowly rotate your foot at the ankle twenty times in either direction. If you like, move it in one direction; pause for ten seconds; then rotate it in the opposite direction.

Do this with each ankle, one at a time, pausing for ten seconds in between each set of rotations.

Then do the same for each knee; for your hips; for each wrist; for each elbow; and for each shoulder. Pause for ten seconds after each set of rotations.

Sometimes trauma energy can get stuck in the joints. These rotations help to release that energy.

OM-ING

The vibration of the word *om* (or *aum*) has a uniquely powerful settling effect on the human body.

Get comfortable and take a few deep breaths. Let your shoulders relax.

Breathe in slowly and deeply. As you exhale, for the full duration of your exhalation, very slowly utter the word *om*. It will sound and feel more like *ohhhhhh-ummmmmm-muhhhhh*.

Pay attention to how your body vibrates to the sounds. Then breathe in and begin again.

Do this for ten long, slow exhalations.

When you are done, pay attention to whatever sensations you experience in your body.

SINGING ALOUD TO YOURSELF

Sing a slow, soothing song to yourself—perhaps a lullaby or a gospel tune—as you work, walk, drive, or exercise.

Afterward, notice what your body experiences.

CHANTING

Chanting usually involves repeating a word, phrase, or line over and over. Most chants contain a mantra, a prayer, a song, or a scripture passage. However, chanting appears to have a settling effect on the body no matter what you chant.

When you're finished chanting, stop and pay attention to the sensations in your body.

BREATHE, GROUND, AND RESOURCE

Take a few deep breaths. Let your body relax as much as it wants to.

Think of a person, an animal, or a place that makes you feel safe and secure. Then imagine that, right now, this person or animal is beside you, or that you are in that safe place.

Breathing naturally, simply let yourself experience that safety and security for one to two minutes.

Afterward, notice how and what you experience in your body. Slowly look around, including directly behind you, and locate yourself in the here and now.

You can do this standing, sitting, or lying down, with your eyes either open or closed.

TOUCHING YOUR DISCOMFORT

This final activity is an especially helpful way of teaching your body to settle during times of stress or difficulty.

Think of a moderately painful *but not traumatic* incident from your past.

Then, for five seconds—no longer, at first—focus your attention on a painful aspect of that incident. As you do, notice all the sensations in your body. Also notice what thoughts, images, and emotions arise—without responding to them in any way.

Without disengaging from that incident or from your body, practice breathing, grounding, and resourcing (from the activity above). Feel your body as it relaxes and settles.

Then let go of the incident from your past. Return to the here and now.

If a part of your body feels sore, or tight, or strange in some way, simply put your hand on it and support it for a few seconds.

Practice this activity every day or two. Over time, slowly increase how long you stay with the painful memory, until you are able to relax and settle while experiencing it for a minute or more.

The soul nerve is not just where we experience our emotions. It's also where we feel a sense of belonging. This is why we can think of it as both a bodily organ and a communal one. More than almost anything else, each of us yearns to belong. Within each human body is this deep, raw, aching desire.

Here is what makes white-body supremacy so pervasive and so intractable: *Beneath all the exclusion and constriction and trauma, white-body supremacy offers the white body a sense of belonging.* It provides a false sense of brotherhood and sisterhood, of being a part of something intrinsically valuable.

A variety of organizations, from the Ku Klux Klan to the NRA, have capitalized on this, offering quasi-community, a manufactured history, respected elders, cohesive symbolism, rules of admonishment, an internally coherent (though toxic) worldview, and so on. White-body supremacy partly soothes white bodies in this way. But white-body supremacy also reflexively triggers the historical trauma embedded in those bodies.

African American bodies also feel a sense of belonging, of course. Ours, however, has its roots in necessity and an actual shared history. American police have their own sense of belonging, too, sometimes called the Blue Brotherhood. But there are many other ways to belong, and many other people and groups we can belong to. We can belong as family, as friends, as intimate partners, as neighbors, as countrymen, and as fellow human beings.

We will not end white-body supremacy—or any form of human evil—by trying to tear it to pieces. Instead, we can offer people better ways to belong, and better things to belong to. Instead of belonging to a race, we can belong to a culture. Each of us can also build our own capacity for genuine belonging.

The next two chapters are about building this capacity. You will learn to feel deeper into your own body, and then to harmonize it with other bodies. When practiced by enough people, these simple, primordial activities can begin to change the world, body by body.

RE-MEMBERINGS

- The soul nerve is the unifying organ of your entire nervous system, reaching into your throat, lungs, heart, stomach, liver, spleen, pancreas, kidney, and gut.

- Your soul nerve is where you experience a felt sense of love, compassion, fear, grief, dread, sadness, loneliness, hope, empathy, anxiety, caring, disgust, despair, and many other things that make us human.

- One of the main purposes of your soul nerve is to receive fight, flee, or freeze messages from your lizard brain and spread them to the rest of your body.

- Another purpose is to receive and spread the opposite message of *it's okay; you're safe right now; you can relax.*

- Your soul nerve is intimately involved with how your body interacts with other bodies.

- Your soul nerve tells most of the muscles in your body when to constrict, when to release, when to move, and when to relax and settle.

- With some attention and patience, you can learn to work with your soul nerve—consciously and deliberately relaxing your muscles, settling your body, and soothing yourself during difficult or high-stress situations.

- Over time, with further practice, you can also learn to use your soul nerve to activate and mobilize your body on demand.

- Your soul nerve is also where you feel a sense of belonging. More than almost anything else, each of us yearns to belong.

- Beneath all the exclusion, constriction, and trauma, white-body supremacy offers the white body a sense of belonging, a false sense of brotherhood and sisterhood.

- We will not end white-body supremacy—or any form of human evil—by trying to tear it to pieces. Instead, we can offer people better ways to belong and better things to belong to. Each of us can also build our own capacity for genuine belonging.

CHAPTER 11

SETTLING AND
SAFEGUARDING YOUR BODY

*"Breathe. Let go. Remind yourself that this very moment
is the only one you know you have for sure."*
OPRAH WINFREY

*"Healing is a practice. It's not a one-time thing or an idea. If I
get up and do a bunch of exercises and repeat them, over time my
muscles will get stronger. Healing is a practice just like that."*
MARNITA SCHROEDL

Few skills are more essential than the ability to settle your body. If you
can settle your body, you are more likely to be calm, alert, and fully
present, no matter what is going on around you. A settled body enables
you to harmonize and connect with other bodies around you, while
encouraging those bodies to settle as well. Gather together a large
group of unsettled bodies—or assemble a group of bodies and then
unsettle them—and you get a mob or a riot. But bring a large group
of settled bodies together and you have a potential movement—and a
potential force for tremendous good in the world. A calm, settled body

is the foundation for health, for healing, for helping others, and for changing the world.

I'm a therapist by profession. I've been trained by many wise elders and other professionals; I've earned a Master of Social Work degree; I know a variety of practices such as talk therapy, EMDR, and multiple forms of healing touch. If you paid me to, I could discuss your inner child, your internal archetypes, your ego and superego and id, Gottman's seven principles for a happy relationship, or any of a hundred other concepts therapists use. Yet none of these has much to do with why clients come to me, or how our work together helps them heal.

Although they don't always realize it, people visit my office to be with my settled, regulated nervous system. At first, clients come in with dysregulated nervous systems. Over time, their repeated contact with my nervous system helps their nervous systems settle. This does not happen through a process of mirroring, or cognitive training, or verbal communication. What takes place is energetic, chemical, biological—a synching of vibrations and energies. My nervous system does not model the way; over time, it helps other nervous systems access the same infinite source that mine does.

My settled nervous system isn't an accident of birth. It's partly the result of my training, my education, my experience, and my long-standing and mindful self-care.

But I didn't wrestle or mold or manage an unsettled nervous system into a settled one. Over time, I learned to access a settledness that is always and already present. I usually call it the Infinite Source, but it doesn't require a name, or an explanation, or a belief.

This settling of nervous systems, and this connection to a larger Source, is vital to healing.

*

If you're white, you may discover that when you can settle and manage your body, you won't feel a need to manage Black ones—or a need to ask Black ones to manage yours. You'll also be better able to manage, challenge, and disrupt white-body supremacy.

If you're Black, you may find that when you can settle and manage your body, you'll be better equipped to not internalize the standards of white-body supremacy. You'll also be more able to challenge it through organized and sustained resistance.

If you're a police officer, you may realize that when you can settle and manage your body, your job will be less stressful. In addition, many of the bodies you encounter will seem less threatening. Some of the law-abiding people you serve and protect may also feel less threatened by you. In addition, you may get sick or injured less often.

In each of these cases, you will discover that when you have regard for your own body, it is easier to have regard for other bodies.

Learning to settle your body and practicing wise and compassionate self-care are not about reducing stress; they're about increasing your body's ability to *manage* stress, as well as about creating more room for your nervous system to find coherence and flow. The activities you'll learn and practice in this chapter won't make your commute shorter, your boss more empathetic, or your child less self-centered. But they will help you be less resentful or reactive when your commute, your boss, or your child makes your life more difficult. As a result, you will lose your cool less often, and stressful situations will be less likely to trigger a fight, flee, or freeze response. In turn, you may develop stronger and more respectful relationships with your fellow commuters, your boss, and your child.

Settling is *not* the same thing as healing; it is an all-important foundation for healing. A settled body invites and accepts efforts to mend it; an unsettled one tends to resist those efforts.

Unfortunately, some people learn to settle their bodies, but misuse that ability. Instead of inviting and accepting healing, they use settling in a neurotic way, to *avoid* healing. When they face a conflict or difficulty, they don't settle themselves and then work through the clean pain. Instead, they flee the situation, and then partly soothe and settle their bodies with meditation, prayer, yoga, hiking, and so on. They use settling as a form of dirty pain, rather than as support for moving through clean pain. (There is nothing wrong with any of these practices. In fact, I often recommend them. For most people, most of the time, they are healthy. But when someone uses *any* activity to avoid growing up or facing clean pain, it's my job as a therapist to call him or her on it.)

Others, in an effort to avoid anxiety and hypervigilance, over-settle their bodies into a state that resembles depression. This, too, can be a flight response.

The activities in this chapter all focus on the body—*your* body. They are not mere exercises in relaxation, mindfulness, or learning to feel good. They are ways to better know, experience, and understand your body. They will make you more aware of your soul nerve, how and where and when it activates, and the many emotions it gives rise to. Most of all, they will help you develop the ability to settle your body whenever you wish.

Try not to view these settling activities as tools to be used only when you're under stress or feeling anxious or upset. These practices are nourishment as well as medicine. Do at least two or three of them regularly—ideally, every day or several times a week. If you like, rotate among several different ones.

Each person's body is unique, so some activities will work better for you than others. At your leisure, test each one. Use the ones that work and feel good; ignore the ones that don't. If an activity stops working or feeling good after doing it for some time, then switch things up. In all of these activities, however, you will learn to slow down, notice your body, and soothe yourself.

The central feature of any trauma response is speed. It has to be; otherwise, in the presence of genuine danger (for example, a snake about to strike), your body wouldn't be able to protect itself in time. This is why, in order to work through your trauma, you need to learn to slow down, reach for an internal resource, and fully experience your body through your soul nerve.

At other times, of course, your body needs to activate rather than settle. It's not that settling is good and activation is bad; each of us needs to be able to do either one on demand, based on the needs of the moment. With practice, these and later activities will help you settle your body *or* activate it whenever you need to.

I recommend initially practicing each activity in a quiet, comfortable, private space, as you did in earlier chapters. Once a practice has become familiar to your body, however, begin using it during difficult moments—including when other people are present.

—BODY AND BREATHING PRACTICES—

BREATHE, GROUND, AND RESOURCE, REVISITED

This is a new way to use an activity you practiced in Chapters 2 and 10.

Take a few deep breaths. Let your body relax as much as it wants to.

Think of a person, an animal, or a place that makes you feel safe and secure. Now imagine that this person or animal is beside you right now or that you are in that safe place.

Breathing naturally, let yourself experience that safety and security for about a minute.

Feel into your body. Where does it seem constricted, uncomfortable, or unwell in any way? Note each of these locations.

Pick one of these locations and focus on it. For a few seconds, let yourself fully experience the constriction or discomfort.

Then, once again, visualize the person, animal, or place that helps you feel safe and secure. Imagine you are in that place or that the person or animal is beside you. Experience the safety and security for a minute or two.

Do this for each part of your body that feels uncomfortable or constricted.

COMING INTO THE ROOM

Sit comfortably in a chair. Close your eyes and take a few deep breaths.

Imagine you're floating in space. Below you, planet Earth turns slowly. Watch it turn for a few seconds.

Slowly descend until the part of the country you're in fills your field of vision. Stay directly above it, like a GPS satellite, so that it doesn't move beneath you.

Keep descending until you're looking down on whatever city, town, mountain, valley, or other area your body is sitting in right now.

Continue your descent until you're looking down at the top of the building you're in. If you're seated outdoors, descend far enough so that you can see your own body below, as if you're viewing it from a helicopter.

Keep dropping slowly and steadily, until you can see your body in detail, as if you're about ten feet above it. Observe your body's posture, any movements it makes, and the clothing it's wearing.

Slowly and smoothly, descend the rest of the way, and slip inside your body.

For a few breaths, simply be aware of being in your body. Relax and let the chair support you.

Then notice the sensation of the chair against your legs and thighs.

Then notice how it feels against your back.

Open your eyes. Orient yourself by looking around you, including behind you. Return to the here and now.

BODY SCAN

Sit comfortably in a chair. Take a few breaths, feeling the air move in and out of your body. Close your eyes.

Notice the experience of the chair against your back. Notice the sensation of your feet on the ground.

Starting with the top of your head, slowly scan your body from top to bottom. Pay attention to each part as you slowly move your attention downward. Notice where there is pain or discomfort, where there is constriction, and where there is relaxation or expansiveness.

First move slowly down your forehead, then through your face, then down your neck.

Follow your attention as it moves across the top of your shoulders and onto your shoulder blades, then down your torso and into and down your arms.

Continue to descend down your torso and arms, through your hips and buttocks, and into your hands. Experience your attention spreading into your fingers and then out your fingertips.

Continue moving down your legs, through your knees, and down to your ankles. Pay attention to your major joints—your ankles, knees, hips, wrists, elbows, and shoulders. These are spots where energy often gets blocked. (If you feel the urge to move any of these, feel free to do so.)

Follow your attention into your feet, then down into your toes, then into the bottoms of your feet.

Take a moment to notice where your soles meet the ground.

For a pleasant and effective variation of this body scan, practice it standing in the shower, as you let the water surround and cleanse you.

SQUEEZE AND HOLD

Stand or sit comfortably. Take a few breaths.

Feel into your body. Where does it seem constricted, uncomfortable, or unwell in any way? Note each of these locations.

Then, one location at a time, gently press your hand against the uncomfortable spot, as if you are holding it lightly in place.

For thirty to forty-five seconds, simply experience that gentle pressure.

Then rub the spot, slowly and gently. If this feels good, keep rubbing for thirty to sixty seconds. If it doesn't, stop.

Next, *gently* squeeze and hold that spot. If squeezing it feels good, continue for thirty to sixty seconds. If it doesn't, stop.

Do this for each part of your body where there is pain, constriction, or distress.

Use this activity whenever a part of your body feels uncomfortable.

FINGER BALANCE

For this activity, buy what's called a *balancing bird*. Google those two words and you'll find a lot of options. Get one that's four to seven inches long; you should be able to find one for a dollar or two. (Prices range widely, but all models have the same basic design.)

Hold out your hand with the palm up. Keep your index finger extended, but curl the rest of your hand into a fist.

Place the beak of the balancing bird gently on the tip of your index finger. The beak will be no wider than a pencil point.

If you keep your hand still, the bird will balance perfectly on your fingertip. The bird will seem to defy gravity and float in place.

Continue to let the bird balance on your fingertip for thirty to sixty seconds, keeping your attention focused on it. If you like, move your hand in small, slow circles while the bird stays balanced.

These birds are more than just cool toys. They can have a profound focusing and settling effect on the body. I first learned about them as part of my training as a somatic therapist.

If you like, carry the bird in your purse or pocket. In moments of stress or difficulty, pull it out and balance it on your finger for a minute or so. (But if you want to be left alone, don't do this in public. There's a good chance someone will come over and say, "Wow, that is *awesome*.")

SOOTHING YOUR HANDS

Find an oil or lotion that smells good and feels good on your skin. This doesn't have to be anything special; many people use olive oil or hand lotion.

Get comfortable. Focus your attention on one hand. Then, very slowly and mindfully, rub it with lotion or oil. Apply it to your fingertips; then to the rest of your fingers; then to the spaces between your fingers; then to your palm; then to the back of your hand. Spend fifteen to twenty seconds slowly and gently rubbing it in.

Notice how each part of your hand feels as the liquid first touches it, then spreads across it, then gets rubbed in.

Now do the same for your other hand.

Safeguarding your body requires self-regard and soft, wise, and compassionate self-care. Caring for your body supports its health, its healing, and its settling. A well cared for body also tends to feel better.

The suggestions on the next few pages will help you create and follow your own self-care *growth routine*. Because each body is unique, there is no one-size-fits-all program. Experiment with different variations and combinations until you find a growth routine that feels good and that you can easily follow day after day. It's best not to be too ambitious at first. Begin with modest changes; then make gradual additions and adjustments over time.

The elements of an effective and gratifying growth routine are:

- *Enough sleep.* For most people, this means seven to eight hours a day; some people need more. Getting sufficient sleep can improve your concentration and memory, help you maintain or lose weight, improve your mood, and bolster your cardiovascular health. Many people find afternoon naps—even brief ones—especially rejuvenating.

- *Good nutrition.* Eat mostly fresh fruits and vegetables, whole grains, and lean proteins. Replace most of the fats in your diet with olive oil and/or butter. Avoid refined sugar and highly processed foods. Limit your daily alcohol consumption to one to two drinks and your caffeine intake to two regular-size coffees or teas. Take healthy supplements.[65] And check your tolerance for gluten by not eating it for a week or two; many of my clients experienced big health improvements when they stopped eating it.

- *Enough water.* Most Americans are chronically dehydrated. Monitor your water intake and make sure you drink at least eight to nine cups a day.

- *Regular exercise* (at least thirty minutes a day, five days a week). Physical exercise can increase your resilience, strengthen your heart, improve your mood, release endorphins and other feel-good chemicals, reduce tension, and support your overall physical and mental health. You don't have to join a gym or buy special equipment or outfits; brisk walking, swimming, biking, and/or jogging are all excellent. Just taking a two-mile walk five days a week can

---

65   I'm a therapist, not a physician or nutritionist, so I can't recommend specific supplements. However, I've seen many people's mental and physical health improve when they followed a growth routine and took some or all of these supplements under the guidance of a qualified nutritionist: a food-derived multivitamin, a food-derived B-complex vitamin, vitamin D3, magnesium, CoQ10, and flaxseed oil.

make a profound positive difference. If you're over fifty, I also recommend half an hour of strength training twice a week.[66]

- **Simple pleasures.** Each and every day, do at least one small, simple, soft thing that feels good to your body: do yoga, watch the sun rise, dig in the garden, play your guitar, take a walk with a friend, or do anything else that brings you joy. To ensure these simple pleasures become a regular part of your life, build them into your schedule.

- **Some form of meditation, prayer, or chanting.** This can be secular (for instance, Mindfulness-Based Stress Reduction), religious, or somewhere in between (such as insight meditation or Zen meditation). I recommend doing this for twenty to forty minutes a day—if possible, in the morning.

When your life is particularly stressful or uncomfortable, you will be tempted to abandon your growth routine. Don't. Do just the opposite: *strengthen your growth routine*. Get an extra thirty to sixty minutes of sleep each day. Eat as healthily as possible. Temporarily avoid all alcohol. Make a point to enjoy a couple of extra small pleasures each day. Be gentle and soothing with yourself. Wear soft, comfortable clothing. Hang out with gentle, friendly people. Spend more time with a loving pet. Listen to music that settles your body. (It doesn't have to be soft and gentle—gospel, country, folk, jazz, and even some R&B and rock can all have a settling effect. If you feel into your body, you'll notice which artists settle it and which ones don't.) The additional support will further strengthen your body's resilience and its ability to settle.

If you're not already convinced of the value of a growth routine, here's what I want you to do: Create a routine, try it for a month, and pay attention to what your body experiences. Then, for the month after that, deliberately *don't* follow the routine. Do whatever you want, whenever you want (so long as it's legal and ethical). Pay close and regular attention to what your body experiences. At the end of that second month, compare your body's responses.

---

66   Before beginning any new exercise routine, consult with a physician.

Here are some other helpful guidelines for keeping your body healthy and resilient:

- *Avoid all forms of tobacco.* Even smokeless tobacco can damage your body. Anything more than a celebratory cigar once or twice a year is too much.

- *Monitor and limit your drug use.* Use prescription drugs carefully. Be alert for drug interactions—the side effects of taking two or more different drugs at once. When taking any medication, use as little as possible to get the desired effect. Avoid recreational drugs in general; some, such as cocaine and marijuana, can impair your judgment; others, such as meth and heroin, can injure or kill you. (If you have strong cravings for drugs and/or alcohol, this craving may point to unhealed trauma. It may also offer a clue as to how and where that trauma got stuck in your body.)

- *Reach and maintain a healthy body weight.* You don't need to be thin to be healthy, but if you're carrying around more than ten to twenty extra pounds, that excess weight puts a strain on your breathing, heart, joints, and spine. If you're heavy, losing even a few pounds may dramatically improve your health.

- *Notice if you fall into a negative feedback loop.* A vicious circle of habits can steadily erode your health. Imagine, for example, that you regularly drink coffee at dinner. As a result, you have trouble falling asleep, so you're tired during the day—so you drink more coffee with dinner. Because you're sleep deprived, your performance at work suffers, and you're sometimes irritable with your kids. If you notice you've slipped into a negative feedback loop, deliberately strengthen your growth routine, and change your habits and schedule to break the negative pattern.

- *Pay attention to your body.* If it doesn't feel right, ask yourself, "Is there something I'm doing—or not doing—that's causing me to feel this way?" Then change that habit or behavior for a few days and see what happens. If you feel better, consider making the change permanent.

- ***Visit your doctor and dentist regularly.*** Get a physical once a year, an eye exam (for both health and vision) once a year, and a dental check-up every six months. These will help you head off potential problems and catch current problems early. (Under US law, your health insurance policy must pay for both your annual physical and your annual eye exam, and neither exam is subject to your deductible.[67]) If you don't feel well for more than two weeks, or if you have some other health symptom that lasts that long, have a physician check you out.

Caring for your body, your psyche, and your soul is not optional. It's crucial to your health, sanity, happiness, and healing, and it is an essential part of being human.

One final point: If you are currently experiencing new or repeated trauma, the best thing you can do to care for your body, psyche, and soul is to *stop the trauma.* Usually this means removing yourself from the situation that creates it. This isn't always possible, of course. Often toxic stress is unavoidable. Your home is destroyed in a hurricane. Your best friend dies. Your partner suddenly and unexpectedly leaves you. In these situations, use the practices in this chapter to settle your body, maintain or strengthen your growth routine, and care for yourself as well as you can.

RE-MEMBERINGS

- Few skills are more essential than the ability to settle your body. When you can settle your body, you are more likely to be calm, alert, and fully present, no matter what is going on around you.

---

67   This applies as of August of 2017. The law may have changed by the time you read this.

- A settled body also enables you to harmonize and connect with other bodies around you—while encouraging them to settle as well.

- A calm, settled body is the foundation for health, for healing, for helping others, and for changing the world.

- Learning to settle your body is *not* about reducing stress. It's about increasing your body's ability to *manage* stress.

- Settling is not the same as healing; it is an all-important foundation for healing.

- A settled body invites and accepts efforts to mend it. An unsettled one resists them.

- The central feature of any trauma response is speed. In order to work through your trauma, you need to learn to slow down and feel into your body, using your soul nerve.

- The ability to settle *or* activate your body on demand is essential for healing trauma.

- Safeguarding your body also requires wise and compassionate self-care. This includes:

  + Getting enough sleep

  + Good nutrition

  + Drinking enough water

  + Regular exercise

  + Enjoying simple pleasures

- When your life is especially stressful or uncomfortable, strengthen your growth routine.

- Caring for your body, your psyche, and your soul is not optional. It's crucial to your health, sanity, happiness, and healing and it is an essential part of being human.

CHAPTER 12

THE WISDOM OF
CLEAN PAIN

"Life is full of pain. Let the pain sharpen you,
but don't hold on to it."
PATRICIA NOMBUYISELO NOAH

"Self-care is the constant practice of not letting more pain
accumulate. It is about continually remembering that our lives are
of value. It is the active process of settling our nervous systems so
that we have more access to the present moment."
SUSAN RAFFO

Healing trauma involves recognizing, accepting, and moving through pain—clean pain. It often means facing what you don't want to face—what you have been reflexively avoiding or fleeing. By walking into that pain, experiencing it fully, and moving through it, you metabolize it and put an end to it. In the process, you also grow, create more room in your nervous system for flow and coherence, and build your capacity for further growth.

Clean pain is about choosing integrity over fear. It is about letting go of what is familiar but harmful, finding the best parts of yourself, and making a leap—with no guarantee of safety or praise. This healing does not happen in your head. It happens in your body. And it is more likely to happen in a body that can stay settled in the midst of conflict and uncertainty.

When you come out the other side of this process, you will experience more than just relief. Your body will feel more settled and present. There will be a little more freedom in it and more room to move. You will experience a sense of flow. You will also have grown up a notch. What will your situation look like when you come out the other side? You don't know. You can't know. That's how the process works. You have to stand in your integrity, accept the discomfort, and move forward into the unknown.

The alternative paths of avoidance, blame, and denial are paved with dirty pain. When people respond from their most wounded parts and choose dirty pain, they only create more of it, both for themselves and for other people.

When white supremacists discuss race in America, many of their arguments and positions are expressions of dirty pain and forms of fighting, fleeing, or freezing. Some common examples include talking but not listening; taking over all the energy in the room; denying other people's lived experience; jumping to statistics (which are often incorrect or misinterpreted); jumping to theory or philosophy or concepts or generalities (that is, fleeing from the body into the head); reframing racialized issues as issues about money or social class; focusing solely on personal responsibility and individualism; reductionism; objectification; false counter-narratives (such as "Black people simply don't work as hard as white people do"); avoidance; defensiveness; denial; blaming and accusations; and violence. This reflexive divisiveness negatively impacts bodies of every color.

White progressives have their own forms of dirty pain. They include white guilt; white savior complex ("Let me help you" and "I can fix this!"); ugly sympathy ("You poor, poor victims"); and taking over all the energy in the room by freaking out or bursting into tears. This last action is white progressives' signature form of white fragility. Many are unable to tolerate even slight discomfort around the complexities of white-body supremacy, trauma, and intersectionality with other forms of exploitation.

Many white progressives imagine they deserve a free pass because they are the "good ones." But white-body supremacy is itself a form of dirty pain. If you are a white progressive, you benefit as much from the structural inequities of white-body supremacy as a white conservative or a white supremacist.

We African Americans have our own forms of dirty pain. They include self-hate; internalized oppression; a bias favoring light skin over dark; a preference for shopping in white-owned businesses because we believe that "white people's ice is colder"; a habit of teaching our kids by "whupping" them; widespread use of the N-word; and a reflexive denigration of brothers and sisters who have achieved success. You'll recognize these as forms of traumatic retention.

Law enforcement professionals also have their own forms of dirty pain. Typically, they involve a reflexive distrust of authority; suspicion of anyone or anything that looks abnormal; extreme reactivity under stress; and a deep conflict between the desire to protect people and the urge to harm real and potential troublemakers. It often involves silence and inaction in the face of wrongdoings by fellow officers.

Because public safety is a profession, not an ethnicity, many police officers routinely experience the dirty pain common to their profession *and* the dirty pain associated with their ethnic background. This makes one of the most difficult and demanding jobs even more difficult.

The particulars of moving through clean pain are unique to each person and each incident. However, the process can be described— and navigated.

The process involves five steps. Each one anchors you in the present and, most importantly, in your body. I refer to them as the *five anchors*.[68]

---

68   One of my mentors, Dr. David Schnarch, has his own version of this process, which he calls the Crucible 4 Points of Balance. You can learn more about Dr. Schnarch and his work at crucible4points.com. (The five anchors stand on the shoulders of the 4 Points of Balance and grew out of some of my work with Dr. Schnarch.)

- **Anchor 1:** Soothe yourself to quiet your mind, calm your heart, and settle your body.

- **Anchor 2:** Simply notice the sensations, vibrations, and emotions in your body instead of reacting to them.

- **Anchor 3:** Accept the discomfort—and notice when it changes—instead of trying to flee from it.

- **Anchor 4**: Stay present and in your body as you move through the unfolding experience, with all its ambiguity and uncertainty, and respond from the best parts of yourself.

- **Anchor 5:** Safely discharge any energy that remains.

You'll know you need to practice the five anchors when you sense a conflict building; when that conflict looks and feels as if it will continue to escalate; and when you feel a growing discomfort in your soul nerve.

Let's move through the process in detail.

ANCHOR 1: SOOTHE YOURSELF TO QUIET YOUR MIND, CALM YOUR HEART, AND SETTLE YOUR BODY.

In an ideal world, when a conflict starts to boil, you'd be able to leave the room, take ten deep breaths, meditate for five minutes, and walk around the block. But in the real world you almost never have that kind of opportunity. In the heat of a conflict, you need to be able to soothe yourself *quickly* in order to move into the second step.

Here are some ways to practice Anchor 1:

- First and foremost, *shut up*. For a few seconds, don't say anything—no matter how much you might want to, or how much you have to say, or how loudly someone else is yelling. Just breathe.

- If you're holding something, let it go or put it down.

- Sit down. Put your hands in your lap or on your knees.

- Mentally tell yourself, *Stay calm* or *Keep it together* or (my own favorite) *Calm the fuck down.*

- Quickly find an internal resource your body experiences as safe, soothing, or pleasurable. Think of this person, place, or animal, and quickly connect to it. For a few seconds, experience this resource (as a sensation, or image, or emotion, or impulse, or vibration).

- Go to the bathroom. Seriously. Say, "I need to use the bathroom. I'll be right back"; then go in and close the door. I know this sounds silly, but in many situations, it's the best way to get two minutes alone to catch your breath and move into Anchor 2. If you just walk away or say, "I need to be alone for a minute," someone might get pissed off or come after you. But they probably won't follow you into the toilet. (Be sure to return and re-engage after a few minutes.)

- Do something else to slow things down without dissing anyone or running away. Say, "Hang on, it's hot in here" and take off your sweater; take a long, slow drink from your mug; open or close a window; reach over and pet the cat.

ANCHOR 2: SIMPLY NOTICE THE SENSATIONS, VIBRATIONS, AND EMOTIONS IN YOUR BODY INSTEAD OF REACTING TO THEM.

This anchor is all about staying in the here and now. Here are some ways to do this:

- Pay attention to your body's experience of simply being in your clothes. Notice how and where your body touches your underwear, your shirt, your pants, your skirt, your socks or stockings, and your hat.

- Notice any other body sensations: your back against the chair, your tongue against the roof of your mouth, the wind blowing against your face. Experience and name each sensation: heat, cold, constriction, relaxation, hollowness, looseness, weakness, trembling.

- As thoughts and emotions and possible reactions arise, don't run off with them. Bring yourself back to your body and its sensations.

ANCHOR 3: ACCEPT THE DISCOMFORT—AND NOTICE WHEN IT CHANGES—INSTEAD OF TRYING TO FLEE FROM IT.

At first this will be difficult, but with practice it will get easier. Here are some ways to practice this:

- When you feel an urge to tamp down or push away the discomfort, don't. Keep your attention focused directly on it. Stay with it and notice when it changes—because, if you don't flee from it, at some point it will.

- When you get the impulse to analyze or think about the discomfort, bring yourself back to the sensation of discomfort itself. Again, notice when it changes.

- When your mind spits out strategies for what to do next, don't grab onto them. Just sit with the discomfort. Notice when the speed, focus, or quality of your thoughts changes.

- When thoughts or images about the past or future pop up, let them float past you. Stay with your body in the present.

- Remind yourself that any discomfort you feel is a protective response, not a defective one. Accepting, experiencing, and moving through that discomfort is the foundation of healing.

ANCHOR 4: STAY PRESENT AND IN YOUR BODY AS YOU MOVE THROUGH THE UNFOLDING EXPERIENCE, WITH ALL ITS AMBIGUITY AND UNCERTAINTY, AND RESPOND FROM THE BEST PARTS OF YOURSELF.

Continue to use the first three anchors to stay in the present and in your body. At the same time, slowly move into the heat, peril, and possibility of the conflict. Feel your way, moment by moment. Here are some tips:

- When you find yourself focusing on the future or the past, use the first three anchors to bring yourself back to your body and the here and now.

- When your attention moves to what's wrong with you or with what a jerk the other person is, use those first three anchors to bring you back to the present.

- Don't try to know what will happen next. It's impossible. If someone asks you a question and your only honest response is *I don't know*, say, "I don't know."

- Don't try to wrest or finagle a particular response from anyone else.

- Act from the best parts of yourself—from your own deepest integrity. As events unfold, you'll sense what these parts are.

Anchor 4 always involves uncertainty. It can take many minutes, sometimes even hours, to play out.

There may be some situations—especially during your first few months of practicing the five anchors—when your lizard brain gets overwhelmed and you temporarily go bonkers. (This happens occasionally to almost everyone, including us therapists.)

If and when you do briefly lose your mind, it doesn't mean you've blown it, that it's too late, or that you might as well smash a window, go berserk, or blow your brains out. *Exactly the opposite is true.* Every new moment is a new opportunity to catch yourself, come back to the here and now, and settle your body.

Whenever you do lose your way—or lose your mind—go back to Anchor 1 and use it to soothe yourself and slow yourself down. Then move forward again into Anchors 2, 3, and 4.

ANCHOR 5: SAFELY DISCHARGE ANY ENERGY THAT REMAINS.

This anchor is underused and poorly understood, but it is no less important than the others. Use this anchor only *after* you have worked through the conflict, or disengaged from it, or agreed to stop focusing on it for now.

If you watch animals in the wild, you'll see that after a high-stress situation has passed, they'll instinctively discharge their built-up energy. A zebra that has just outrun a lion will vigorously shake itself or ripple the skin along its back. Other animals will roll on the ground or run in a circle or pick brief mock fights with each other.

After you have been in the heat of a conflict, its energy remains bottled up in your body. For your physical and emotional well-being, discharge it as soon as you reasonably can. Allow yourself to experience your body's natural defensive and protective urges—and then discharge them. Here are some good ways to do this:

- Most forms of exercise, including walking.

- Playing most sports.

- Dancing.

- Physical labor—heavy yard work, construction, snow shoveling, etc.

- Follow your body's moment-by-moment guidance. You might experience a sudden urge to push your hands in the air, or run around the block, or shake your head vigorously and shout. Let your body do whatever it wants to do. (Unless, of course, it wants to do something harmful, such as putting a fist through the wall. In that case, discharge the energy in a harmless way—by punching a cushion, for example.)

Here are some things that will *not* help:

- Playing sports that don't make you move your entire body for at least twenty consecutive minutes—ping pong, golf, bowling, softball, etc.

- Doing yoga, tai chi, qigong, or meditation. These will stretch and/or relax you, but they will gather rather than disperse your energy.

You'll learn this process by going through it, time after time and experience after experience. Sometimes you'll make mistakes—perhaps even big ones. But, over time, you'll get better at using all of the five anchors, and at handling each part of the process as it unfolds.

*

In previous chapters, we covered a range of practices for settling your body and staying in the here and now. Here are two other processes that can help you settle and stay present in painful situations *as they unfold*. Use them separately, together, or in combination with the five anchors.

—BODY PRACTICES—

STOP, DROP, AND ROLL

Whatever you're doing, thinking, or saying, *stop*. Don't go any further down the same emotional and mental path.

Drop back. Pay attention to what you experience in your body; to what is going on around you; to where the situation seems to be headed; and to how you're helping to push it in that direction. Then ask yourself: "Is that where I want this interaction to go?" If not, say so out loud: "Let's not go where I think we're headed. Let's figure out something different."

Roll with whatever happens next in your body, but without fighting, fleeing, or freezing. Don't try to control it, or run from it, or squelch it, or tear it to pieces. You might suddenly weep, or laugh, or shudder, or moan, or hug yourself. If so, let go and do it. (Unless it will harm you or someone else, in which case channel the energy so that it doesn't, as in Anchor 5.)

This process is especially helpful when your situation looks like it's escalating toward a crisis.

CHECK YOUR BODY'S CHECKPOINTS

Your body has internal checkpoints—physical sensations that activate when something feels unfair, frightening, dangerous, or otherwise not right. These are signals from your soul nerve. They might alert you to something real, something perceived, something possible, or something imagined. (To your body, these are all identical.)

These signals might include a tingle at the back of your neck, a sinking feeling in your belly, a tightness in your shoulders, or some other unpleasant sensation. You'll know these sensations when you experience them. These checkpoints are your body's early warning signals. They alert you when you are headed for a fight, flee, or freeze response.

If you're paying attention, when one of these signals goes off, you can stop what you're doing and take steps to settle your body. This helps you avoid a fight, flee, or freeze response. It also gives you a chance to change the dynamic of the situation by leaving it, stepping back, or saying something like, "You know what? I'd like to do this differently."

Whenever one of your body's checkpoints signals you, investigate it. What do you experience? Where do you experience it? What emotions, thoughts, or images are arising with it?

Then ask yourself, "What is this sensation telling me? What is it urging me to do? What movements do I need to make? What action needs to be completed? How can I respond from my deepest integrity—the best parts of myself?" The answer to this last question will point a way forward.

With practice, you'll get more familiar with your body's checkpoints. Over time, you'll learn to recognize each signal as soon as it activates, and you'll know what it's telling you.

RE-MEMBERINGS

- Healing from trauma involves recognizing, accepting, and moving through pain—clean pain.

- Healing does not happen in your head. It happens in your body.

- The process of moving through clean pain involves five steps, or anchors:

    + *Anchor 1*: Soothe yourself to quiet your mind, calm your heart, and settle your body.

    + *Anchor 2*: Simply notice the sensations, vibrations, and emotions in your body instead of reacting to them.

    + *Anchor 3*: Accept the discomfort—and notice when it changes—instead of trying to flee from it.

    + *Anchor 4*: Stay present and in your body as you move through the unfolding experience, with all its ambiguity and uncertainty, and respond from the best parts of yourself.

    + *Anchor 5*: Safely discharge any energy that remains.

- Two other processes can help you settle your body and stay present in painful situations as they unfold: *Stop, Drop, and Roll* and *Check Your Body's Checkpoints*.

CHAPTER 13

REACHING OUT TO
OTHER BODIES

*"We never know how our small activities will affect others through
the invisible fabric of our connectedness."*

GRACE LEE BOGGS

Events don't just happen. We experience them in our bodies—which
means we need to metabolize them in our bodies as well. Talking with
someone you trust about your experience can help you complete this
metabolic process.

This isn't something to do only after a difficult and stressful event.
It's something we all need to do on a regular basis. Talking with
another person to process what you learned or experienced doesn't
mean having a friendly chat with them. It means *describing an event that
had meaning for you, while the other person listens with caring, full attention, a
calm presence, and a settled body.* This might involve both of you letting you
tremble, cry, sway, shake your head, or move your body in some other
way as it metabolizes the experience.

Therapists call this *active listening*. Being an active listener involves
not interrupting; not making judgments; not asking questions other

than to make sure you understand; not giving advice or offering explanations; and not jumping in with a story of your own.

It's important to reach out to others for this type of support. It's just as important to allow others to reach out to you for it.

In therapy a traumatic experience is sometimes described as an attempted action that got thwarted and became stuck in the body. For example, you tried to cross a street but got injured by a bicyclist; you tried to explain to your uncle why you were late, and he hit you or shamed you; as you walked to work, you saw a man attacking a woman. A common first step in the mending of trauma is *completing the action that was thwarted*. This releases the trauma energy stuck in your body. You can then use this energy to metabolize the trauma.

Most actions can be completed either literally or symbolically. You could certainly call up your abusive uncle and respectfully but firmly tell him off. But you don't have to. You might instead hold such a conversation with an imagined version of him, in your head, while staying aware of what your body experiences as the conversation unfolds. You might also maintain a firm protective boundary whenever you're with him. And the next time you sense someone is thinking about hitting or shaming you, you might take a step forward and say firmly, "No. Don't you *dare*." Thus you complete the action you were unable to complete at an earlier time.

However you choose to complete an action, throughout that experience you also need to slow yourself down; use the five anchors to stay in your body and in the present; pay close attention to what you experience in your body; and notice any changes that occur in it.

Completing an action isn't always deliberate, or even cognitive. Your body may even complete an action without you consciously noticing it. This might involve a small gesture such as brushing something away or holding out your hand. Your thinking brain may completely miss it. But to your body, that simple movement may have profound meaning.

For example, the next time you cross the street at the corner where the bicyclist hit you, your body may naturally turn aside as traffic approaches. You might automatically hold up your hand in a *halt* gesture as you step into the street. You might stop and wave an oncoming bicyclist through. These are all movements you didn't have a chance to make during the original event, so they got stuck in your body. Now it is safe for you to complete any or all of those movements. In completing them, they will get unstuck; energy will be released; and your body will no longer need to harbor such a strong and reflexive protective response.

Completing an action sets up the conditions for healing. But that healing doesn't just occur in the present. It also moves backward and forward in time. When you heal a soul wound, you heal the people who came before you. You heal their presence in your life, in your memory, and in the expression of your DNA. This opens up a bit more room for flow and compassion inside you. You also heal the generations to come, because your healing means that you will not pass on your trauma to your descendants.

In the healing of intergenerational trauma, you may also complete an action that was attempted and thwarted by a traumatized ancestor. The trauma got stuck in their body, and then passed down to you. Even though you may be cognitively unaware of this trauma—or of your ancestor's experience and incomplete action—your own efforts simultaneously heal your trauma and release future generations from its grip.

As you mend your trauma, you'll notice two opposing forces— two different gravitational pulls in your body. The first is your body's natural urge to settle and relax. The second is your body's equally natural urge to protect itself. This can manifest as activation, an urge to move. It can also appear as constriction. During the early stages of healing, you may feel far more protective energy than settling energy. You may find it difficult to settle your body. Protective energy may suddenly surge through you, making you antsy or anxious. All of this is common and normal, and there is no need to do anything about it. Just be patient with yourself. As you practice the activities in this book, your body will naturally build its capacity to settle.

Remember: it's not that settling is good and activation is bad. Your body needs to be able to do either one, based on the needs in the moment. Ultimately, your body will learn to activate, or settle, or move back and forth between the two as you need to, whenever you need to.

RE-MEMBERINGS

- We experience events in our bodies—which means we also need to metabolize them in our bodies.

- Talking with someone you trust about your experience can help you complete this metabolic process.

- It's important to reach out to others for their support in this way. It's just as important to allow others to reach out to you in this same way.

- A common first step in the mending of trauma is *completing the action that was thwarted*. This releases the trauma energy stuck in your body. You can then use this energy to metabolize the trauma.

- You can complete most actions either literally or symbolically.

- Completing an action isn't always deliberate, or even cognitive.

- When you heal historical and intergenerational trauma, you heal the people who came before you. You also heal the generations to come, because your healing means that you will not pass on your trauma to your descendants.

- As you mend your trauma, you'll notice two opposing forces: your body's natural urge to settle and relax and its equally natural urge to protect itself.

- During the early stages of healing, you may feel far more protective energy than settling energy. This is normal.

- Ultimately, you will learn to activate your body, or settle it, or move back and forth between the two states as you need to, whenever you need to.

CHAPTER 14

HARMONIZING WITH OTHER BODIES

*"An individual has not started living until he can rise above
the narrow confines of his individualistic concerns to the
broader concerns of all humanity."*
MARTIN LUTHER KING, JR.

Healing with other human beings requires us to respect, regard, and
be in harmony with other bodies. Black, white, and police bodies all
need to learn to be more comfortable and settled with one another.
That is a key focus of this chapter—and the rest of this book.

Unfortunately, much of what Americans say and do is designed to
keep our bodies out of harmony with each other. Our public discourse,
our media, and our policing all unsettle our bodies far more than they
help us settle them. This is especially true around issues involving the
myth of race.

The first step in changing this dynamic is settling our own bodies,
one by one. Earlier chapters laid out various activities to help us do
just that. The next step is bringing that settling out into the world and
getting our bodies in sync with others.

I've discussed how a settled body helps other bodies it encounters to settle as well. Give bodies the right context and encouragement, and they will begin to harmonize as well. When, over time, enough bodies heal from historical, intergenerational, and personal trauma and learn to harmonize, that harmony can turn into a culture of resilience and flow.

If this sounds touchy-feely, that's because it *is* touchy-feely. It's grounded in the body—and the body is all about touch and sensation. But I'm talking about a resilient and grounded touchy-feely, not a "Kumbaya" touchy-feely. No one heals from generations of trauma through warm fuzzies or smiley faces. In the coming pages, you won't find rainbows, organized group hugs, or pleas to just love one another. There may be an opportunity to add love in a decade or two. For now, though, we need to simply get our bodies more in sync.

This chapter offers a menu of straightforward, everyday activities you can do to help harmonize your body with other bodies. Some of them build on (or are variations of) activities in earlier chapters.

Practice these activities *only* with people and groups you already know and trust. If they're all the same race, that's fine; if they're a variety of races, that's fine, too. (In later chapters, I'll offer some other, more focused activities for white bodies to do with other white bodies, for Black bodies to do with other Black bodies, and for police bodies to do with other police bodies.)

Many of the practices may seem absurdly simple—and many of them are. But each one can have a profoundly positive effect on your body, and on other bodies that are nearby.

Keep in mind that these are *everyday* activities—things to be done briefly, in the moment, with one or more other bodies. For example: "Before we begin our meeting, let's all hum together for about ten seconds to help harmonize our bodies." Or, "Can we try something? For the next few minutes, let's try walking silently, side by side, keeping our footsteps in sync." Or, "Wow, you look really beat. Want me to massage your feet for a couple of minutes?" Or, "Before I begin my sermon, let's all settle our bodies. Everyone please rise. Now, if you would, for about fifteen seconds I'd like each of you to just rub your belly, slowly, like I'm doing now."

Don't over-think, over-plan, over-emphasize, or over-organize these activities. Keep them simple and friendly. Just add them to other interactions and events; don't make them the focus of anything. As you do them, pay close attention to your body and to what it experiences. Notice where and how it constricts, and where and how it settles. Be aware of any impulses, urges, emotions, thoughts, and images that arise. Use the five anchors to stay present and in your body.

Immediately after completing an activity, check in with your body to see if anything feels different. Then orient yourself to the space around you. Look around, including behind you.

A few other things to keep in mind before you begin:

- Set aside any goals and personal agendas, especially agendas involving power, sex, or money.

- Don't expect or try to evoke a particular response from anyone.

- Don't take on the role of schoolmaster, making sure everyone does an activity the *right* way. Sometimes the "wrong" way will be better.

- Whenever possible, turn off your cell phone before you begin. Urge others to do the same.

- You never know how someone will react to any of these activities. They might be pleased, grateful, amused, delighted, confused, suspicious, wary, afraid, offended, or angry. They might think the activity is silly.

- Whatever they do, be as present as you can, and use the anchors from Chapter Twelve to hold yourself steady as you move through the situation.

- Above all, don't try to convince or coerce anyone into any of these activities. If he or she is not interested or refuses to participate, simply say, "No problem. It was just an idea. Never mind."

—BODY PRACTICES TO DO TOGETHER—

THINGS TO DO WITH FRIENDS, FAMILY MEMBERS, AND OTHERS YOU KNOW AND TRUST

Hum or keen together. This can be a single tone, a series of tones, or a tune all of you know.

Hum and touch. Pair up with someone you trust and respect. Before you begin humming, have the other person face away from you; then *gently* cup your hand around the base of their skull, where their soul nerve begins. Keep your hand there as you hum together. After a few minutes, switch places.

***Om* together.** You may first need to briefly train people, especially in stretching out the sound into three syllables. If necessary, explain that this is a harmonizing practice, not a religious one.

Sing a lullaby (or any other song) together. Lullabies are ideal because they help bodies settle as well as harmonize. Louder and more energetic singing can harmonize bodies, too, but may not help settle them.

Rock back and forth together, without touching. You can do this while singing or humming; to music, without vocalizing; or silently and mindfully. Holding hands or draping arms over each other's shoulders is optional. (This activity can have more power when people *don't* touch because it simultaneously affirms individuality *and* connection.)

Rub your bellies, breastbones, or solar plexuses at the same time. Each person of course rubs his or her own.

Take a silent walk together; after a few steps, deliberately keep your footsteps in sync. Walking side by side is ideal, but one person can also walk in front of the other. Silence is an important part of this activity.

Take someone's hand and gently massage it for one to two minutes. First ask his or her permission, of course. Do this with either or both hands.

Wash or massage someone's feet. You may be surprised at what a profound experience this is for some people. They may (or may not) melt or swoon or cry. You may also be surprised at how few people will agree to it—even though it is almost universally pleasurable—and deeply settling. Always ask for permission first.

Simply stand and breathe quietly together, with gazes cast slightly downward. Option 1: stand in pairs, back to back. Option 2: stand in a circle, facing front to back, with each person's hand placed gently on the shoulder or midback of the person in front of him or her.

When someone is in emotional distress, simply be settled and present with the person. If he or she cries or wails, cry as well. If the person needs to talk, simply listen mindfully and respectfully, without passing judgment, or interrupting, or asking a lot of questions.

THINGS TO DO IN GROUPS WHOSE MEMBERS KNOW AND TRUST EACH OTHER (CHURCH GROUPS, BLOCK CLUBS, ETC.)

Hum together, as described earlier.

Group hum and touch. Have five or more people stand in a circle, with each person facing the next person's back. Have each person cup his or her hand gently around the base of the next person's skull. Then hum together.

Sing together.

Rock back and forth together, without touching. You can do this with or without music and with or without singing. Have people stand in a circle or, if that's not possible, a line.

Rub bellies, breastbones, or solar plexuses together. Again, each person rubs his or her own.

Line dance or folk dance together as a group. (*Not* as partners.)

Sit silently together in a circle for ten to fifteen minutes, simply resting and breathing. Ask people *not* to make eye contact. Instead, ask them to cast their gazes down or close their eyes.

Our bodies guide and follow other bodies; a settled nervous system encourages other nervous systems to settle. This is why a calm, settled presence can create room for a multitude of possibilities, and become the foundation for changing the world.

RE-MEMBERINGS

- Our public discourse, our media, and our policing all unsettle our bodies far more than they help us settle them.

- The first step in changing this dynamic is settling our own bodies, one by one.

- The next step is bringing that settling out into the world and getting each of our bodies in sync with others.

- A settled body helps other bodies it encounters to settle. Give those bodies the right context and encouragement, and they will begin to harmonize as well. When, over time, enough bodies heal from trauma and learn to harmonize, that harmony can turn into culture.

- Because a settled nervous system encourages other nervous systems to settle, a calm, settled presence is the foundation for changing the world.

CHAPTER 15

MENDING THE BLACK HEART AND BODY

"When I dare to be powerful—to use my strength in the service of my vision—then it becomes less and less important whether I am afraid."

AUDRE LORDE

"I have learned over the years that when one's mind is made up, this diminishes fear; knowing what must be done does away with fear."

ROSA PARKS

When my brothers and I were little, we spent a lot of time at our grandmother's house. She was always happy to have us, but sometimes, when we got into serious trouble, she would whup us. She used a switch braided from the branches of a willow tree that grew in her backyard. A portrait of her and my grandpapa, painted many years earlier, hung in her living room. She kept the switch behind the portrait.

My brothers and I were normal boys, so we probably did what adults expected of us about half the time. The rest of the time we did whatever we pleased. Sometimes my grandmother would get upset with us. Her most common complaint went like this: "What did I *just* tell you? Y'all don't listen *at all*. You boys don't realize you're eatin' fat till your faces are *covered* in grease."

Like most young boys, we'd listen politely while she chewed us out. Then we'd be obedient for the next fifteen minutes. Then we'd go back to doing whatever we wanted.

About once a year, though, we did something that seriously upset her. When that happened, she wouldn't even bother chewing us out. She'd just say, "That's it" and head toward the portrait in the living room. When she wanted to, that woman could move *fast*.

My brothers and I would freeze in terror. We knew what was coming next.

If you've never been whupped with a willow switch, let me tell you this: It's something you want to avoid. When the switch strikes you, it wraps *around* your arm or leg. It doesn't usually break the skin, but it leaves welts that last—and sting—for a couple of days.

On at least two occasions, my grandmother was so upset at us that she made us go into the backyard, cut branches off the willow tree, and bring them to her. Then, as we watched in dread, she braided a new switch right before our eyes.

My grandmother grew up in a sharecropping family in Round Lake, Mississippi. *Her* grandparents spent much of their lives on a plantation. You don't need a degree in psychology to recognize my grandmother's whupping us with a switch as a traumatic retention.

The term *whupping* is a slightly sanitized version of *whipping*, which for centuries was a standard practice in America. Overseers on plantations routinely whipped Black bodies, both to punish them and to control them. The apparatus used to inflict pain has also been somewhat sanitized, from a whip to a switch.

But there was another aspect to my grandmother's whuppings. She never got any pleasure out of whupping us. In fact, sometimes when she did it, there were tears in eyes. Always, after she had hit each of us a few times and put the switch away, my brothers and I would sit on her living room floor, sobbing. She would sit down with us and tell us, "What did I tell you boys? Y'all got to listen when I tell you somethin's dangerous. If I tell you to stay away from somethin', *you need to stay away from it.* I don't want y'all gettin' hurt. You understand?"

My grandmother never whupped us because she was angry or just because we had been disobedient. If we broke a vase or a window, she'd give us a talking to or, at worst, deny us peach cobbler at supper. She only whupped us when she felt we had put ourselves in danger, either physically or socially. (At the time, of course, I didn't realize this.)

Afterward, she would always explain why she whupped us and why we needed to be more careful. This gave us context, safety, and security; it helped us process what had happened; and it helped instill more resilience in our bodies. She whupped us in an attempt to protect us from what she knew could easily harm the young Black bodies in front of her. Her whuppings may have been misguided, but they were well intentioned—done out of her love for us.

As a father and a therapist, I can't condone any of my grandmother's whuppings.[69] Yet I understand them. I also recognize that what she did was a partial mending of her own trauma.

She should not have whupped us in the first place, of course. But, truth be told, at times my brothers and I were some pretty hardheaded, bad-ass kids. Still, because of her loving explanations afterward, something deeply healing occurred: *she did not pass on her traumatic retentions to any of us.*

*

I've never whupped my son, Tezara, who is now sixteen. But there have been times when I've had to hold him close to me, press my face up close to his, and announce, "You . . . are . . . going . . . to . . . have . . . to . . . get . . . your . . . shit . . . together."

The times when I've gotten most upset at Tezara—and the moments when I've most had to override the temptation to whup him—have usually been when he was about to put himself in danger.

---

[69]   In 2014, Minnesota Vikings running back Adrian Peterson, who is African American, was arrested for whupping his young son with a switch. The arrest and indictment were entirely warranted. But the painful irony is that, for hundreds of years, it was legal in many American states for white slave owners to whip enslaved Black people. For an insightful discussion of the use of the switch in African American families, read DeNeen L. Brown's *Washington Post* article, "A Good Whuppin'? Adrian Peterson Child Abuse Case Revives Debate" (September 13, 2014).

Long ago I stopped worrying about him running out into the street without looking both ways or putting his eye out with a bow and arrow. But I do still worry that he will get hurt—mostly at the hands of strangers.

Tezara is a normal teenager. He wants as much freedom as possible, and he simply doesn't understand the dangers that await him out in the world. This is the unsettling and unavoidable paradox of creating a loving home: parents raise kids whose bodies are unprepared to protect themselves from all the evils they will eventually face. I can't tell you how many times I've had some version of the following dialogue with my son:

Tezara: "Daddy, why can't I? You're just being mean. Hayden's parents are letting him do it."

Me: "I'm not being mean. I'm trying to protect you."

Tezara: "Hayden's parents don't think he'll be in any danger."

Me: "I don't think your friend Hayden will be in any danger, either."

Tezara: "So why can't I go with him?"

Me (sighing): "Because Hayden has a white body and you have a Black one. You're subject to dangers that he isn't. That's just how it is. I'm your daddy, and part of my job is to keep you from getting hurt or killed. That's why my answer is no."

Tezara: "Oh, come on, Daddy. Who would want to kill me?"

This is when I often blink back tears and think of Tamir Rice and Emmett Till.[70] I want to tell my son, "Tezara, the list of people who want to kill you is *long*." Of course I don't. I usually just say, "This conversation is over" and leave the room.

*

The rest of this chapter, while applicable to bodies of all colors, is especially relevant to African Americans.

---

70   After writing this in early 2017, I googled Emmett Till and learned of a story that had broken the day before. It involved Carolyn Bryant Donham, the woman who claimed in 1955 that Till had followed her, grabbed her around the waist, used vulgar language, and told her that he had had sex with other white women before. She now publicly admitted that she made up all those details. Soon after Donham first made her accusations, Till was kidnapped, tortured beyond recognition, and shot in the head. His body was tied with barbed wire and thrown into the Tallahatchie River. The two white men who killed him both later admitted their guilt in a *Look Magazine* interview. Both were acquitted by an all-white, all-male jury.

In Chapter Thirteen, you read about things you can do to harmonize your body with those of others, regardless of their backgrounds or skin colors. Now I'd like to suggest some activities to help you harmonize your body with other *African American* bodies, and to help each other heal. I encourage you to practice these activities often—with friends, family, and trusted groups in safe settings.

All of these activities will seem familiar, which is exactly why I recommend them. They are family and communal strategies that African Americans have used for generations. They helped us and our ancestors to survive, remain resilient, settle our bodies, and alleviate trauma for hundreds of years. When you practice these activities with others, you also recognize a shared history.

Each activity is listed separately, but people often do two or three of them at the same time.

—BODY PRACTICES TO DO TOGETHER—

Sing together. Not just any songs, but gospel songs, call-and-response tunes, and other uniquely African American music.

Group drumming. Anyone who can move at least one limb can drum. If you don't have drums, a tabletop will do.

Rhythmic group clapping. This is basically drumming on our own bodies.

Hum in sync with others. This is ideal for when groups are cleaning, packing, cooking, or doing some other chore together.

Brief, secure, caring touches. Of course, only give such touches to people who welcome and appreciate them.

Braiding or combing each other's hair. Although this is typically a woman-to-woman activity, there's no reason why men—or men and women—can't do it together.

Cook together. This can also include eating together; feeding each other; bringing food to others in difficult times; serving or delivering meals to people in need; trading recipes; teaching others (especially young people) to cook; feeding each other's babies or children; cooking new dishes or cuisines together; volunteering to cook together as a family at a church supper or charitable event; or hosting or sponsoring a giant potluck. Let me state the obvious: for such gatherings, you can't go wrong with soul food.

Hug people mindfully. Before you give a hug, do your best to settle your body. As you hug the other person, pay close attention to your body—*and* to their body, too. This transforms a greeting ritual into a practice for settling and harmonizing bodies. (Of course, only hug people who are okay with being hugged.)

Offer supportive touch. Gently but firmly, simply hold a part of someone's body to support it. This might be a person's elbow or their shoulder or the back of their neck. This can be especially settling for someone who is distraught or shaken. Of course, always ask the person for permission first. To provide additional support and settling, also hum softly.

Cry or wail together in times of grief, tragedy, or death. Host a wailing circle or set up a wailing room. There can be great healing in the shared expression of suffering or misery.

Provide (or create) reprieve spaces—places and situations where people can take temporary shelter from the ravages of white-body supremacy. While these can be officially designated spaces in African American homes, community centers, businesses, or houses of worship, they don't have to be. Reprieve spaces can also be created spontaneously, as needed. You can let someone spend an afternoon alone in your spare bedroom, or allow them to sit for two hours in a quiet booth in the back of the restaurant where you work. You can even create a temporary reprieve space simply by sitting with someone and listening to him or her with a settled body and a mindful presence.

One way to begin to mend your heart and heal your trauma is to observe yourself carefully, and notice when and how white-body supremacy operates inside you. In particular, be alert for these two characteristics:

Traumatic retentions. Historically, many of the practices African Americans developed to survive are coupled with these. The most common is whupping our kids, but there are dozens more. With practice, you can learn to settle your body, observe your own impulses, and then decouple what is valuable (for example, helping your kids survive and be resilient) from what is harmful (for example, the traumatic retention of beating them). You can then maintain or grow the valuable aspects and let go of the harmful ones.

When you see yourself begin to slide into a traumatic retention, stop yourself in your tracks. Use the five anchors to stay in your body and in the here and now. Look at what you're about to do and why you're about to do it. Notice what you experience in your body, and what images, emotions, and impulses arise. Then choose a path forward based on the best of who you are.

Reflexively making white people feel safe and comfortable. There's nothing wrong with either safety or comfort. But you are not white people's one-stop comfort shop. Nor is it your job to soothe white people whose lizard-brain fears get activated by the color of your skin.

White fragility screams this message to people of all colors: *Whenever a white body feels unsafe or uncomfortable, it's everyone's job to soothe it down ASAP. If they don't, a dark body may need to get broken.* This message gets broadcast twenty-four/seven to (and through) millions of white bodies. But it's a flat-out lie. And the best response to any lie is to call it out and counter it with the truth.

Here is the truth about white bodies: They are resilient, just like yours and mine. They can heal, just as you and I can. They do not require special attention and care—from you or anyone else—simply because they are white. *All* adults need to learn how to soothe and anchor themselves, rather than expect or demand that others soothe them. *All* adults need to heal and grow up. Nevertheless, many African Americans have become so habituated to soothing white bodies that it has become reflexive for us. We need to unlearn this reflex.

In any situation, you can start by settling your own body; paying attention to what it experiences; slowing down your internal processes; and using the five anchors to help you stay in your body and in the moment. You can then discern what people genuinely need at that moment, in that situation.

At the same time, you can notice your own impulses and where they come from. Are they responses to the actual circumstances? Or are they reflexive responses arising from your (or your ancestors') prior experience? Either way, your task is to act from the best parts of yourself.

There will surely be times when soothing someone is exactly the right thing for you to do. Sometimes that person will be white. But from now on, when you soothe another body, I encourage you to do it *by choice*, not out of reflex.

—BODY PRACTICES—

Imagine the following scenario. At each moment, observe your body closely. What does it experience? Where does it constrict? Where does it relax? What does it want to do? What emotions, thoughts, images, or words bubble up?

You're walking in a busy shopping mall. Outside a jewelry store, two white cops—a man and a woman—stand side by side. Both catch your eye, lock gazes with you, and stare grimly at you as you walk closer. As you near the store, the male cop moves his hand and lets his palm rest lightly on the butt of his gun.

Stop.

What do you experience in your body? Where is there constriction? Where is there settling? What does it want to do? What impulses, emotions, images, or thoughts arise—or flood in? Does time speed up, slow down, or keep the same pace?

Use the five anchors from Chapter Twelve to settle your body and slow yourself down.

Now, act from the best parts of yourself. What do you do?

Here's another scenario. As before, observe your body closely, moment by moment. What does it experience? Where does it constrict? Where does it relax? What does it want to do? How does it want to move? What emotions, thoughts, images, or words bubble up?

You've been invited by a white friend to her company's Christmas party. When you get to the party, it is in full swing, with about sixty people talking, eating, drinking, and milling about. As you enter, you notice four things: everyone in the room is white; almost all of them are in suits or cocktail dresses, while you are in casual clothes; you don't see your friend anywhere; and, as you enter the room, many of the people turn and look at you.

Stop.

What do you experience in your body? Where is there constriction? Where is there settling? What does it want to do? What impulses, emotions, images, or thoughts arise?

Use the five anchors from Chapter Twelve to settle your body and slow yourself down.

Now, act from the best parts of yourself. What do you do?

Here's a simple practice I encourage you to develop into a habit:

Starting now, each time you encounter a white (or yellow or red or police) body, pay attention to *your own* body. What do you experience in it? Where does it constrict? Where is it relaxed? What does it want to do? Does it sense a threat? If it does, work with the practices in Chapter 12 to slow yourself down and notice what's actually happening.

Use your discernment to evaluate the situation. If you experience a sense of danger, is this a reflexive response, or is the threat real? If your body's response is a reflex rather than a response to the unfolding situation, use one or more of the strategies you learned earlier to help your body settle. If the threat seems genuine, use what you learned in Chapter 12 to move through the situation as mindfully as you can.

Afterward, orient yourself to the space around you. Look around, including behind you.

This activity is not meant to encourage you to reflexively trust all white bodies. At this point in time, that may not be too wise. Instead, it's designed to help you notice any reflexive distrust and to replace that reflexive response with presence, observation, and discernment.

RE-MEMBERINGS

- Activities that can help you harmonize your body with other African American bodies—and help all of you heal—include:
    - ✦ Singing together
    - ✦ Group drumming
    - ✦ Rhythmic group clapping
    - ✦ Humming in sync with others
    - ✦ Brief, secure, caring touches
    - ✦ Braiding or combing each other's hair
    - ✦ Cooking together
    - ✦ Hugging people mindfully
    - ✦ Crying or wailing together in times of grief, tragedy, or death

- One way to begin to mend your heart is to observe yourself carefully, and notice when and how white-body supremacy operates inside you. In particular, be alert for traumatic retentions and the reflexive urge to make white people feel safe and comfortable.

- All adults need to learn how to soothe and anchor themselves, rather than expect or demand that others soothe them. And all adults need to heal and grow up.

CHAPTER 16

MENDING THE WHITE
HEART AND BODY

*"There's a perception that whiteness is working for white people.
It's not . . . White people must join the world in fighting the
pernicious ideas that created their category."*

QUINN NORTON

*"Healing is about taking the time to notice what gets in the way
of feeling connected to your life, your community, and your sense of
possibility. Healing, at its core, is about slowing down so that we
can better listen, to ourselves and each other."*

SUSAN RAFFO

Imagine I hand you a month-old puppy. Its tail is wagging wildly, and
as you take it into your arms, it eagerly licks your face. You can feel the
softness of its fur and the warmth of its body. As you hold it, you can
smell its puppy breath. After a minute or two of its wiggly affection,
you hand it back to me. I place it gently on the ground, where it sits
down, wagging its tail.

I reach into my backpack and pull out a hammer. "Here, buddy," I say to the puppy, and it turns to look at me.

I smash its head with the hammer. It yelps once, whimpers, and falls on its side. I kneel beside it and beat it with the hammer, over and over, until it stops breathing and blood oozes from its still body.

—BODY PRACTICES—

What did you experience in your body when I handed you the puppy? When you held it in your arms? When you gave it back to me? What happened in your body when I first struck the puppy with a hammer? When I kept striking it? When you realized I was murdering it? When you knew for certain it was dead?

What did your body want to do? Try to stop me? Grab for the hammer? Punch me in the face? Run away? Freeze in terror? Dial 9-1-1?

Had I actually beaten a puppy to death in front of you,[71] you might have suffered vicarious trauma. That trauma could stay stuck in your body—possibly for months, years, or even decades—until you addressed it and mended it. And in order to mend it, you would first need to recognize it as trauma.

I suggest you take a break from this book for at least half an hour. During that time, consider using one of the many techniques you've practiced for settling your body. Once your body experiences a difference and a settledness, resume reading.

*

For the next activity, you'll need access to a computer, smartphone, or tablet with Internet access. Go to the Wikipedia page for the 1920 Duluth lynchings (https://en.wikipedia.org/wiki/1920_Duluth_lynchings). Take a close look at the photograph of three mutilated Black bodies, one of which has been decapitated.

---

71   It goes without saying that I've never done—and would never do—any such thing. I adapted this thought experiment from a story told by Joy DeGruy.

As you look at this picture, what does your body experience? Where do you feel constriction or release?

What other sensations does your body experience? What does it want to do? What impulses, emotions, or images arise? Do these feel fresh and new, or old and historical?

Which parts of your body want to fight? Which parts want to flee or turn away? Which parts want to freeze?

Does a part of you want to shut down and override what you're experiencing? Is a potentially soothing thought going through your head, such as, *Hey, it's just history*, or *Thank God people don't do this anymore*, or *This is just bad people doing bad things*?

Now look at the two dozen or so white bodies that are posed around the lynched Black bodies. Look at the expression on each man's face.

What do you experience now in your body? Where do feel constriction or release? What other sensations do you feel? What impulses, emotions, or images arise?

Does the experience you are having right now seem new and fresh, or ancient and historical?

What does your body want to do? Which parts of it want to fight? Which parts want to flee? Which parts want to freeze?

Now imagine you're one of those men, standing close to three mutilated corpses that are being displayed for the camera. What do you imagine he experiences in *his* body? What might *he* be feeling and thinking? What might he be smelling, hearing, or seeing?

Finally, imagine you live in Duluth, Minnesota, in 1920. You're walking home from a friend's home one night. You turn the corner and suddenly see three dead Black bodies—and thirty men posing beside them.

Now what does your body want to do?

What would you say to the men, if anything? Would you confront them? Would you keep walking? Would you hurry to a police station? Would you bend over and throw up? Would you stay silent?

If you did choose to stay silent, what do you imagine would get passed down to your children in your DNA?

What do you imagine any Black bodies in the vicinity would experience? What do you think would get passed down through *their* bodies to the bodies of their descendants?

The image from the 1920 Duluth lynching wasn't a standard news photo. It was made into a postcard that was sold as a memento. In fact, images from many lynchings were made into postcards. People collected them, like baseball cards. (The US Postal Service banned the mailing of these cards in 1908; thereafter, though, people continued to buy and keep them as souvenirs.)

In 1920, lynching was not an aberration; it was a fairly common practice.[72] For some white people, it was also a celebratory event, like fireworks on the Fourth of July. Nor was lynching a strictly white-on-Black activity. In Minnesota, for example, white people lynched more white people than Black ones.

White-body supremacy alone does not explain the popularity of lynching. Neither does the idea that white people in 1920 were somehow fundamentally different from white people (or people of color) today. This is a dodge. Many of us use it to flee from our own pain around lynching. I urge you not to fall into this trap.

I also urge you not to flee into relativism: *Times were different then. So were cultural norms.* That's a dodge, too. When a cultural norm is inhuman and evil, it's our obligation as human beings to do our best to put a stop to it. This was as true in 1920 as it is today. (If smashing puppies' heads with hammers were to become a standard practice, should anyone accept it as normal and reasonable?)

---

72   In 1920, there were sixty-one lynchings in the United States. Fifty-three of the victims were Black.

The white people posing in the photograph were born with human bodies just like yours and mine. They had the same physical, mental, and spiritual wiring you and I do. But something happened to them—and to their ancestors. That something enabled them to override the human body's normal reaction of shock, horror, terror, and disgust—the very emotions you likely felt when you imagined watching me bludgeon a puppy to death.

What happened to the men in the lynching photo—and to many, many other men and women like them—was deep and persistent trauma. This trauma got transmitted and compounded through multiple generations; eventually, it began to look like culture.

I live in Minnesota, about two hours from Duluth. Some of the children and grandchildren of the men in that postcard probably live nearby. It's possible that I know one or two of them, but don't realize it. What do you imagine is stuck in *their* bodies? What got passed down in and through them?

There is an image from the Middle Ages,[73] showing a man being drawn and quartered—that is, being dragged by horse or carriage to the execution site, then pulled apart into four quarters by four horses. In it, a crowd has gathered to witness the execution.

Drawing and quartering was a fairly common punishment in England. The first recorded instance was in 1241, and it continued to be practiced in England until 1820—sixteen years after the creation of the first steam locomotive railway, and over two centuries after the first Africans arrived in the United States.

Drawing and quartering was used most famously in England on Guy Fawkes, who was convicted of treason in 1603. Here is a description of the practice by Fawkes' contemporary, Edward Coke:

> . . . he shall be strangled, being hanged up by the neck between
> heaven and earth . . . Then he is to be cut down alive, and to have
> his privy parts cut off . . . After, to have his head cut off . . . And,
> lastly his body to be quartered and the quarters set up in some high
> and eminent place, to the view and detestation of men.

---

73   A 1610 painting depicting the execution of Francois Ravaillac in France. Ravaillac had murdered French king
Henry IV.

Such punishments were very much public performances. In an entry in Samuel Pepys's famous diary, dated October 13, 1660, he writes: "I went out to Charing Cross, to see Major-General Harrison hanged, drawn and quartered; which was done there, he looking as cheerful as any man could in that condition."

Is this how you would respond to witnessing a drawing and quartering? What would your body have had to do to itself to respond the way Pepys does?

Lynchings are a gruesome and shameful part of American history, but they were not an American invention. They were a European import on which we put our own local spin. The bodies that brought these practices to America also brought with them the centuries-old traumatic retentions that enabled those bodies to see torture and decapitation as normal human behavior; to accept them and comply with them; and to view them as forms of public entertainment.[74]

Don't think for a moment this phenomenon is a thing of the past. In 2017, in some parts of the world, public beheadings are common events. The Islamic State routinely beheads people publicly. Saudi Arabia has done so for many years and continues to do so repeatedly.[75] Also don't assume we Americans are necessarily more enlightened than we used to be regarding such practices. Here's an excerpt from an article in the *Atlantic*, published in 2017:

> The Trump administration is looking into bringing back torture, according to a draft order published by the *New York Times* and the *Washington Post* . . . Torture was a key part of Trump's national-security platform as a candidate. He publicly defended torture on the trail, proclaiming that "torture works" and "only a stupid

---

74   The term *lynching* is thought to be named after Charles Lynch, an eighteenth-century Virginia planter, politician, and militia officer in the American Revolution. Lynch, along with other militia officers and justices of the peace, often rounded up undesirables—typically, people suspected of being English loyalists—and meted out their own extralegal forms of justice, including whipping, confiscation of property, and forced conscription into the revolutionary army. So far as we know, however, they never murdered anyone. The original term was *Lynch's law;* over time, it morphed from the noun phrase into a verb.

75   A 2016 article in *The Guardian* describing Saudi Arabia's ongoing program of beheadings suggests that medieval thinking—and medieval punishments—remain an ongoing feature of twenty-first-century life (Associated Press, January 1, 2016, https://www.theguardian.com/world/2016/jan/02/saudi-arabia-beheadings-reach-highest-level-in-two-decades).

person would say it doesn't work." Even if it didn't work, Trump concluded, "They deserve it anyway, for what they're doing."[76]

How much of this is public policy? How much is a traumatic retention?

*

Everyone is welcome to read this chapter, but it's intended primarily for white Americans. To all my white readers: welcome. Of all the chapters in this book, this is the most important one for you to read. I'm glad you're here. Let's get to work.

It's important to begin with the following observations: Trauma is never a personal failure, nor the result of someone's weakness, nor a limitation, nor a defect. It is a normal reaction to abnormal conditions and circumstances.

Nevertheless, "I had been traumatized" is never a valid excuse for murder, or any other crime. Neither is "My ancestors were traumatized." These statements are calls to heal, not to cause harm.

Your white body was not something you chose. But the imaginary construct of whiteness is something you *can* change. Simply because you have a white body, you automatically benefit from white-body supremacy, whether you want to or not. Even if you're the most fair-minded person on Earth, at times certain privileges will be conferred upon you because of the color of your skin. Your whiteness is considered the norm, and the standard against which all skin colors—and all other human beings—are compared. That alone provides you with a big advantage.

I'm not blaming you for this, or asking you to feel guilty or ashamed about it. But you *do* need to be aware of what those privileges are and how they function. You need to *not* take those privileges for granted as your birthright. You were granted those privileges, but you did not earn them. Great harm was done to other human beings to secure those privileges for you, and for others with white skin. The presence of these privileges in your life—and of white-body

---

76   Adam Server, "Can Trump Bring Back Torture?" *The Atlantic* (January 26, 2017).

supremacy in general—is not benign. It's your responsibility to not merely enjoy those privileges, but to share them with others—and, ultimately, with everyone.

If you're like many white Americans, the presence of an unfamiliar Black body may sometimes trigger an alarm in your lizard brain. This may be the case even if you're a lifelong progressive who has many Black friends and relatives. If so, you need to get to work on healing and growing.

Stop for a moment. Did your body recoil or constrict as you read the previous paragraph? If so, notice how reflexive that response was and how quickly it happened.

As you now know, your body doesn't give a rat's ass what your cognitive brain thinks or believes. Your soul nerve and lizard brain either feel safe or they feel threatened. You can think one thing, and your body can simultaneously respond as if you had exactly the opposite thought.

Your body puts each new body it encounters into one of two categories: *safe* or *dangerous*. And many white Americans—no matter what they think or believe—put unfamiliar Black bodies into the *dangerous* category. This makes it difficult for their bodies to settle when Black bodies are nearby.

This sense of danger does not come out of nowhere. But it also doesn't come from Black bodies—even though, to white bodies, it *feels* like it does. It comes from the ideas and images that were created, perpetuated, and institutionalized over hundreds of years—all for the benefit of powerful white bodies.

—BODY PRACTICE—

The most important thing you can do to unravel white-body supremacy—and to mend your own personal, historical, intergenerational, and secondary trauma around the myth of race— is to notice what your body does in the presence of an unfamiliar Black body. Whenever you encounter an unfamiliar Black body, pay attention to your own body. What do you experience in it? Where and how is it constricting?

Where and how is it released and open? Does it sense a threat? What emotions, images, or impulses arise?

If it does sense a threat, work with the activities in Chapter Twelve to slow yourself down and notice what's actually happening. Use your discernment to evaluate the situation. Is the sense of danger you experience a reflexive response, or is the threat potentially real? Ask yourself: "If this body were exactly the same, but white instead of Black, how would I experience it right now?"

If your body's threat response is reflexive, use one or several of the activities described throughout this book to help it settle and relax. If the threat seems genuine, use the five anchors from Chapter Twelve to stay in your body and remain in the here and now. Then move through the situation as mindfully and compassionately as you can, while acting from the best parts of yourself.

This activity is not meant to encourage you to reflexively trust Black bodies. Like white (and other) bodies, not all Black bodies are trustworthy. Practice discernment, just as you would with any encounter with a stranger. As you practice this activity, day after day, eventually your lizard brain will stop seeing unfamiliar Black bodies as foreign bodies, and start seeing them as human beings.

Confronting white-skin privilege—and sharing that privilege—often involves small, everyday courageous actions. As you'll discover, these courageous actions will also benefit you. As you practice them, over and over, they will help your body experience more settledness in the presence of Black (and other non-white) bodies. Here are some examples:[77]

---

77   I've used Blacks in these examples because of the ways in which many white bodies reflexively respond to Black ones. I encourage you to share your privilege in these same ways with other people of color—and to call out white-body supremacy when you observe it harming any non-white human being.

- When there's no line in a store and a Black and a white salesperson are both equally available, choose the Black salesperson.

- If you have a retail or service job, and a Black customer and a white customer walk in at the same time, assist the Black customer first.

- When you're waiting to be served (for example, at a bakery or butcher shop), and a Black person arrived at the same time as you, let them be served first. If the person behind the counter offers to help you first, shake your head and say, "I believe it's her (or his) turn."

- When deciding how much of a tip to leave for a Black server in a restaurant, imagine they are white. If this inclines you to leave a bigger tip, do so. Also take note of that inclination.

- When you see a Black person in distress or in need of assistance, don't assume it's not your problem. Offer your help if you can. (Ask yourself, "What would I do if this person were white?")

- If you can choose between two equally good dentists (or gardeners, guitar teachers, math tutors, personal trainers, and so on), one white and the other Black, select the Black one.

Here are some additional practices to help your body settle in the presence of Black bodies:

- When you get on a bus or train—or enter the waiting area of a train station or airport or doctor's office—and you can choose between sitting next to a Black body or a white one (or between sitting next to a Black body and standing), sit next to the Black body.

- Join a gym (or church, running club, weight-loss group, etc.) with a clientele of mixed ethnicities.

- If you live in a place where you rarely encounter many Black bodies—for example, in many suburbs, Wyoming, Vermont, and so on—visit safe places where Black bodies congregate, such as African and Caribbean restaurants and boutiques, African American churches, concerts by Black musicians, and book readings by Black writers.

It's not enough to simply notice your own white-skin privilege. It's important that you also call out white-skin privilege, white-body supremacy, and white fragility when you encounter them outside of yourself. In particular, call them out in the presence of other white people.

This doesn't have to mean creating a confrontation or a scene, playing the hero, or otherwise making a big deal out of the incident. It's usually enough to make a brief but pointed comment—a simple response that challenges the historical habit of silence. This may also create some additional room for growth in your body and nervous system—and, perhaps, in the bodies and nervous systems of others around you. Here are some examples:

- When someone uses code words (often called "dog whistles" or "dog-whistle words"[78]), ask him or her for clarification. For example, when someone talks about "inner city youth," for example, ask, "Do you mean Black kids? Or poor Black kids? Or kids from central Burlington, Vermont?" Politely but firmly keep pushing that person until you get a clear answer.

- When you hear someone use a dodge, challenge him or her on it. For example: "No, we *don't* need to wait until all the facts are in to discuss Philando Castile's death. You and I aren't a jury that's been charged with rendering a legal verdict. We're two citizens having a discussion, and we both saw the video his girlfriend took as he died." (Noticing that something is a dodge means you're beginning to find your way out of the fog of white-body supremacy. Keep going, though, because you're only getting started.)

---

78   Dogs can hear frequencies human beings can't. *Dog-whistle words* are words and phrases some white people use that are intended to have alternate, racialized meanings. Ostensibly, only other white people can hear and decode those meanings. But Black people hear those meanings loudly and clearly.

- If you're attending a meeting or forum and a white person keeps talking on and on, not allowing others to speak, while some Black folks wait their turns, speak up. Say firmly, "Excuse me, but I believe others have things they need to say as well. I'd like to hear their thoughts."

- As you're browsing in a store, if you see a salesperson ignore a Black customer and begin to wait on a white one who arrived later, say to the salesperson, "Excuse me, but I believe this customer was here first."

- If you see a store employee following a Black customer to make sure he or she is not pilfering merchandise, go up to the employee and say, "Excuse me, but it looks to me like you're shadowing that customer. Is it because the person is Black?"

As you move through these encounters, it's important to have a settled body and a calm presence. Some white people will be shocked and bewildered that another white person is confronting them. These initial responses may quickly give way to anger—which is precisely why many white people who notice these micro-aggressions don't publicly call them out.

Use the five anchors to slow yourself down and stay present in your body and in the moment. Then respond from the best parts of yourself.

Throughout each encounter, also pay close attention to what you experience in your body. Where and how is it constricting? Where and how is it released and open? Does it sense a threat? What emotions, meanings, images, or impulses arise?

Also notice when white-skin privilege, white fragility, or white-body supremacy reflexively arises inside yourself. (This will happen. How can it not? All of these things are in the air we breathe.) When it occurs, simply notice what you're doing (or what you're about to do). Notice the sensations, images, urges, impulses, meanings, and emotions you experience. Don't try to override them and get past them as quickly as possible. Instead, use the five anchors to slow yourself down and stay present in your body and in the moment. Simply observe each impulse or concept or image, without doing anything about it.

If it makes your body feel uncomfortable, just stay in that discomfort for a time. Let your body settle into it. Then choose a course of action that comes from the best parts of yourself. Throughout it all, keep your body as settled as you can.

*

We all need to grow up if we are to live full, meaningful lives. A pernicious side effect of white-body supremacy is that it allows (and sometimes encourages) white Americans to choose not to grow up. They can stay purposely blind to their own white-body supremacy and trauma; repeatedly deny or refuse to address it; socialize almost solely with other white people; root for their favorite sports team (perhaps one with a racialized logo); watch cable TV; and probably get through life just fine.

For generations, white-body supremacy allowed many white Americans to avoid developing the full range of necessary skills for navigating adulthood. Instead of building resilience, and accepting the full pain and grief and disappointment of human existence, they outsourced some of that pain, grief, and disappointment to dark-skinned bodies. They also hired (or forced) dark bodies to protect them. At the same time, many white Americans tried to protect themselves by retreating to all-white or mostly white enclaves.

Paradoxically, these efforts made many white Americans more vulnerable to trauma and caused them to feel more fragile and threatened, in the same way that overprotecting a child encourages him or her to become a helpless, frightened adult. This is the ultimate irony of white-body supremacy: in the name of protecting and serving white Americans, it has done immense harm to them.

Until recently, hiding behind the curtain of white-body supremacy has been an option for many white Americans. But not anymore. For many reasons—some demographic, some financial, some cultural, and some political—retreating into a cocoon of white-skin privilege is no longer possible. The game is up.

You, and millions of other white Americans, now have to make a choice. You can opt for clean pain and work to heal the trauma of white-body supremacy, both in yourself and in others. In moving through this process, you will help create a saner and more compassionate America. Your other option is to choose dirty pain, double down on white-body supremacy, deepen the trauma for everyone, and create far more—and far worse—suffering.

You have the power to stop intergenerational and historical trauma in its tracks, and to keep it from spreading from your body into others. Above all, you have the power to heal. But first you have to *choose* to heal.

This book is dedicated to supporting that healing. In Part III, we'll look at practices that can help you and others heal collectively.

RE-MEMBERINGS

- "I had been traumatized" is never a valid excuse for committing a crime. Neither is "My ancestors were traumatized." These statements are calls to heal, not to cause harm.

- If you have a white body, you automatically benefit from white-body supremacy, whether you want to or not. Even if you're the most fair-minded person on Earth, at times certain privileges will be conferred upon you because of the color of your skin.

- If you have white skin, you have a responsibility to share your privileges with others.

- The presence of an unfamiliar Black body may sometimes trigger an alarm in your lizard brain. This may be the case even if you're a lifelong progressive who has many Black friends and relatives.

- The most important thing you can do to unravel white-body supremacy—and to heal your own historical and secondary trauma around race—is to notice what your body does in the presence of an unfamiliar Black body, and then learn to settle your body in the midst of that presence.

- Much of white-skin privilege involves small, everyday actions. So it's possible to share your privilege with others through such actions.

- It's also important to call out white-skin privilege, white-body supremacy, and white fragility when you encounter them in others. You don't need to make a scene or be a hero; it's enough to make a brief but pointed comment.

- You, and millions of other white Americans, have to make a choice. You can opt for clean pain and work to heal the trauma of white-body supremacy, both in yourself and in others—or you can choose dirty pain, and deepen and perpetuate that trauma.

- You have the power to stop trauma in its tracks, to keep it from spreading from your body into others.

- Above all, you have the power to heal.

CHAPTER 17

MENDING THE POLICE HEART AND BODY

"I must undertake to love myself and to respect myself as though my very life depends upon self-love and self-respect."

JUNE JORDAN

"It seems that it's either pro-cop and anti-Black or pro-Black and anti-cop, when, in reality, you can be pro-cop and pro-Black, which is what we should all be."

TREVOR NOAH

"You can have great regard for law enforcement and still want them to be held to high standards."

JON STEWART

"There is a big difference between learning about trauma and learning a practice. There is a big difference between learning a practice and actually making that practice become a practice."

AUTUMN BROWN

This chapter is written especially for law enforcement professionals—beat cops, mall cops, security guards, police detectives, county sheriffs, state troopers, truancy officers, precinct captains, police chiefs, members of the National Guard, and anyone else in America whose job it is to protect and serve its people.

I also hope that *everyone* will read this chapter, so they will better understand and support those professionals, both on and off the job. This includes encouraging them to consistently act from the best parts of themselves.

*

To everyone in America who works in law enforcement, there are three things you need to hear:

First, you need to take better care of yourselves, both individually and collectively. You *deserve* to take better care of yourselves. You deserve bodies that are healthy and whole, that feel good, and that can operate at their best. America's current police culture does not support this.

Your job is often stressful, difficult, and sometimes dangerous. Yet you've likely been given little training and support in helping you handle that pressure. After each workday, you're expected to go home, get a night's sleep, and report for work the next day feeling refreshed, relaxed, and alert. This does not happen automatically; it requires strong and consistent self-care.

Many law enforcement professionals live day after day with the chemicals of chronic stress in their bloodstreams. This is bad for your body, sometimes traumatic, and occasionally tragic. It is also why *you need to learn to manage and care for your body.* No one else can do this for you. Caring for your body may save your life. It may also keep you from unnecessarily taking the life of a stranger.

Second, to do your job well, you need to metabolize your trauma and move through it. If you don't, you may find yourself blowing that trauma through some of the very people you vowed to protect and serve.[79] Too many cops have ended their careers prematurely in just this way.

Third, like it or not, being a public safety professional in America means being an apparatus of white-body supremacy—a manager and controller of Black bodies. When you first became a cop, you probably did not sign up for this. Yet, no matter what hue your skin is, it may now be a routine part of your job.

Many Americans think of today's public safety professional as the modern-day descendant of the heroic Wild West sheriff: someone who protects residents, maintains order, and guns down outlaws who would disrupt the community and/or rule of law. This is also how some law enforcement professionals see themselves, especially during the early years of their careers.

In fact, however, American policing has many of its historical roots in slavery. As early as 1704, long before many settlements had anything like police, the colony of Carolina created a slave patrol. The patrol's job was to assist wealthy landowners in capturing and punishing enslaved people who had run away. The people in those patrols were tools of the colony's landowners. Their job was to round up other tools that had gone astray. As Victor Kappeler notes in the journal *Police Studies Online*,

> The use of patrols to capture runaway slaves was one of the precursors of formal police forces, especially in the South. This disastrous legacy persisted as an element of the police role even after the passage of the Civil Rights Act of 1964.

Even today, some elements of slave patrols remain entrenched in the police forces of a number of American cities and towns. If you work in one of these communities, you must acknowledge and rise above these ancient, toxic influences.

This chapter will help address all of these challenges. It offers a range of activities designed to help you manage your own body and take better care of yourself. It provides some strategies for beginning to

---

79   If you've already done this, I urge you to meet with a therapist—preferably one who has experience working with law enforcement professionals. They can assist in two ways: they can help you develop strategies to ensure that you don't blow your trauma through others again, and they can help you heal that trauma.

move through trauma—especially racialized trauma. And it will help you shake off the influence of white-body supremacy without reducing your ability to protect and serve your fellow human beings.

Of all the bodies you protect and serve, the most important is your own.

USE THE FIVE ANCHORS

When you find yourself in a stressful or potentially dangerous situation, practice the five anchors from Chapter 12 (unless the situation calls for immediate, split-second action), repeated below:

- **Anchor 1:** *Soothe yourself to quiet your mind, calm your heart, and settle your body.*

- **Anchor 2:** *Simply notice the sensations, vibrations, and emotions in your body instead of reacting to them.*

- **Anchor 3:** *Accept the discomfort—and notice when it changes—instead of trying to flee from it.*

- **Anchor 4:** *Stay present and in your body as you move through the unfolding experience, with all its ambiguity and uncertainty, and respond from the best parts of yourself.*

- **Anchor 5:** *Safely discharge any energy that remains.*

Use the five anchors when you feel stress or conflict building; when that stress looks and feels as if it will continue to escalate; and when you feel a growing discomfort in your soul nerve.

It's especially important to practice Anchor 5. After you've been through a dangerous or high-stress encounter—such as seeing a dead child, attending to a gaping wound, being shot at, or shooting someone—your body needs to discharge any excess energy. If it doesn't have that opportunity, the energy may stay stuck in your body—possibly as trauma. Here are some ways to discharge that energy:

- Most forms of exercise, including walking.

- Playing most sports.

- Dancing.

- Physical labor—heavy yard work, construction, snow shoveling, etc.

- Following your body's moment-by-moment guidance. You might experience a sudden urge to push your hands in the air, or run around the block, or shake your head vigorously and shout. Let your body do whatever it wants to do—so long as it doesn't harm you or others.

LEARN TO SETTLE YOUR BODY

Practice some of the activities in Chapters 11 and 12 regularly. They will train your body to settle whenever you need it to.

A settled presence is vital to effective on-duty encounters with other people. A settled body also feels better, reduces your on-the-job stress, and can help you do your job better. Sometimes a settled presence can save your life—or keep you from needlessly harming or killing someone else.

ADD SOFTNESS TO YOUR LIFE

Since your job is often difficult and hard-edged, it's important to build some soft things into your life—on a regular basis. I don't mean teddy bears and rainbows, but simple, everyday practices that help your body feel good and stay (or get) healthy. Here are some options:

- **Get enough rest.** Every human body needs sufficient sleep and relaxation.

- **Learn and regularly practice a form of silent meditation.** This can be secular (Mindfulness-Based Stress Reduction), religious, or something in between (insight meditation or Zen meditation).

- **Do yoga.** I recommend basic, easy stretching poses—not hot yoga, Power Yoga, Ashtanga yoga, Bikram yoga, or anything else difficult or expensive.

- **Get plenty of pleasurable physical exercise.** This can be anything from walking to boxing to competing in triathlons, as long as it feels good to your body.

- **Get regular massages.** Massage therapy feels wonderful and is excellent for reducing stress. Many health clubs offer massages at reasonable prices. Get massaged at least once a month if you can.

- **Take long walks.** Ideally, walk in the neighborhood where you work. This will help you get to know the people you have pledged to protect.

- **Go dancing often.** Line dancing, ballroom dancing, square dancing, folk dancing, and ordinary boogying all count.

- **Download and use a stress-reduction or grounding app.** Some examples include Inner Balance; Stop, Breathe & Think; My Calm Beat; Calm; and Mindfulness Training. A related app, Daylio, can quickly and easily track your mood and energy—and, perhaps, help you discover rhythms and patterns in them that can support your health, sanity, and relationships.

- **Listen to "Weightless" by Marconi Union.** Working with sound therapists, British band Marconi Union created this eight-minute song to relieve listeners' anxiety and help them relax. In lab tests, the song worked as promised: people's breathing and heart rates slowed, and their blood pressure went down.

- **Listen to music with female vocalists—and the bass turned down or off.** This appears to have a unique ability to settle the soul nerve.[80]

- **Get regular manicures and pedicures—especially if you're male.** Pedicures feel particularly good. Charles

---

80 Initial experiments suggest this, though we don't yet know why it works. It appears to work equally well with Beyoncé, Madonna, Dixie Chicks, Aretha Franklin, and Joanna Newsom.

Barkley, Shaquille O'Neal, Tim Tebow, Dwayne Wade, and 50 Cent have all reportedly received (or given) pedicures.[81]

- **Apply essential oils to your body.** I recommend this for both men and women. It's surprisingly soothing. Potential bonus: applying oil to someone else, or having them apply it to you, can be a turn-on. So can the sight of an oiled body.

- **Add soft, pleasant scents to your home with candles, essential oils, or scent plug-ins.** These can evoke spices, flowers, the ocean, or the woods. Visit a specialty candle, soap, or fragrance shop, and follow your nose.

- **Take long, relaxing baths in bath salts (Epsom salts, for example) or bubble baths.** Some of the best bubble baths are the ones supposedly formulated for kids.

- **Spend time in nature.** Surfing, hiking in the woods, hang gliding, napping on the beach, and sitting on a park bench all qualify.

- **Laugh regularly.** Spend at least an hour a week watching funny films, standup comedians, cat videos, late-night comedy shows, or anything else that makes you laugh out loud.

- **Hug and kiss your parents, grandparents, and siblings—and, of course, your partner and kids.** If you don't already do this regularly, start now.

- **If you have a dog or cat, spend regular time with it.** Pet it, play with it, run with it, train it, etc.

- **Volunteer at a hospital neonatal intensive care unit to touch and hold newborns.** Hold babies of every color.

Practice some of these activities regularly—ideally, both before and after work each day. When possible, do some of them at work, too. For instance, as part of your patrol, hang out at the corner park for a few minutes to chat with people and pet their dogs. Or, when you see

---

81   See Autumn Whitefield-Madrano, "A Partial List of Male Celebrities Who Have Given or Received Pedicures," *The Beheld: Beauty and What It Means,* May 24, 2012, http://www.the-beheld.com/2012/05/partial-list-of-male-celebrities-who.html.

a group of kids dancing, pull over and dance with them. If you don't know the dance, ask them to teach you.[82]

Here's another profound thing you can do to reduce harshness and add softness to your life: when you're off duty, leave your gun at home (if you're permitted to).

All of this is especially important if, as is the case in some American police forces, your professional culture rewards and elevates alpha males. These are people (of any gender[83]) who see the world in terms of dominance and submission, winning and losing, overpowering or being overpowered.

There are times in police work when dominating or overpowering someone is a necessary tactic. But as the basis for police culture, it does far more harm than good. It can turn law enforcement professionals into storm troopers—and ordinary citizens into victims and losers whom police ultimately look down upon.

FOLLOW A REGULAR, CUSTOMIZED GROWTH ROUTINE
Look back at Chapter 11 for detailed guidance on creating such a routine.

TALK TO SOMEONE WHO KNOWS HOW TO LISTEN
Have honest, straightforward conversations with someone about your life, your work, and your personal and professional challenges. This person doesn't have to be a therapist. He or she can be a minister or priest (or rabbi or imam); a social worker; a body worker or healer; or someone with a background in counseling. (This person should *not* be a bartender. Bartenders are trained to soothe their customers, not help them heal.) Have such conversations regularly—at least every month or two.

---

82   This simple, fun act of harmonizing bodies can quickly build trust and rapport with the people you serve and protect. If you don't believe me, google "police Nae Nae," and you'll find news reports and videos from Utah, Texas, North Carolina, and Washington, DC, about cops and kids dancing the Nae Nae together. The results of these encounters are uniformly positive. As one teenager said, "I never expected cops to be that cool. There are some good cops." As then-former President Barack Obama once tweeted, "Great example of police having fun while keeping us safe."

83   One of the biggest, baddest, most relentless, and best-known alpha males in American history was a woman: the writer Ayn Rand. I have raised my children to be as unlike her as possible.

A good therapist can help, of course, especially if you find yourself reflexively doing things that aren't good for you (or for other people). If possible, find a therapist who has worked with cops before, so they understand many of your concerns from day one.

*

As I've mentioned, my brother, who lives in Dallas, is a police officer. He has trained cops in Texas and Wisconsin, as well as nationally and internationally. He often sings the praises of the Dallas Police Department. As of this writing in early 2017, the DPD is widely seen as a model for successful police reforms. Its former chief, David Brown—who retired a few months earlier—was a national leader in the effort to reduce officer-involved violence.

Like all human organizations, the department also has its problems. My brother told me recently, "Resmaa, all kinds of crazy shit happens to us cops before we even hit the streets. I don't mean just here in Texas; I mean everywhere in this country. Nasty stuff gets forced into us as part of our standard training. Sometimes when I go in front of a group of cops, a piece of my job is to *untrain* and retrain them."

Most of us need to untrain ourselves from white-body supremacy because it is in the air we breathe, the water we drink, and the very bodies we inhabit. As a police officer, you need to bring the best of yourself to your job at all times. Most of the time this means following your training. But sometimes it means being better than your training. You have an obligation to treat every human being you encounter *as* a human being. You do not have a free pass to needlessly harm anyone. The following practice can help you avoid inflicting such harm:

When you encounter an unfamiliar Black body, quickly use your discernment to assess the person and the situation. If there appears to be an actual or clearly imminent threat, respond to the situation in a professional manner.

If not, stop for a moment and pay attention to your own body. What do you experience in it? Where and how do you experience constriction? Where and how do you experience relaxation and settledness?

Does your body sense a potential threat? If so, ask yourself if what you're experiencing is likely a reflexive response, or an intuition of something real but unseen.

Then ask yourself: "If this body was exactly the same, but white instead of Black, how would I feel about it right now?" If your body's response seems to be reflexive, use one or more strategies to help it settle and relax. If the threat seems genuine, respond to it appropriately.

This process is *not* meant to encourage you to reflexively trust Black bodies. But do notice any reflexive *dis*trust. Over time, focus on replacing that reflexive response with being present, observing, and using your moment-by-moment discernment.

This simple practice will help you better protect and serve bodies of all colors. It will help your body feel more settled during those times when you need it to be. And it will help you be a better and more honorable cop—someone who consistently brings integrity to his or her work.

You deserve better than to be an apparatus of white-body supremacy. The people and community you serve deserve better as well.

IF YOU HOLD A LEADERSHIP ROLE[84]

If you're a leader in your department or unit, here are some things you can do to support the physical and mental health of your officers:

- Set up a police officers' running (or walking, biking, or rollerblading) club.
- Offer exercise classes every morning.
- Offer yoga sessions once or twice a week.
- Offer silent group meditation for fifteen minutes every morning (all you need is an empty room and some chairs).
- Bring in a massage therapist to give officers free twenty-minute chair massages.
- Offer classes in stress management and reduction.

---

84   If you don't hold a leadership role, ask your superior to provide some of the items on this list.

- Get the precinct office its own treadmill. Better yet, put in a mini-gym with weights and mats.

- Ask a local fitness center to provide free or reduced-price gym memberships for officers.

- Provide your officers with fitness trackers, such as Fitbit, to help them track their bodily rhythms—and their fitness in general. The Fitbit breathing app is an especially valuable tool for helping bodies settle, stay anchored, and be present. If there's no money in your budget to buy Fitbits, talk to local merchants and/or service clubs about donating the devices— or raising the money to buy them.

- Bring in an outside social worker for a few hours a week, and allow your officers to sign up for free thirty- or sixty-minute appointments.

- Two or three times a year, bring in healers—volunteer physicians, nurses, physician assistants, psychologists, and/or social workers—to help your officers create their own custom-designed self-care plans and growth routines. These should take into account the times before, during, and after shifts; downtimes within shifts; and off-duty hours.

- Hold monthly (or bimonthly, or quarterly) listening sessions facilitated by consultants, therapists, or social workers. In these, allow people to speak safely, anonymously, and off the record about their job-related concerns. You and other leaders should of course *not* attend these sessions. However, have people's anonymous comments brought to you and other leaders, so you can better take the pulse of your department.

- Create a policy that automatically gives officers an hour or two of recovery time following any traumatic incident— for example, a death, a disaster, a serious injury, or a confrontation at gunpoint. This will enable your officers to avoid responding to back-to-back high-stress calls, which can encourage a fight, flight, freeze, or annihilate response.

- If an officer shoots, kills, or injures someone—or if he or she becomes the subject of a serious complaint or investigation—don't leave the officer in the lurch to find emotional support on his or her own. Bring in a social worker or psychologist to help him or her move through his or her pain and confusion. (This should *not* be handled through your office of internal affairs, which may reflexively put the protection of the department ahead of the mental health and welfare of your officer.)

- Keep a close eye on each officer's morale and his or her physical, mental, and emotional health. When you see something of concern, speak with the officer about it—in a curious rather than a punitive way—and work to address it. (Depending on your organization, this might be an official early intervention program or it might be less formal and official.) Some things to look for include excessive drinking, drug use, isolation, burnout, chronic anger, compassion fatigue, depression, major weight gain or loss, physical health issues, or taking medical leave or a lot of sick time. Any of these can be an indicator of trauma or extreme stress. Do your best to catch and deal with problems early on. (These efforts should not involve your office of internal affairs, for the reasons mentioned above.)

- When one or more of your officers is involved in a high-profile event—for example, a deadly shootout, a major natural disaster, a suicide bombing, or a hostage situation—the bodies of everyone in your department or unit will remember that event for years to come. As each anniversary of that event nears, people's bodies will automatically become constricted or activated—usually without anyone cognitively understanding why. Tempers will flare; people's trauma will be triggered; and your officers will be more likely to respond to stressful events with fight, flee, freeze, or annihilate reactions. To help settle your officers' bodies and avoid such potentially deadly situations, create a brief remembrance ceremony on (or just before) the anniversary of the original high-profile event. Announce the ceremony at least a month in advance. If the original event involved not only an officer, but many community members—for example, in the case of a major fire, a hurricane, an earthquake, a terrorist attack, etc.— open the ceremony to the public. If the original event was particularly deadly, painful, or tragic, hold such a ceremony annually for two, three, or even five years afterward.

- Lobby the people you report to for money to spend on the wellness of your officers.

- If you can't get any public money, raise it privately. If you can get ten $500 donations from service clubs, businesses, and well-to-do people in your community, you'll have $5,000 for a mini-gym. In the process, you'll also improve relations between your officers and the community.

Any of these changes and additions can help your officers feel better and do their jobs better. For your department, they can reduce turnover and the amount of medical leave and number of medical retirements your people take. For the community, they can help prevent the tragedy of one of your officers unnecessarily killing or injuring someone.

While any of these individual changes can be of value, I urge you not to view them as mere add-ons. Think strategically rather than tactically: carefully choose from these options to create an organized, coordinated structure that consistently supports the health, sanity, and resilience of your officers. Better still, develop an official organization or precinct-wide care strategy for your officers that begins with their training and continues until (and perhaps well into) their retirement.

*

Based on the results of my work with police officers and departments, I strongly recommend two (and perhaps three) forms of additional training for all your people.

First, train your officers in basic psychological first aid, not just bodily first aid. This involves assisting people who get caught in a dangerous or high-stress situation—an accident, a disaster, a riot, a violent crime, and so on. Teach your officers to assess people's mental and emotional states, and then assist them appropriately—for example, by helping their bodies settle; asking the right questions in the right way; and helping them find shelter, a lost companion, or a route to leave the area.

Train all the people and units that report to you in the essentials of trauma—spotting it, understanding it, and responding appropriately to it. Part of this training should cover secondary and vicarious trauma, which often occur in people who witness a crime, accident, or disaster. It should also involve training police to spot, understand, and address trauma in themselves and their fellow officers.

Second, train your people in the use of the five anchors in Chapter 12, and in some of the body-settling activities in Chapter 11.

Third, carefully and thoroughly examine all other forms of training your department or unit provides. Does any aspect of it create unnecessary risk for officers? Does any of it encourage them to unnecessarily harm people they have pledged to serve and protect? In part, this means helping your officers not get dragged by their lizard brains into a fight, flee, freeze, or annihilate response when such a response isn't warranted.

Think back to the incident discussed in Chapter 8, in which officer Lonnie Soppeland unnecessarily shot and wounded Matthew Hovland-Knase, who was sitting quietly on his motorcycle by the roadside. How might your officers be trained differently to help them avoid Soppeland's error?

Now think back to the other incident described in Chapter 8, in which officer Jeronimo Yanez unnecessarily shot Philando Castile seven times, killing him. How might your officers be trained differently to help them avoid Yanez's error? How many lives—in particular, how many Black lives—might be saved through such training? How many police careers might also be saved?

Avoiding an unwarranted lizard-brain response is just one piece of the puzzle. Another involves acknowledging and calling out white-body supremacy—which lives deep in our bodies. Why, for example, did Officer Soppeland wound the calm and compliant Hovland-Knase with a single shot, while Officer Yanez shot the equally calm and compliant Castile seven times, killing him? Why did Soppeland's body go into a fight response, while Yanez's went into an annihilate response?

This isn't about pointing fingers and calling cops racist. It's about training your officers to do their jobs better—and to avoid needlessly hurting or killing someone.

Finally, take a close and careful look at your organization. Is there anything about its norms, structures, processes and procedures, codes, or expectations that exposes anyone—citizens, officers, or anyone else—to unnecessary risk? If so, shine light on it—and do what you can to change it.

*

Most police training is tactical. It teaches people when to attempt to de-escalate a conflict, when to draw their guns, when to shoot, when to call for backup, and so on. This kind of training is necessary, but it is never sufficient.

If you just rely on tactical training, the result may be civilians who are shot unnecessarily, ruined police careers, and public disgust, distrust, and unrest.

When one of your officers is on trial for shooting someone, and his or her defense is "I was simply following my training," something is clearly wrong with that training.

Law enforcement professionals need more than just tactical training. They also need skills to slow themselves down, be present, pay attention, and exercise discernment. They need practice in unthawing themselves from a freeze response without going into a fight or annihilate response. They need practices to help their nervous systems settle, so they don't plunge unnecessarily into a lizard-brain reaction.

Most of all, public safety professionals need experience being with the people they serve and protect. When their lives intersect with the lives of people in the community, they don't need to rely just on training.

They can trust their lived experience with the people they talk with, sing with, make jokes with, share food with, and solve problems with.

One Minneapolis police officer I know coaches football at the high school in his precinct. Sometimes he has kids from the team over for meals because their families don't have enough food. Sometimes he lets kids stay overnight at his home. He's out in the community without his gun or uniform, browsing at garage sales and watching parades and pushing kids on swings in the park.

Experience trumps training. In fact, training is just a temporary measure for people to rely on until experience gives them the wisdom to do their jobs well. Encourage your people to start with the necessary training, but to grow beyond that training through hands-on experience.

My brother the police trainer once told me this: "Resmaa, so many officers are told, over and over, 'Hesitation will get you killed. The faster you react, the more likely you are to go home alive.' Some cops are *trained* to let their reptilian brains take over. Back when I was first getting started, I was also told, 'Once you draw your gun, empty your clip.' The idea is that if a threat is so big that I have to pull my gun, I'm going to need to annihilate that threat." He paused. "Resmaa, that—" He paused again. "—is fucked up."

*

Too many Americans reflexively support their police officers, seeing them as noble protectors who can do no wrong.

Too many other Americans reflexively oppose the police, seeing them as enemies—members of an occupying force.

Meanwhile, too many public safety professionals reflexively distrust some of their fellow officers. A cop who gets close to people in the community may be looked on with suspicion by his or her peers. The thinking goes: *It's us cops against the world. We're the line of protection against chaos. If you hang out with community members—and if those community members like and appreciate you—you must be untrustworthy and possibly a snitch. You won't have other cops' backs when the chips are down. We don't want you hanging out with those community people. You need to make a choice—either us or them. Whose side are you on?*

Each of these views is simplistic and unrealistic. Each can also be a trauma response.

You *don't* have to choose between being a loyal cop who enforces white-body supremacy or a traitor who protects and serves the community. There is a third option: you can be a justice leader. You can be a police officer who is also a grown-up human being. You can care for, serve, protect, and be responsible to the community. You can *also* care for, and be responsible to, your fellow officers and your department. And you can *also* be responsible to your own conscience and your own physical, mental, and spiritual well-being. You can consistently act out of the best parts of yourself.

At times, this might involve calling someone out—a community member, a fellow cop, or even a chief—who acts badly. It might also mean challenging yourself, your fellow officers, and your organization around the norms and standards of white-body supremacy. Consider this chapter a heartfelt invitation.

RE-MEMBERINGS

- Law enforcement professionals need to take better care of themselves, both individually and collectively. American police culture today does not support this.

- Of all the bodies you protect and serve, the most important one is your own—so you need to learn to manage and care for your body. No one else can do this for you.

- To do your job well, you will need to metabolize your trauma and move through it. If you don't, you may find yourself blowing your trauma through some of the very people you've vowed to protect.

- When you find yourself in a stressful or potentially dangerous situation, practice the five anchors from Chapter 12 (unless the situation calls for immediate, split-second action).

- Regularly practice some of the activities in Chapters 11 and 12. They will help you settle your body whenever you need to.

- Because your job is often difficult and hard-edged, regularly add some softness to your life. Ideally, practice these before and after work each day. When possible, do some of them at work, too.

- Follow a regular, customized growth routine, as described in Chapter 11.

- At least once every month or two, have an honest and straightforward discussion about your life, work, and challenges with someone who knows how to listen. This can be a therapist, a member of the clergy, a social worker, a body worker or healer, or someone with a counseling degree.

- You need to bring the best of yourself to your job at all times. Usually this means following your training. But sometimes it can mean being better than your training.

- You have an obligation to treat every human being *as* a human being. You do not have a free pass to needlessly harm anyone.

- If you are a leader in your department or unit, do what you can to support the physical and mental health of your officers.

  + Train your officers in the basics of trauma and psychological first aid.

  + Encourage them to use the five anchors from Chapter 12 and the body-settling activities in Chapter 11.

  + Revamp their training so they don't needlessly hurt or kill someone.

  + Create an organized, coordinated structure that consistently supports the health, sanity, and resilience of your officers. Ideally, this begins with their training and continues until (and perhaps well into) their retirement.

- You do not have to choose between being a loyal cop who enforces white-body supremacy and a traitor who protects and serves the community. You can choose a third option: being a justice leader.

PART III

MENDING OUR COLLECTIVE BODY

CHAPTER 18

BODY-CENTERED ACTIVISM

"Healing must be collective, both in its process and benefits."
WILLIAM OLIVER

"No matter what accomplishments you make,
somebody helped you."
ALTHEA GIBSON

"Protest is this idea of telling the truth in public . . .
arrests will not stop people from telling the truth."
DERAY MCKESSON

"The future belongs to those who prepare for it today."
MALCOLM X

Healing from white-body supremacy begins with the body—*your* body.
But it does not end there. In order to heal the collective body that is
America, we also need social activism that is body centered. We cannot
individualize our way out of white-body supremacy. Nor can we merely
strategize our way out. We need collective action—action that heals.

We need to join in that collective action with settled bodies—and with psyches that are willing to metabolize clean pain. I can't stress this enough. Bringing a settled body to any situation encourages the bodies around you to settle as well. Bringing an unsettled body to that same situation encourages other bodies to become anxious, nervous, or angry. That discomfort, in turn, can sometimes activate people's lizard brains and create a fight, flee, freeze, or annihilate response. In America, all too often this results in an injured or murdered Black body.

I'm looking at two photographs of civil rights actions taken in the 1950s. The first is of the Greensboro Four—four African American students from North Carolina Agricultural and Technical University. In 1960, they sat down at a whites-only lunch counter in a Woolworth store and refused to leave until they were served. The second is Elizabeth Eckford, a fifteen-year-old girl carrying a notebook. In 1957, she tried to enter the all-white Little Rock Central High School, in order to receive the same education as white fifteen-year-olds. The students in both photos have bodies that are settled and minds that are focused.[85] When I watch a video of the late James Baldwin or Malcolm X, I see the same things: a settled body and a focused mind.

Before *you* show up for any social action—a rally, a march, a demonstration, a talk, a concert—first do what you can to settle your own body and nervous system. Use some of the grounding and settling activities in Chapters 10, 11, and 12. If your body simply won't settle, remove yourself from what's happening for a few minutes. Find a relatively quiet and private spot; resettle your body; and then return.

Remember that it's unwise to strive to have a body that is *always* settled. You also need the ability to shift into an activated state when the situation requires it.

IF YOU'RE AN EVENT ORGANIZER, PLANNER, LEADER, OR SPEAKER
In any social action, your task is to communicate with others—not just

---

85   "Settled" does not mean "unworried" or "unfrightened." It means the person's body is able to access its resilience. A human body can be frightened, angry, or filled with dread *and* settled at the same time. (In Elizabeth Eckford's photo, she is being pursued by a furious, jeering mob, so she would have been foolish not to have been frightened.) I suspect this occurs during many heroic acts.

mind to mind, but body to body. This includes helping to harmonize as many bodies as possible. This process begins with all event-planning gatherings. Begin each of these with one or two of the activities in Chapter 14. Have the group hum or buzz together, sing together, *om* together, rock back and forth together, or rub your own bellies at the same time. Feed your bodies together. Make some of these planning gatherings into potluck meals. Better still, precede them with meals that attendees cook and eat together.

If some of your organizers or planners are not from the community, give them a walking tour of it, so it will feel more familiar to them. If *you* are not from the community, orient yourself by strolling through it for an hour or two. Stop in at local businesses. Hang out for twenty minutes in a park or coffee shop. If there's a concert or block party or street festival, drop in for a few minutes.

As you plan the event, remember that it will involve a large number of human bodies, each of which has needs and vulnerabilities. Be sure to arrange to have people on hand who are trained in first aid and well equipped with first-aid supplies. Also have on hand people who are trained in psychological first aid (described in more detail later in this chapter).

As part of your planning, create an *incident command system* (ICS)—a set of protocols and relationships that determines, in advance, who is in charge of what in the event of a crisis or emergency. Incident command systems can prevent chaos, save time, and, most important, prevent panic, injury, and death. Your ICS does not have to be complicated, but it does need to be crystal clear—and well understood by all event organizers, planners, leaders, and speakers. For many events, it may be important (or essential) to include local law enforcement in your planning.

If possible, also plan to set up a quiet *reprieve space* near the edge of the gathering. This is where someone can go if he or she experiences trauma (whether it is new or historical), serious distress or anxiety, disorientation, or some other mental or emotional problem triggered during the event. This reprieve space can be a tent or other temporary shelter; a roped-off area; an area created by a circle of parked cars;

or even the back of a parked cargo van. Staff this reprieve space with someone trained in psychological first aid.[86]

If you plan to set up stations with food, water, toilets, and/or first aid, set these up near the edges of the gathering, *not* near the center. This minimizes the flow of bodies at the event's center, creates more bodily harmony, and enables participants to be more focused and less distracted. This arrangement also makes it easier to move people out of (or into) the crowd in an emergency.

An hour or two before the actual event begins, bring together your key people—all the speakers, leaders, marshals, ushers, and/or observers. Settle and harmonize your bodies using one or two of the activities in Chapter 14. At first, some people may laugh or roll their eyes at these activities—but remember that they can be immensely valuable. The settling and harmony they encourage will in turn help settle the bodies of other people in attendance—including police, public officials, onlookers, passersby, and media people. This can do far more to bring people together than any cogent argument.

Whenever possible, also incorporate some of the following body-centered activities into the event itself:

- Get the crowd humming (or buzzing) loudly together; encourage *everyone*—onlookers, police, public officials, media people—to join in. I often do this as soon as I'm in front of a microphone. The first thing I say is, "Let's all take a moment to harmonize our bodies. I'm going to start to hum. For fifteen seconds—just fifteen seconds—I want everyone to hum along with me. Police, media folks, everyone—hum with me."

- Have everyone in attendance rub their own bellies slowly, in harmony. In an assertive but friendly way, call out folks who don't ("I see two police in the back with their hands on their hips. I'm gonna call them Nelly and Shelly. Everybody—keep rubbing and turn around and look at Nelly and Shelly. Now

---

86   Times of civil restlessness and unrest, and actions of protest and civil disobedience, can be re-traumatizing for some African Americans. Present experience and media images can meld with historical, intergenerational, institutional, and personal traumas of our past. As a result, some Black bodies may experience rage and horror as if the year were 1820—or 1619. Reprieve spaces thus become especially valuable—and especially protective—for African Americans.

repeat after me: Nelly and Shelly, rub your bellies! All right! Everyone, let's give a big cheer for Nelly and Shelly!")

- As part of a march, have everyone smile, nod, and make brief eye contact with each police officer as they pass them.

None of this is even remotely as lighthearted as it may appear. Nor is it for the benefit of the police. These practices are ways to harmonize and settle all the bodies at an event—including the folks whose job is to keep you safe and treat you in a safe manner.

It helps in two important ways. First, someone whose body has recently harmonized with yours may be less likely to arrest you or crack open your head. Second, a crowd of harmonized bodies is far less likely to turn into a mob—or turn on each other.

If you are speaking at an event and event organizers don't do any of the things in the bulleted list above, add one or more of them to your own presentation.

Consider one other activity that has a profound effect on the human soul nerve: foot washing. Washing someone's feet creates deep harmony and a strong body-to-body connection. It is an immediate, tactile, visceral expression of caring, respect, empathy, humility, and service. It is simple and wordless, yet its message is unmistakable: *You matter to me.* When you wash someone's feet, his or her heart naturally opens a bit.[87] And when someone washes yours, your heart naturally opens a little as well. Foot washing tends to settle the bodies of both the recipient *and* the giver. It also feels deeply pleasant, nurturing, relaxing, and calming.

Perhaps more important, after you have washed someone's feet— or after he or she has washed yours—the two of you are no longer strangers, no longer *others*.

This can also be true when you have simply *offered* to wash the feet of someone (a neighbor, a reporter, a skeptical onlooker, or a police officer who doesn't look or act like a soldier), even if that person has said no. Just by having made the offer, it is now harder for him or her

---

87   While I'm sure there are some people who are exceptions, in general our soul nerve is wired to respond positively to having our feet washed—and to washing the feet of others. Only a great deal of training—or a great deal of trauma—can blunt this natural response.

to see you as less than a fellow human being. The same is true for how you see that person. Even just watching someone wash another person's feet can have a profound settling and harmonizing effect on the human body. It may also create a little more room for growth in the observer's body and nervous system.

In addition, some folks will surely video the foot washing and upload that video to the Internet. Who knows how many people might be curious enough to watch?

There are of course a lot of religious implications to foot washing—but I suggest not invoking them. They will be clear to people with religious backgrounds.[88]

It's up to you to decide how to best use foot washing (and whether to use it at all) as part of your own social action. It requires water, containers,[89] and towels, and it takes a bit of time, so you need to plan thoughtfully. The process should not distract large numbers of people from the event or create clots or long lines of bodies. One option is to have volunteers stand at the edges of the crowd with basins and water jugs, and offer to wash the feet of random attendees. Another is to limit the foot washing to people on the stage at the front of the event. Each speaker might briefly wash the feet of the person who follows (or precedes) him or her.

IF YOU'RE A FREQUENT OR SERIOUS ACTIVIST

Take a class in basic first aid and CPR. This will enable you to offer potentially life-saving help if someone needs swift medical attention. Your local branch of the Red Cross and/or the American Heart Association either sponsors such a class, or can refer you to another organization that does. In-person classes typically run about six hours; classes are also offered online (or as a combination of online and in-person training.)

Also take a basic class in psychological first aid (PFA). This will enable you to assist people who are stunned, overwhelmed, or seriously

---

88   On the last evening of his life, Jesus washed his disciples' feet. The Old Testament has multiple references to foot washing. In 2016, as part of the Holy Thursday celebration at a refugee center outside of Rome, Pope Francis washed the feet of Muslim, Hindu, Catholic, and Coptic Christian immigrants.

89   I suggest reusing ordinary plastic water bottles, which can be refilled with tap water. If you are feeling adventurous, add some scented Epsom salts.

distressed in the wake of a disaster (a terrorist attack, an earthquake, the shooting of a police officer, etc.), civil unrest, or some other potentially traumatic experience. It may also teach you how to organize and set up an incident command system before an event begins. Basic PFA classes are available both in person and online. (You can enroll in an interactive six-hour online course by visiting the website of the National Child Traumatic Stress Network. The Network also offers a free basic PFA handbook.) As a PFA instructor myself, I can attest to the great value of this training.

Lastly, a note of caution: It's easy to get caught up in social activism to the point where you allow yourself little or no down time. There is always much to be done—and much that needs doing. But no human body can be activated all the time. Your body's abilities are finite. Like every other human body, it needs regular periods of rest. Listen to your body. Give it adequate rest, recovery, leisure, relaxation, and rejuvenation. Help it settle, over and over. Have a bit of fun now and then. All of this is required, not optional.

As you will discover, self-care will help you be a more effective activist—and a better human being. You will bring a healthier body and nervous system to your activism. You will also lead a happier and more balanced life.

Burned-out activists show up in my therapy office all the time. For years—sometimes decades—they push themselves hard, because they see what they do as so important. But they refuse to face the fact that the well being of their own bodies is also important. Exhausted and unhappy, many of these people ultimately drop out of activism altogether. They move to a different city, start over, and raise a family. Their children are shocked when they discover that mom the prof or dad the piano tuner used to lead marches—and was arrested four times for civil disobedience.

For some people, intense activism is actually a dodge—a way to try to avoid some of their own pain or personal trauma; a way to flee a conflict with their partner, parent, child, or other relative; or a way to avoid addressing some other difficult personal issue. These folks need to step back from activism for a time; slow themselves down; face what is bothering them; move through clean pain; and resolve the issue.

At its best, activism is a form of healing. Activism is not just about what we do; it is also about who we are and how we show up in the world. It is about learning and expressing regard, compassion, and love—for ourselves and for our fellow human beings.

RE-MEMBERINGS

- Healing from white-body supremacy begins with your body—but it does not end there. We cannot individualize our way out. We also need social activism that is body-centered.

- As we engage in collective action, we need to do so with settled bodies.

- Before you show up for any social action, first do what you can to settle your own body and nervous system, using some of the activities in Chapters 10, 11, and 12.

- If your body simply won't settle, remove yourself from what's happening for a few minutes. Find a relatively quiet and private spot; resettle your body; and then return.

- In any social action, do what you can to help settle and harmonize as many bodies as possible. Do the same in any event-planning gathering.

- If you're a frequent or serious activist, take a class in basic first aid and CPR, as well as a class in psychological first aid.

- Never forget the importance of rest, leisure, and good self-care.

- At its best, activism is a form of healing. It is about what we do and how we show up in the world. It is about learning and expressing regard, compassion, and love.

CHAPTER 19

CREATING CULTURE

"You're not obligated to win. You're obligated to keep
trying to do the best you can every day."
MARIAN WRIGHT EDELMAN

"Children have never been very good at listening to their elders,
but they have never failed to imitate them."
JAMES BALDWIN

"Without inner change, there can be no outer change.
Without collective change, no change matters."
ANGEL KYODO WILLIAMS

Culture is how our bodies retain and reenact history—through the foods we eat (or refuse to eat); the stories we tell; the things that hold meaning for us; the images that move us; what we are able (and unable) to sense or feel or process; the way we see the world; and a thousand other aspects of life.

Because culture lives in our bodies, it usually trumps all things cognitive—ideas, philosophies, convictions, principles, and laws. In many cases, it even supersedes human desires and needs.[90]

Change culture and you change lives. You can also change the course of history.

Many well-meaning social activists overlook this essential fact. They focus relentlessly on strategy, but strategy means nothing to our bodies and our lizard brains. When strategy competes with culture, culture wins—every time. This is one of the reasons why the most brilliant anti-white-supremacy strategies in the world have failed to dislodge white-body supremacy from our culture.

The Boy Scouts and Girl Scouts have their own cultures. The National Rifle Association has a culture. The Mafia has a culture. Each organized street gang has a culture. The Ku Klux Klan has a culture—one that has lasted over 150 years. Each of these organizations has elders, rituals, symbols, uniforms, displays, shared terminology and language, stories, mentoring, roles, titles, awards, codes of behavior, rules of admonishment and belonging, a shared history, a communal vibe (a shared vibrational language), and an explanation of the world and our place in it. These can be deeply soothing to the human body—especially a traumatized body. They can also create a deep sense of harmony with other bodies that belong to the organization. And all of these cultural trappings—and the powerful sensations and experiences they engender—are immediately available to anyone who becomes part of the group and adheres to its structure.

More than anything, culture creates a sense of belonging—and belonging makes our bodies feel safe. This is why culture matters to us so deeply.

We humans want to belong. We experience belonging—or the lack of it—in our bodies. We experience it deeply. When we belong, we feel that our life has some value and meaning.

But we can never belong to a strategy. We can never belong to a movement, either, though we can be part of it. We can only belong to a *culture*.

---

90   Consider how hungry you'd have to get before you'd eat beetles or moths—even though they're highly nutritious, routinely eaten by people in other cultures, and, reportedly, quite tasty.

Social activism is necessary for changing the world in positive ways. But if our collective body is to fully heal from the trauma of white-body supremacy, we must create cultural shifts as well.

White-body supremacy is already a part of American culture—in the norms we follow, the assumptions we make, the language we speak, the water we drink, and the air we breathe. This is the case no matter the color of our skin. This means we must create new expressions of culture that call out, reject, and undermine white-body supremacy.

This won't be quick or easy—but there is no other way.

The good news is that American history is full of such profound cultural changes. If enough people do the same thing over and over, or if they share something with each other enough times, eventually it becomes culture.

Our culture has been radically changed by the sale of new products, such as the birth control pill, the personal computer, and the smartphone. It is about to be changed radically again by the self-driving car.

Culture has been radically changed through the creation of new or expanded public utilities—from rural electrification, to radio and TV airwaves, to the Internet, to Wi-Fi.

It has been radically changed through the creation of new social programs. Social security, for example, profoundly changed how we view and experience retirement. When the program was enacted in 1935, the poverty rate among our elderly citizens was over 50 percent; in 2013, it was 10 percent.

Culture has also been radically changed through advertising campaigns. One of the most successful was the Don't Mess With Texas campaign, which began in 1985. Designed to reduce roadside littering, the campaign targeted Texas residents (mostly young men, ages eighteen to twenty-four) who routinely threw litter out of car and truck windows—and who considered littering to be part of their identities as Texans. The campaign redefined littering as *anti*-Texan—and it defined people who *didn't* litter as proud, authentic Texans protecting their state and culture. The campaign has been hugely successful: in its first four years it reduced roadside litter by 72 percent.

While we need to promote cultural change, the place for us to begin is *not* with the broadest aspects of American culture, such as casual clothing, barbecues, and superhero movies. Because Black Americans, white Americans, and police have each developed their own subcultures, each group first needs to create profound change *within* its own culture. This means that each group needs to develop its own new stories, symbols, rituals, role models, elders, and so on.

This is especially important for us as African Americans. We need to be solely in charge of our own cultural shifts. Otherwise we run the risk of being co-opted yet again by the pervasive (and often subtle) influences of white-body supremacy.

There's another important reason why white Americans, African Americans, and police need to transform their own cultures first: right now the three cultures simply cannot work together on a large scale. Some observers say this is because there is too much tension, and not enough trust, among the groups. That's true, but the real issue is more elemental: right now, if we attempted to work together, we would regularly trigger the trauma in each other's bodies.

First, each of our separate communities—African Americans, white Americans, and American police—needs to learn and practice the settling of our bodies. We can also learn and practice the five anchors from Chapter 12. We can steadily make our bodies more resilient and less constricted. Many of us—most of us, I hope—can mend our trauma and create more room in our nervous systems. Over time, and with practice, all of this will enable us to better regulate our responses to discomfort and challenge when it comes to white-body supremacy and racialization.

Once this occurs—whether it's years or decades or generations from now—the three groups may be ready to work together as one. Our first step together will need to be harmonizing our bodies. Right now, our bodies are not ready for this.

I don't see this timeline as a cause for despair; it's simply a recognition of where we are—and where and how we need to begin.

Black bodies have suffered repression, torture, and murder by white bodies for four centuries. During medieval times, white bodies suffered repression, torture, and murder by other white bodies for a millennium. In comparison, a healing process that evolves over a generation or two (or three or four) is not so long.

Let me be clear that I'm talking about *parallel* processes, not isolated ones. Simultaneously, there needs to be collaboration, coordination, and cooperation among the three groups—especially when it comes to social activism. It's a classic both/and situation.

Until then, it's important to recognize that all three cultures share many of the same attributes—especially when each group is at its best. These include strength, resilience, courage, creativity, perseverance, and achievement. They need to be recognized, highlighted, lifted up, and passed on *within* each group, along with supportive stories and practices that are unique to that group.

None of the three groups needs to start from scratch. Each can draw on, build on, and, in some cases, rediscover its existing talents and achievements.

I especially want to draw white Americans' attention to this. White fragility is a lie, a dodge, a myth, and a form of denial. White Americans *can* create culture that confronts and dismantles white-body supremacy. Any suggestion that they are unable to rise to this challenge is a lie. White Americans are anything but helpless or fragile; they are (of course) precisely as capable as other human beings. But they need to refuse to dodge the responsibility of confronting white-body supremacy—or the responsibility of growing up.

In the three chapters that follow, I suggest some possible directions and activities for each of the three cultures. First, though, let me call out a few essential aspects of creating culture:

- Developing and uplifting elders (and eldership) is especially important, because elders provide mentoring and guidance for the next generation. Elderhood isn't an entitlement that comes with age or a position that individuals can claim. Someone becomes an elder because a community gives that authority to that person, based on who he or she is and what he or she has done.

- The creation, telling, and passing on of new stories is crucial. The stories should be narratives of resilience, compassion, achievement, and transformation.

- The most effective leaders lead by example and model the way for others. The most effective followers *also* model the way for others.

- Cultural change takes hold through consistency and repetition. When enough people do the same thing, in the same way, over and over, eventually those actions become culture.

- Everyone needs to learn to take care of themselves—and to help care for others. To support this, each culture needs to create body-centered rituals and practices that promote self-care *and* collective wellness. These practices, too, need to be passed on from person to person—particularly from parents to children.

- These practices help our bodies to slow down and settle. They help us have fewer and less intense reflexive responses. And they help us give more energy to love, compassion, and regard.

- You already know what needs to be at the center of all these efforts: an individual and collective willingness to be in our bodies, accept and metabolize clean pain, and heal.

RE-MEMBERINGS

- Culture is how our bodies retain and reenact history.

- Because culture lives in our bodies, it usually trumps everything cognitive.

- Change culture and you change lives. You can also change the course of history.

- When strategy competes with culture, culture wins every time.

- Culture involves elders, rituals, symbols, uniforms, displays, rules, stories, mentoring, roles, titles, awards, codes of behavior, and a shared history. These can all be deeply soothing to a human body—especially a traumatized body.

- Culture matters deeply to human bodies because culture creates a sense of belonging—and belonging makes our bodies feel safe. More than almost anything else, we humans want to belong.

- If enough people do the same thing over and over, or if they share something with each other enough times, eventually it becomes culture.

- Social activism is necessary for changing the world in positive ways. If our collective body is to fully heal from the trauma of white-body supremacy, we must also create new expressions of culture that call out, reject, and undermine white-body supremacy.

- Because Black Americans, white Americans, and police have each developed their own subcultures, each group first needs to create profound change *within* its culture. This means each group needs to develop its own new stories, symbols, rituals, role models, elders, and so on.

CHAPTER 20

CULTURAL HEALING FOR AFRICAN AMERICANS

"Give light, and people will find the way."
ELLA BAKER

"Healing is not just about what we experience in the present, it's also about how we understand the past, how we name our histories and frame the times in which we live."
SUSAN RAFFO

Someone needs to write a detailed guide to cultural healing for African Americans. That guide needs to be both visionary and practical—and it needs to catalyze social activism. I may attempt to write that book at some point—but not this year. For now, let me highlight what I see as the most important focuses of this cultural healing—and what I see as the most promising places to begin.

Raise up African American leaders, artists, writers, speakers, activists, and elders who have addressed some of their own racialized trauma. When someone has metabolized much of their clean pain around race, you can see it in their eyes, face, and body. The person exudes a presence, a conviction, a *knowing*. You can sense the added clarity and space in their body with *your* body. Their body is calm and settled—but ready to activate at their own discretion when circumstances warrant. Such people have the potential to be some of our greatest heroes and leaders.

Among people alive today, this includes DeRay Mckesson, bell hooks, Alice Walker, Congressman John Lewis, Toni Morrison, and many others. Among people who are no longer with us, it includes James Baldwin, Maya Angelou, and Malcolm X, to name just a few. Watch some videos of these folks; as you do, don't just listen to their words (though their words are often deeply insightful). Also pay attention to their bodies. Let your own body experience the settledness and self-awareness of these men and women. Then share these videos with other people you know—and call out that settledness and self-awareness to them.

The people in these videos are and were imperfect. We should not hold them up as gods, but as human beings like us who have done the necessary personal work of healing and growing—the work each of us needs to do as well.

Learn and teach about traumatic retentions—and grow out of them. Like all human beings, we African Americans need to hold onto the strongest and most resilient parts of ourselves, and grow out of the weakest ones. We need to do this as individuals, as a group, and in our culture.

Traumatic retentions often stay with us because they combine both strengths *and* weaknesses. With time, careful attention, and practice, we can tease out—and teach others to tease out—what is beneficial from what is harmful.

Think of my grandmother whupping me and my brothers to help us learn to be safe. We *definitely* needed that lesson—but my grandmother could have taught us without using the willow switch.

Like most other traumatic retentions, the act of whipping Black bodies—first by white bodies, then by other Black ones—was passed down through the generations, until it looked like culture.

We African Americans also need to grow out of any traumatic retention around our African bodies—thinking darker skin is inferior to lighter skin, curly hair worse than straight hair, a wide nose less attractive then a narrow one,[91] and so on. We would also be wise to stop calling each other by the N-word, even in an affectionate or ironic way. (Jews do not call each other kikes in any context. Latinos do not call each other spics. Native Americans do not call each other redskins.)

We need to call out all such traumatic retentions to each other— and recognize them in ourselves. Then we need to settle our bodies, anchor ourselves, and move through the clean pain of growing out of them.

Learn and teach about historical and intergenerational trauma. A basic understanding of inherited trauma can help people put their lives in context; comprehend why they experience some of the things they experience and do some of the things they do; and begin the process of healing. All of us African Americans—especially our children—can benefit from an awareness of the trauma pyramid (see page 46).

Learn and teach about African history and cultures. It's common for African Americans to trace back our bloodline only as far as our ancestors' arrival in America. When we do this, though, we may unconsciously equate our entire history as Black human beings with oppression and violation. This is of course not the case. In doing this, we diminish our lineage by limiting it to a dozen or so generations.

Let's enlarge our history to include those times and places in which our ancestors' bodies were free of racialized trauma. This means teaching our children about the art, stories, and histories of African cultures.

Life in Africa before our enslavement was hardly idyllic, just as life in Africa is not idyllic today (for reasons involving corruption, dictatorial leaders, geopolitics, globalization, and so on). Our task is not to create some illusory ideal past, but to pass on genuine knowledge and wisdom about our actual shared history.

---

91   Wide noses have not only been racialized; but they also have been falsely identified with African bodies. Black people from Ethiopia, Eritrea, and Somalia (and their descendants), for example, rarely have wide noses.

Modern human beings have been on this planet for about 200,000 years; civilization as we know it is roughly 6,000 years old. The first modern human beings were Black; so were the first civilizations. We need to teach our children this as well.

Invoke the power of names. We can name our children after Black men and women we admire—and want our kids to admire. When your son or daughter asks you, "Where did my name come from?" you can use this teaching moment to explain a bit of Black history, and to sing the praises of a human being whose life contributed to our well-being and sanity. You might add, "We gave you that name to encourage you to be like your namesake, and make a positive difference in the world."

We can also continue to create unique names for our sons and daughters. When you tell your daughter Sarahnita or Shaquilina (or your son LeThomas or Brondell), "We created your name just for you because of how much we love you," you send a deeply empowering message—one that may encourage resilience and self-confidence for a lifetime. It can also create a bit more room in that child's body and nervous system for growth and possibility.

Any of us can also choose to rename *ourselves*. This is not some hard-to-achieve fantasy. In America, you can legally change your name quite easily. My own name, which is from the Kemetic tradition, is not the one on my birth certificate, but one I chose to legally adopt as an adult. (I received the name from elders, who received it from our ancestors.)[92]

Naming—and renaming—are powerful acts of reclamation. They reestablish a form of personal agency that white-body supremacy denied our ancestors for many generations, because others named us. After enslavement was abolished in 1865, many African Americans renamed themselves—often with first names that resonated with dignity, such as Prince, Noble, or Mister. Because many white folks refused to address Black people by their surnames—as Mrs. Garnet,

---

92   I was born Chester Mason, Jr. When I was young, people called me Little Chet. Now that I have a different name—one that I chose to adopt as an adult—calling me Chester would be disrespectful. The name Resmaa has a dual benefit: it connects me to an ancient tradition, and it's unusual enough to make me easy to find online.

Miss Graham, Mr. Simms, etc.—these first names forced white people to be respectful when speaking with African Americans.

There's also a practical reason for giving your child—or yourself—a unique name: that person will come up first in any online search. When Sarahnita grows up and applies for a high-powered job, her potential employers will be able to easily research her on the web—and they probably won't confuse her with someone else. A unique or unusual name is helpful for authors, artists, and performers for the same reason.

Teach our children the basics of body awareness and somatic healing. Think how much more resilient, focused, and mature your children will be if you teach them some of the activities in Chapters Ten and Eleven while they are small—and if you instruct them in the anchoring practices in Chapter Twelve when they turn eleven or twelve.

This is not pie-in-the-sky thinking. Many schools now teach mindfulness and somatic practices to young children—with excellent results.[93] As pediatrician Nadine Burke-Harris observes of mindfulness practices in general,

> There's good evidence that those therapies can help to counter the effects of trauma on the developing brain and body of a child . . . Some of the best practices can be to incorporate stress-reduction techniques into the school day, particularly if they are in a school that is in a community where there's a high degree of stress involved. Some of the best practices include things like mindfulness-based stress reduction. There are a number of schools that are using mindfulness-based meditation in class, moments of quiet, helping kids regulate their behavior and kind of settle and land in the classroom so they're able to focus and pay attention better.[94]

---

93   See Donna St. George, "How Mindfulness Practices Are Changing an Inner-City School," *The Washington Post* (November 13, 2016), which describes one of many such initiatives, at Robert W. Coleman Elementary School in West Baltimore.

94   From "A Conversation with . . . Nadine Burke-Harris, MD," *California School Boards Association,* Summer 2013.

Practice and teach the art of disruptive healing. Genuine healing is a temporarily disruptive process. This is true not only for individual bodies, but for the collective Black body—and the collective American body—as well. Just as the human body creates inflammation to heal, wise social activism creates the social and cultural disruptions needed to help a culture heal and grow up. These disruptions might also be called *compassionate agitation.*

We can also teach the history and value of disruptive healing in the collective body, so that many more Black Americans recognize—and sense in their bodies—the through-line shared by Harriet Tubman and John Brown, Medgar Evers and Ella Baker, bell hooks and Cornel West, and Alicia Garza and DeRay Mckesson.

More African Americans also need to know that Black Lives Matter is not a historically isolated movement; it is the most recent manifestation of a resistance movement that goes back centuries.

Indeed, more African Americans (and more Americans of all colors) need to become aware that history is ongoing. Now is always part of its flow. In every new moment, each of us creates history—through the choices and decisions we make, and the things we say and do.

It's often said that Americans care little about history. "That's in the past," white Americans often say. "Let's focus on the here and now—or, better yet, on the future." This is just another dodge created by white-body supremacy. It is yet another attempt to avoid growing up and healing from racialized trauma. History matters, and an awareness of it puts our lives into a context. A disdain for history sets us adrift, and makes us victims of ignorance and denial. History lives in and through our bodies right now, and in every moment.

Encourage and support eldership. Encourage wise and loving Black adults to take on mentoring roles. Actively support them in those roles. Encourage our children to find, work with, and learn from African American mentors.

Learn and teach regard for one another. Regard is the foundation of all cooperation, all growth, and all positive social change. Let us make it the foundation of our lives as well.

RE-MEMBERINGS

- Some suggestions for promoting social and cultural healing among African Americans:

  + Raise up African American leaders, artists, writers, speakers, activists, and elders who have healed their racialized trauma.

  + Learn and teach about traumatic retentions.

  + Learn and teach about historical and intergenerational trauma.

  + Learn and teach about African history and cultures.

  + Name our children after Black men and women we want our kids to admire—or create unique names for them.

  + Rename *ourselves* after Black men and women we admire—or create unique names for ourselves.

  + Teach our children the basics of body awareness and somatic healing.

  + Practice and teach the art of disruptive healing, as well as the history of such healing.

- These practices can help us create more room for healing and resilience in our children. They can also help us heal and grow up.

CHAPTER 21

WHITENESS WITHOUT SUPREMACY

"Nobody's free until everybody's free."
FANNIE LOU HAMER

"To sit back and do nothing is to cooperate with the oppressor."
JANE ELLIOTT

"White people . . . have quite enough to do in learning how to accept and love themselves and each other, and when they have achieved this . . . the Negro problem will no longer exist, for it will no longer be needed."
JAMES BALDWIN

"You need not carry the heavy, hollow burden of racism any longer. Leave it behind. Be for something, and not because it's easy."
JESSE WILLIAMS

If America is to grow out of white-body supremacy, the transformation must largely be led by white Americans. This transformation cannot rely primarily on new laws, policies, procedures, standards, and strategies. We've already seen how these are no match for culture.

For genuine transformation to take place, white Americans must acknowledge their racialized trauma, move through clean pain, and grow up. African Americans and American police need to do the same. And, for now, we each need to do it in our own culture, and in our own way.

When I explain this to groups, some earnest white folks in the audience often ask me some variant of this question: "Resmaa, I'm totally up for this. But I have no idea what to do or where to start, or what the next steps are. Can you lead us or offer us a set of next steps?"[95] My answer, of course, is no. The question is itself just one more expression of imaginary white fragility. It is white Americans turning yet again to a Black body and saying, "Help us. Serve us. Save us. Bail us out. Do our work for us. Above all, don't make us stand on our own two feet and grow up." But growing up is exactly what all of us—individually and collectively—need to do.

I can't grow you up. You can't grow me up. Adulthood can't be outsourced. Each of us needs to do it on our own—by accepting and moving through clean pain. Nor can I force you to grow up. You—and I, and everyone else—have to do it willingly. Nor can I create a new form of white culture for you. The very notion is absurd. Imagine a roomful of African Americans in 1970 asking Tony Bennett to invent hip-hop for them.

There are no shortcuts or workarounds. There is simply a choice: clean pain and healing, or dirty pain and more trauma. There is possibility and there is peril.

To all my white countrymen, I say this: Not only is it not my business to lead you out of white-body supremacy, but I would do you a profound disservice by trying to do so. You need to develop, lift up, and follow your own leaders in the work of dissolving white-

---

95   Sometimes white folks ask reflexively, "Why can't we all just sit down and talk, and then do it together? I mean, we're all the same, aren't we?" I explain that, more often than not, *sit down and talk* means either *Black people spend many, many hours getting white people up to speed* or *White people refocus all the energy and attention on themselves.* Sometimes it turns out to mean both.

body supremacy. If you don't—if you choose to follow a Black Pied Piper—you will collectively reaffirm the myth of white fragility and helplessness in racialized contexts. You will also have no one to pass the baton to when your Black savior retires, dies, or moves on (or turns out to be flawed, like all human beings).

If you think you don't already have people who can lead these efforts, google Tim Wise. Or Robin DiAngelo. Or Peggy McIntosh. Or Jim Wallis. They're just a small part of the front row of a roomful of such folks. These people continue to do their own work around white-body supremacy, while helping other white folks do the same work collectively.

Then there are all the capable and inspiring white leaders who may live in your community, but whom you've ignored or haven't noticed. Plus all the talented white leaders who are yet to emerge—and yet to be born.

Read about people like Wise and McIntosh. Read their books and blogs and articles. Listen to them speak, in person and in audio recordings. Watch videos by and about them on YouTube.

This chapter offers no blueprint or list of proposed steps for working with your fellow white Americans to dismantle white-body supremacy. Instead, I offer some observations, suggestions, possibilities, and things to avoid or be wary of. At best, these are a handful of threads that can be woven into a much larger tapestry. While I urge you to take them to heart, I also urge you to amend them, build on them, be inspired by them, ignore them, or create something better.

You know how crucial culture is to human life—and to the human body. Yet white Americans have not yet created any form of anti-white-supremacy culture. White Americans who seek to undo white-body supremacy have organizations; they have ideas and strategies and goals; they have initiatives; and they have energy, conviction, and hope. But they have little sense of community—and no culture to build and support such community. This needs to change. White allies must build culture, because culture trumps almost everything else. You can start by creating:

- A brief but compelling narrative that links the past, present, and future; that acknowledges the unique responsibility of white allies as a separate cadre of activists; that pledges to work with and alongside African American (and other non-white) change makers; and that offers a compelling, positive vision of a future world.

- Credos that emerge from a combination of language, support, love, and regard.

- Past and present heroes, heroines, role models, leaders, and elders.

- A system for mentoring people (especially young people) who want to get involved.

- Study groups and classes on the subjects of racialization, white-body supremacy, trauma and its healing, and psychological first aid.

- Symbols and icons.

- Rituals and ceremonies, including for births, deaths, and elderhood.

- Clear, established practices of rejuvenation and good self-care, so people don't burn out or routinely fall ill.

- Rules of belonging and admonishment.

- Names, naming practices, and naming ceremonies.

- Awards that strengthen the bonds between recipients and the new culture.

- Clear roles, positions, titles, and ways of giving authority to leaders.

- A sticky name for the new culture and/or the people in it ("white allies" and "white progressives" lack energy and stickiness).

As leaders emerge, each one can (and should) create his or her own unique style, from both his or her own experience and the collective experience and knowledge of the new culture. This may include a unique catchphrase, hairstyle, or item of clothing.

For example, DeRay Mckesson almost always wears a blue down vest—not because his body is cold, but so he can be easily spotted, identified, and remembered. Google images of him and you'll see that in most of them he's wearing that vest.[96]

The late film critic Gene Shalit understood the importance of a unique item of clothing. He almost always wore an outrageous bowtie. Eventually, any time an American saw a bowtie on anyone, he or she thought of Shalit.

Signature details don't have to involve clothing. The late actress Tallulah Bankhead was widely recognizable through her use of the word *darling*, which she pronounced *DAHH-ling*. The late scientist Carl Sagan was immediately identifiable from his repeated use of the phrase *billions and billions*. Any sticky—and benign or appealing— sensory image will do.

For a sane culture to take hold and prosper, there needs to be more than just an emphasis on the individual and individual achievement. There also needs to be an equal emphasis on cooperation, and on the collective good. Indeed, in building culture, one good place to start is by letting go of a focus on oneself, and re-centering the focus on benefitting one's fellow human beings. (Some of the shared cultural elements I discussed above may also help white Americans grow out of the extreme imbalance toward individualism that white-body supremacy fosters.)

If all of this sounds daunting, it is only because the task of culture building may feel so unfamiliar. People are not often urged to build a new culture. However, white Americans—and their European forbears before them—have done it many times before.[97] This time, however, white Americans need to create new culture without murdering, enslaving, or debasing others.

---

96   So far, people have been wise enough to not emulate Mckesson. The blue down vest is a symbol of Mckesson himself, not of the Black Lives Matter movement. If a lot of other folks were to wear similar vests, Mckesson would become far less visible—and, perhaps, a less influential leader. (In that case, he'd probably replace the vest with a different visual trademark.) On a related note, you'll notice that my list of suggested cultural trappings doesn't include a uniform or mode of dress. That's because, outside the professions and ancient religions, uniforms on adults are often a hallmark of cults. Think of the Ku Klux Klan, or the Hare Krishnas, or the Gloriavale Christian Community.

97   Most notably, of course, with the creation of white-body supremacy itself.

A stellar example of such a successful (and generally healthy) new culture is twelve-step programs: Alcoholics Anonymous, Al-Anon, Alateen, Narcotics Anonymous, Overeaters Anonymous, Codependents Anonymous, and dozens of other, related recovery programs. Though these groups are now a common part of our cultural landscape, they did not spontaneously appear. In the 1930s, twelve-step culture was created by a small (and overwhelmingly white) group of Americans. Building on earlier work by others, the founders of Alcoholics Anonymous created the twelve-step principles, traditions, slogans, group meeting structure, mentoring relationships, and other elements of culture. Today, many millions of people from around the world attend twelve-step groups. While twelve-step culture is no magic bullet—and, like all human creations, is less than perfect— it has supported the recoveries of tens of millions of people, and has saved millions of lives and relationships.

For individual white Americans who see the value of growing out of white-body supremacy, I offer the following thoughts: Don't expect to be guided by others at all times. Notice for yourself the persistent and ever-present ways in which white-body supremacy provides advantages to white people. Whenever you spot a manifestation of white-skin privilege or protection, note it and name it (at least mentally, and sometimes verbally). When you can, extend that privilege to others.

Study yourself, your ancestors, and your people. What are their stories, both in America and before they arrived here? How did they end up in the New World? How did their lives lead to yours?

Also, study the world. In particular, study history, so that your understanding of white-body supremacy becomes part of a larger context.[98] Read some sociology, anthropology, and psychology as well.

Changing culture will take a lot of time and a lot of effort—on your part and on everyone else's. This means *years* of observing, questioning,

---

98   One example: In the 1930s, Nazi leaders closely studied America's race laws, which they deeply admired, to help them create their own Nuremberg Laws in 1935. One of the laws stripped Jews of their citizenship; another prohibited sex or marriage between Jews and people with "German or related blood." See James Q. Whitman's eye-opening book, *Hitler's American Model: The United States and the Making of Nazi Race Laws* (Princeton, NJ: Princeton University Press, 2017). In addition, some of South Africa's and Australia's forms of white-body supremacy were informed by American practices.

reflecting, and learning. Not eight hours a day, of course, or even an hour a day—but a serious and extended commitment.

Consider Malcolm Gladwell's observation that it takes about 10,000 hours of practice to become highly proficient in almost any serious endeavor.[99] By the time African Americans reach adulthood, many have spent 10,000 or more hours learning how to navigate the dangers, constrictions, and contradictions of white-body supremacy. They have done this not by choice, but as a matter of survival. In comparison, most white Americans have spent zero time in such endeavors, for the obvious reason that they haven't needed to navigate white-body supremacy, but have received support and assistance from it. White people who want to grow out of white-body supremacy now need to put in a similar amount of time and effort in order to change themselves and create new culture. (Gladwell's 10,000-hour figure has been challenged by some authorities, and needn't be taken literally. The point is simply that if white-body supremacy is to be dissolved and replaced with sanity, respect, and regard, many white Americans will need to expend considerable effort toward those goals, both individually and collectively, over an extended period of time.)

It also means thinking and acting in terms of community, not mere transactions or tactics. Don't just show up at a meeting or class at its starting time, participate, and go home. Come early; talk with people and get to know them; ask questions; stay afterward to talk further and help clean up. You are helping to build something bigger than yourself. This needs to be reflected in what you do and how you treat and respond to other people.

There will surely be many setbacks and frustrations and failures. White-body supremacy has arranged your world so that many things in your life have been easy. This will no longer be the case for you. Accept and expect this.

Often, when the topic of white-body supremacy is raised, one common trauma response in white bodies looks and sounds like this: "I'm not racist! Back off!" Or, "I'm not racist! How dare you?" Another common trauma response looks and sounds like this: "I'm not racist!

---

99   Malcolm Gladwell, *Outliers: The Story of Success* (New York: Little, Brown and Company, 2008).

My daddy marched with Martin Luther King, my sister-in-law is Black, and I donate to the NAACP." This response is especially common among white progressives. A third familiar trauma response—also common among white progressives—looks and sounds like this: "I know! I feel so guilty! Oh, I'm going to break down and cry now." A fourth is, "I'm an exception to everything you're talking about because I'm biracial," or "I was born and raised in Patagonia," or "I grew up in an orphanage run by progressive Black nuns."

All of these responses focus attention away from any potentially meaningful discussion about white-body supremacy. Then they re-center the discussion on the reflexively defensive—or reflexively guilty—white person. None of these responses serves anyone.

Honestly, I don't care if your sister-in-law is Black; if you used to cut Martin Luther King's hair; if you adopted nine Black babies; if you gave $50,000 to the NAACP's Legal Defense Fund last year; or if you're a sax-playing ex-president. I do not keep a scorecard on you and your life. As an adult, neither should you.

I also don't give a rat's ass how guilty—or how offended and falsely accused—you feel. (As a therapist, I'd better not. If I did, I'd need to find a new line of work.) What I *do* care about is what you do with your life *now*. Are you treating all human beings with genuine regard? Are you calling out evil and immorality when you encounter it? Are you serving your fellow human beings? Are you acting out of the best parts of yourself? Are you working with other white people to develop culture and dismantle all forms of white-body supremacy?

Lastly, you're not an exception, no matter how much you think you are. As I said at the beginning of this book, white-body supremacy is part of the operating system of America. It is in the air you and I breathe and the water you and I drink. And it is literally in our blood. You (or I or anyone) can't opt out of breathing or drinking water or circulating blood throughout our bodies.

Here's something else: white Americans as a group do not get to make their own historical and intergenerational trauma the center of national attention. That trauma is real, and white Americans need to acknowledge it, face it, and mend it. But this shouldn't involve putting whiteness front and center yet again. For example: *Oh my God. White bodies traumatized each other for more than a millennium. We're a collective wreck. We need help. Let's bring as much media attention as possible, and as many government dollars as possible, to addressing white trauma.* This only reinforces the practices and institutions of white-body supremacy.[100]

The previous chapter discussed the power of naming for African Americans. Names can play a powerful role in the lives of white Americans as well. If you're white, here are some ways you might use names to help dissolve white-body supremacy:

- Name your kids after African Americans you admire—for example, Fannie Lou Zaleski, Thurgood Goldstein, Maya Angelou Rizzoli, John Audubon Osborne, or Marlon James O'Malley.

- Better yet, name your kids after white Americans who have worked hard and sacrificed to dismantle white-body supremacy—for example, Jane Elliott Wheatley, John Brown Kowalski, or Anne Braden Murdoch. This will help you pass on context to them.

- Raise your kids with respect and appreciation for their namesakes. Tell them that you hope they will grow up with some of the same qualities that made their namesakes great.

- When your kids first ask where their names come from, teach them a bit of history, psychology, and sociology, and introduce the topics of racialization and white-body supremacy.

- If you're not satisfied with your own name, change it—for example, from Betty Lou Johanssen to Rosa Parks Johanssen.

- If you are in a position to name (or suggest a name for) a street or a building, propose the name of a white anti-white-

---

100   In the late 1980s and early 1990s, during America's crack epidemic (which overwhelmingly involved African Americans), crack use was treated almost solely as a criminal justice issue. Much money and effort were poured into policing, particularly in Black neighborhoods and communities, and an enormous number of dark-skinned Americans were arrested and jailed. As of this writing in 2017, America faces another drug epidemic, this one involving opioids. This time, however, the great majority of addicts are white—and this time the call is not to arrest people, but to build treatment centers. Dr. Andrew Kolodny, executive director of Physicians for Responsible Opioid Prescribing, explains the difference: "I think it was pretty clear that our response during the crack cocaine epidemic was largely a criminal justice response. Whenever you hear people talking about our opioid crisis, within the first few minutes you hear someone say something to the effect that we can't arrest our way out of this problem" (see Steven Ross Johnson, "The Racial Divide in the Opioid Epidemic," *Modern Healthcare* (February 27, 2016).

supremacy ancestor, such as John Brown, or the name of an African American whom you admire. It's especially helpful to suggest such names for streets and buildings in mostly-white neighborhoods and downtown areas. Encourage a W. E. B. Du Bois Avenue in Beverly Hills or a Harriet Tubman Building in Scottsdale.[101]

An often-overlooked group of American organizations has great untapped potential for helping to dismantle white-body supremacy. These are service organizations for European immigrants and their descendants. In my hometown of Minneapolis, for example, we have the Germanic-American Institute, the Swedish Institute, the Italian Cultural Center, the Polish American Cultural Institute, the Ukrainian American Community Center, and several others. As you now know, at one time immigrants to America from these and other European countries were not considered white—or even fully human. As a result, some of their descendants—the vast majority of whom are white—are well aware of the harm white-body supremacy did to their ancestors. If you're a member of one of these organizations, you might lead an effort to issue a collective public statement like this one:

When our ancestors came to America, they were looked down upon and denied opportunities because of where they came from. Eventually they were accepted as full citizens and normal human beings—but at the cost of diluting their heritage and becoming "white" people. We reject that identity. We are not content to passively accept the identity and perks of whiteness. We are proud to be German Americans (or Italian Americans, Polish Americans, Irish Americans, etc.[102]), and we stand together with African Americans, Chinese Americans, and the descendants of immigrants from any other nation against the constraints and dehumanization of white-body supremacy.

---

101   To quickly recognize the pervasiveness of white supremacy in America, study street names. Many American streets are named after Martin Luther King, Jr.—almost all of them in mostly-Black (and poor) neighborhoods. If white Americans genuinely admired Dr. King as much as they claim to, they would also rename streets in wealthy, mostly white neighborhoods in his honor.

102   In 1988, when Jesse Jackson encouraged Americans to use *African American* rather than *Black, Negro, Afro-American,* or *colored,* the idea was to deliberately echo the names of groups such as Irish Americans and Italian Americans. While these groups had formerly been looked down on and considered non-white, by 1988 they were relatively free of discrimination. The term *African American* did catch on, as Jackson hoped, but for these Americans a much smaller amount of discrimination melted away—simply because, unlike Italian and Irish immigrants and their descendants, African Americans never had the opportunity to become white.

You might also encourage your organization to make the dismantling of white-body supremacy part of its mission. This is not that much of a stretch. Many religious organizations, and many service organizations serving immigrants from non-European nations and their descendants, are already doing similar things. It would not take a great deal of effort for European-focused service organizations to follow their lead.

Whiteness and white-body supremacy began as a scam, a myth, a shell game. But, false as they are, they are also part of American culture. We can't all just rub our eyes, admit that we believed in a phantasm, and move on.

For white Americans, then, the most important task in dissolving white-body supremacy involves separating whiteness from supremacy. Over the centuries, American leaders have welded the two concepts together in millions of white minds—or, more accurately, millions of white lizard brains. This has resulted in large numbers of Americans who are white, racist, and proud to be both; an even larger number who are white, racist, and in reflexive denial about it; and another large number who are white, progressive, and ashamed of their whiteness. All of these are forms of immaturity; all can be trauma responses; and all harm African Americans *and* white Americans.

White supremacists created whiteness and then defined it as something childish, selfish, and closed-minded. But it doesn't have to be. Whiteness can mean taking responsibility.

White activists can deliberately reclaim whiteness. They can first call it out as the sleight of hand and the swindle it has always been. Then they can publicly redefine it as something caring, open, and grown up.

This gives them an opportunity to say to America's overt white supremacists, "You're a bunch of spoiled children. You think your whiteness makes you special. You aren't. You think your whiteness entitles you to privileges and respect. It doesn't. Grow up, start caring for your fellow human beings, and earn the respect you crave."

In her essay "The Role of European Americans in a Decolonization Process," Sara Kolstad Axtell, adds these useful suggestions:

We need to work in partnership with other European Americans and people from other cultural communities to change institutions, so that they stop claiming authority over people's lives . . . another path is to look to our own past for at least part of our means of transformation. . . . we, as European Americans, need to help our people see themselves as having a culture. This is a powerful way to disrupt whiteness, not just to rid ourselves of something that is destructive, but to reclaim/reconstruct something that is positive, that fills a void, that has the potential to create health and harmony.[103]

This is not some fanciful dream or idealistic vision. White Americans across the country are already beginning to create new culture that redefines whiteness and works to dismantle white-body supremacy.

Just in Minneapolis, we have several organizations and initiatives—and plenty of white Americans—moving in that direction. These include Healing Roots (healingrootscommunity.com) and The Tree and the Well (treeandthewell.wordpress.com). No doubt there are dozens, if not hundreds, of parallel groups and initiatives across America.

There are also many proven and widely used initiatives that can be used (or adapted) to dissolve white-body supremacy and build healthy white culture. One example is the Trauma Resource Institute's Community Resiliency Model. This model teaches people personal and communal wellness skills; helps them better understand resiliency and their own nervous systems; and encourages mutual support, the building of community, and individual and collective healing

Efforts to dissolve white-body supremacy do not (and should not) focus on taking anything away from white people. Instead, they focus on extending white Americans' rights, privileges, and opportunities to people of all colors, so that all Americans get to enjoy them in equal measure.

103   Sara Kolstad Axtell, "Comments for 'Tearing Down the Myths' Panel Overcoming Racism" Conference, October 29, 2010, St. Paul, MN, http://www.cehd.umn.edu/FSoS/people/faculty/pdf/Axtell-panel.pdf.

No one can guess which of these efforts will catch on and thrive, and which ones will fall by the wayside. I do know that any new culture will need to require that white Americans tolerate discomfort, move through clean pain, and grow up. When white Americans learn to manage their own bodies, they will no longer feel a need to manage Black ones. When white Americans build culture that is sane and loving, they will no longer feel a need to exclude people of color from it.

Ultimately, whiteness must transform from race to culture. Once this has been achieved, it can begin to transform from culture into community.

RE-MEMBERINGS

- If America is to grow out of white-body supremacy, the transformation must largely be led by white Americans.

- The engine of this transformation will be the creation of new culture, which will ideally include:

  - A brief, compelling narrative of hope and possibility.

  - One or more credos.

  - Past and present heroes, role models, leaders, and elders.

  - Mentoring.

  - Rules of belonging and admonishment.

  - Study groups on white-body supremacy, trauma, and psychological first aid.

  - Symbols and icons.

  - Rituals and ceremonies.

  - Practices of good self-care and rejuvenation.

  - Awards that strengthen the bonds between recipients and the culture.

  - Clear roles, positions, and titles.

+ Names, naming practices, and naming ceremonies.

+ A sticky name for the new culture and/or the people in it.

- For this new culture to take hold and prosper, there needs to be an emphasis on cooperation and the collective good, as well as on the individual and individual achievement.

- Re-imagined names can help drive or exemplify this new culture.

- Some organizations that serve European immigrants and their descendants may publicly embrace this new culture.

- Whiteness itself can be redefined—so that it gets equated with taking responsibility and growing up.

- None of this will be easy. It will take great effort from many white Americans, individually and collectively, over a period of years. Yet the only alternative is the perpetuation of white-body supremacy and a great deal of dirty pain for all.

CHAPTER 22

RESHAPING POLICE CULTURE

"Healing isn't fully healing if it doesn't in some way connect the individual to the community . . . We heal so that communities can take on healing as part of their everyday ways of being."

SUSAN RAFFO

"Sometimes you have to raise a little hell to get some heaven."

JOE MADISON

"Truth demands a voice: speak up."

ROLAND MARTIN

To every member of the law enforcement profession, I propose this opportunity and challenge: *You can be a genuine hero.*

To every police chief, department head, precinct captain, or other public safety leader, I offer this vision: *Your organization can command widespread respect, appreciation, and gratitude.*

All of this is possible because it is already the case in many, many communities across America—but not in a lot of communities where many residents have dark skin.

In most of these, you may be viewed not as a hero, but as a soldier on patrol, and your precinct house may be viewed with fear and suspicion—in many cases, for good reason.

This is a predictable outcome of the neo-Crow era. For the past several decades, policing in America has routinely meant targeting, accosting, searching, convicting, incarcerating, shooting, and killing large numbers of African Americans and other dark-hued human beings. It has also created a generous—and reliable—income stream for the prison industrial complex, which profits from the corralling and incarceration of Black bodies.

This dynamic will not fundamentally change through interventions instituted from the top down. It will primarily change through you and your colleagues—through how each of you views Black bodies, Black lives, and Black communities. Until you consistently recognize these bodies as human, these lives as human, and these communities as human, no progress can be made in your relationship with them.

There has been a great deal of talk and writing about *community policing*, which is widely seen as a key to improving relationships between public safety professionals and "communities of color" (that is, locales with a lot of dark-skinned residents). But can community policing actually work? It depends. Here is how the US Department of Justice defines *community policing* in its document *Community Policing Defined*:

> Community policing is a philosophy that promotes organizational strategies that support the systematic use of partnerships and problem-solving techniques to proactively address the immediate conditions that give rise to public safety issues such as crime, social disorder, and fear of crime.[104]

Memo to the Department of Justice: That is not community policing. Or justice. Or clear writing.

---

104   US Department of Justice, "Community Policing Defined" (2012, revised 2014), https://ric-zai-inc.com/Publications/cops-p157-pub.pdf. While the Department of Justice badly missed the boat in this instance, it has nevertheless done some important and highly commendable work on community policing—as we'll touch on later in this chapter.

Community policing is not a philosophy. It is not an idea. It is a set of ongoing actions. It is *making your body a part of the community—and then wholeheartedly serving, protecting, and assisting the human beings in that community.*

Community policing includes such things as:

- Calling the city to report an unrepaired pothole or a broken streetlight.

- Providing a ride or an escort to someone in an emergency.

- Helping to push a car out of the snow.

- Responding to calls for assistance.

- Helping residents plant a community garden.

- Waving to residents, saying hi to them, and stopping for friendly chats with them (preferably because you enjoy it).

- Talking with kids in the community; telling them stories or jokes; letting them ask you questions; and perhaps letting the smallest ones sit on your lap.

- Getting a cat out of a tree or a sewer.

- Picking up an overturned trash can on the corner.

- Pulling over drivers who violate the law—always in a professional and respectful way.

- Assisting a resident who appears to be in distress or difficulty.

- Talking with residents about their concerns, their families, and their lives.

- Calling the city a second time if the pothole or streetlight hasn't been promptly repaired.

In a 2016 *Slate* video, Michael Wood, Jr., a retired Baltimore cop, eloquently describes how real community policing works:

If we actually did a community policing model, designed to have decentralized power, so that the patrol officer can take care of things in his or her responsibility area. So, in a true community policing model, if I came down here and I see this overgrown brush, I have the power and the resources to get city workers or something like that down here to fix that. I should have the ability to get weed whackers and recruit people in the neighborhood. And maybe for that day of work, instead of locking people up, I came out with the neighborhood and did this, because that would have some kind of improvement overall . . . We have to start thinking about what are we actually doing and what are our goals. So if our goals are to reduce violent crime, we have to change our metrics. Right now our metrics are arrests. . . . We have to change the metrics to crime reduction, to justice, to problem solving . . . You should be focused on improving your post, not on locking up many of those people on your post, because if you're taking their freedom away, how are you not going to be their enemy?[105]

There's no simple, straight-line route from where American police are now to the kind of community policing model Wood describes. But here are some potential first steps:

IF YOU'RE A PATROL OFFICER OR SOME OTHER ON-THE-GROUND PUBLIC SAFETY PROFESSIONAL

- Consider yourself a member of the neighborhood or community where you work; think of its streets as your workplace—not a war zone that you patrol. Wherever you work, never forget that it is a home for other human beings.

- View yourself as an advocate and ombudsperson who can help residents connect with any services they might need.

- Get out of your patrol car often; walk the streets.

---

105   Leon Neyfakh and Aaron Wolfe, "Why Police Are So Violent Toward Black Men: In the Words of a Baltimore Ex-Cop," *Slate.com*, August 6, 2015. *The Washington Post* and the BBC have also run interviews with Wood. Wood's website, michaelwoodjr.net, contains interviews and articles on this and related subjects.

- Hang out in a local park for a few minutes at a time—not to look for trouble, but to chat with residents, ask them about their families, pet their dogs, and encourage their resilience.

- Hang out in a community coffee shop while you read your newspaper or tablet or emails.

- Regularly volunteer in the community—at a church or other religious organization, in a school, or at a nonprofit in the area you work in. (If you're an effective and well-liked football coach or Sunday school teacher in the community, this alone will profoundly shift your relationship with the people who live in it.)

- Whether you're in or out of your car, smile, nod, and wave at residents. If someone smiles back, ask them how they're doing. If they look like they want to talk, stop and ask in a friendly tone, "Is there something I can help you with?"

- Talk to people; introduce yourself by name; find out their names; laugh and tell stories with them; sit on their front stoops with them; find out if they have any requests you can help with.

- Occasionally shop, eat, take walks, or visit a church, mosque, or temple in the community—ideally both in and out of uniform.

- Meet with leaders of schools, churches, mosques, temples, and businesses in the community. Ask them how you can best be of service. Also ask them for calendars of upcoming community events.

- Stop in at community events such as bake sales, rummage sales, concerts, outdoor dances, street festivals, school fundraisers, parades, church suppers, etc.—again, both in and out of uniform. On occasion, bring one or more family members with you.

- Play, dance, or jump rope with kids in the park; buy small bags of snacks in bulk, keep them in your car, and hand them out. If a small child is sitting on a swing, ask them if they'd like a push.

- Help out with community projects, such as picking up trash during a neighborhood cleanup, weeding a community garden, or painting a fence around a churchyard, mosque, or temple.

- Go to worship services in the community.

- When you see something that needs to be taken care of—a leaking hydrant, an abandoned car, a tree that's fallen over—call the appropriate office and report it; tell the people nearby that it's going to be handled; ask nearby residents and business owners to call the city about it as well; and check on it later to be sure the problem has been addressed.

- When someone you know in the community has a birthday, or gets married, or has a baby, or suffers the loss of a family member, send them a card.

- Recognize that *protecting and serving*—and even *law and order*—should not be forms of dogmatism. You don't serve the community—or other human beings—when you issue citations for jaywalking, or littering, or failing to signal a lane change.

- If you see that a headlight or taillight on a car is out, it's fine to pull the car over. But you don't have to write a ticket. Simply inform the driver in a friendly way that the light is out and needs to be fixed promptly; then wish them a good night and return to your car. (This is what cops routinely do in affluent neighborhoods; why do otherwise where you work?)

- Recognize that laws are often applied more deliberately, harshly, and sometimes brutally to Black bodies. Remind yourself that your job is to enforce the law equally, fairly, and humanely in every situation.

- Think about these statistics: in 2014, about 1,100 people in the United States were killed by police; in 2015, about

1,200 were. In comparison, in 2011, German police killed six people; British police killed two; Australian police killed six; and Japanese police killed zero human beings.

- Do all of this regularly, so that everyone—including you—sees you as part of the community.

- Continue to prevent and fight crime.

When you show up and help people plant a garden or clean up a vacant lot, no one cares whether you're a cop or not. What they see is that you're working and helping out. They see that you care. After a few minutes, your bodies will harmonize. And maybe after a few minutes more, you and the other folks will start talking.

I'm looking at a photo of a smiling white cop in uniform. He's sitting down and talking with a group of small Black kids. One is leaning on him and eating potato chips; another is sitting between his legs. Everyone looks relaxed and happy. Their bodies are obviously harmonized.

This didn't happen automatically. It happened because that cop is regularly out in the community, day after day—sitting and talking with people, listening to stories and jokes, telling stories and jokes of his own, buying things in the local stores, and being a consistent part of that world.

IF YOU'RE A PRECINCT CAPTAIN, POLICE CHIEF, MAYOR, OR OTHER LEADER

- As much as possible, create and maintain a genuine community-policing model—even if you need to buck the system (and you probably will).

- Get rid of all arrest quotas; instead, track each officer's performance by neighborhood improvement, crime reduction, and citizen connection and satisfaction.

- Train police officers, not soldiers; when an officer consistently acts like a soldier in spite of this training, counsel him or her into a military career.

- Train your officers to follow a community-policing model from the moment they come in the door until the moment they leave—including every moment in between.

- Establish clear channels of communication with other community offices, so if an officer calls in and asks for a street light to be repaired, or for a wandering deer to be caught and relocated, the issue is handled promptly.

- As much as possible, recruit, train, and hire police from within the community or neighborhood (or, in the case of a large city, at least from within the city limits).

- Encourage your officers to focus on improving neighborhoods. Make sure they understand that this includes, but is not limited to, reducing crime.

- Honor, reward, and showcase officers who take such a focus in their work.

- Tie community-policing expectations to annual reviews and advancement opportunities.

- White-body supremacy routinely operates—sometimes invisibly—in everyday processes, policies, and procedures. So closely examine each one of your own to make sure that it genuinely serves the community and its residents, and that it doesn't—whether by design or default—elevate whiteness.

- At least once a year, require each officer to complete a survey that tracks their community skills and interactions; this should be tied to performance reviews.

- Coach and train your officers to treat community residents fairly and respectfully. Reprimand, cite, punish, or dismiss any officer who fails to do so.

- Partner with churches, schools, and other local organizations to host community events for residents. This might include concerts, open houses, meet-and-greet sessions with officers, picnics, softball games, movies, and so on.

- Partner with professionals in the community to offer free personal services on a walk-in basis to community members one evening or afternoon a week. These might include haircuts, massages, basic medical and dental exams, etc.

- Arrange and host occasional suppers at the precinct house. Invite people from local religious organizations, schools, businesses, and nonprofits. Also invite people from the community to help cook. If your budget can handle it, pay for the food (and buy it from a community business); if it can't, host potlucks.

- When you need to buy office supplies, janitorial supplies, furniture, or almost anything else for the precinct house, buy it from a community business whenever possible. This means getting to know local business owners.

- Partner with the American Civil Liberties Union (ACLU) to offer regular workshops in the community—perhaps even at the precinct house—on citizen's rights, and on what to do when a police officer appears in your life. Think about the powerful and supportive message this sends to residents. Furthermore, such a workshop will be profoundly helpful and practical, because most Americans haven't a clue about what to do in the presence of a police officer. Such a workshop may also reduce friction between officers and residents; help people avoid misunderstandings and escalation; and result in fewer unnecessary arrests, injuries, deaths, and other tragedies.

- In addition to (or, at minimum, instead of) offering these workshops, have your officers hand out the ACLU's free (and very helpful) pamphlet, "Know Your Rights: What to Do If You're Stopped by the Police." Again, this will help your officers and make their jobs easier, because more residents will know how to respond appropriately in an encounter with an officer. Keep a stack of these cards in a visible location in the precinct house, so anyone can easily take one. (Next to them, perhaps also keep a stack of free pocket-size copies of the US Constitution.)

- Ask or lobby for support from leaders, top managers, and elected officials for all of the above.

- Visit the Campaign Zero website at joincampaignzero.org. The goal of Campaign Zero is to reduce to zero the number of deaths caused by police each year in America. The site offers many excellent, practical suggestions, which I urge you to read and take to heart.

- In May 2015, the Department of Justice released its *Final Report of The President's Task Force on 21st Century Policing,* which provides useful insights and suggestions for effective community policing. In this report, the US Department of Justice has done some of its best work. I strongly urge you to read it and implement some of its suggestions.[106]

- Also visit the website of the National Initiative for Building Community Trust and Justice at trustandjustice.org, which has many helpful articles and other resources.

You will know that you are making progress when your officers are regularly invited to graduations, weddings, christenings, and other social events in the community. You'll know that you are doing many things right when some of your officers are dating community members and leaders (including some active and/or vocal ones); when some have become coaches, Big Brothers, Big Sisters, or adoptive parents for community kids; when some move to the community, or to a community nearby; and when some marry people who live or work in the community. If some of these weddings are held at venues in the community—and you or some of your other officers are invited—then you can be pretty confident that you have been practicing genuine community policing.

Imagine that one of your officers shows up one morning looking sad and exhausted. You ask her what's wrong, and she says, "My son got hit by a car last night. He's going to live, but he needs major surgery." You commiserate for a few minutes; then she heads out to

---

106   The report is available at https://cops.usdoj.gov/pdf/taskforce/taskforce_finalreport.pdf.

begin her shift. A few hours later, Gwen Pritchard, a retiree who lives a block away from the station, walks in carrying a casserole dish covered with aluminum foil. She puts it on the front counter and says to the officer behind it, "I heard that Hannah's son is in the hospital. I hope he gets better. I made this peach cobbler for her and her husband."

When scenarios such as this one become regular occurrences, you'll know that you and your officers are doing your jobs well.

RE-MEMBERINGS

- For the past several decades, policing in America has routinely meant targeting, accosting, searching, convicting, incarcerating, shooting, and killing large numbers of Black bodies.

- This dynamic will not fundamentally change until you and other police officers consistently recognize Black bodies, lives, and communities as *human* bodies, lives, and communities.

- Community policing is not a philosophy or an idea. It is a set of ongoing actions that involve making your body a part of the community—and then wholeheartedly serving, protecting, and assisting the people in that community.

CHAPTER 23

HEALING IS IN OUR HANDS

*"I have come to the conclusion that human beings are born
with an innate capacity to triumph over trauma. . . . In so
doing, we will significantly increase our ability to achieve both
our individual and collective dreams."*

PETER LEVINE

"The triumph can't be had without the struggle."

WILMA RUDOLPH

*"Unarmed truth and unconditional love
will have the final word in reality."*

MARTIN LUTHER KING, JR.

*"Forget the R or the D or the liberal or the conservative.
Are you for right or are you for wrong? Are you for
humanity or are you not? . . . Are you for brown people
to be treated fairly or are you not?"*

D. L. HUGHLEY

Mental illness runs in my grandmother's family.[107] When her sister became schizophrenic and had to be hospitalized, my grandmother willingly took in her two young children and raised them as her own.

My other grandmother did the same thing with my aunt's four kids. When my aunt became a cocaine addict and lost most of her ability to be a caring parent, my father's mother didn't hesitate to take over.

When I witnessed both of these changes in our family, I thought it was because my grandmothers were kind, loving, generous women. That was generally true, of course. But something else was involved—something more important. Both of my grandmothers recognized the need for someone to step in and fulfill a parental role. Both also had the capacity to wholeheartedly take on that role.

They didn't have to do this. They could have let my cousins be shipped off to other relatives, or allowed the county to place them in foster homes. Instead, they drew on their own resilience and stepped forward. This helped create room for growth in the bodies and nervous systems of their grandchildren.

I didn't realize it until I was in my early fifties, but both of my grandmothers also helped to create greater room and resilience in *my* body and nervous system. Their actions taught me to willingly shoulder responsibility.

When my wife Maria and I first started dating, she had a daughter, six-year-old Brittney. After Maria and I had gone out a few times and it was clear that we were serious about each other, I took on the role of Britt's father. This felt completely natural and comfortable to me. My body told me it was the right thing to do.

This sense of naturalness, comfort, and rightness came from my grandmothers. Their willingness to take on a parenting role with their grandchildren helped me to do the same thing as a new parent. This in turn helped create still more room for growth in Brittney's body and nervous system.

You're almost done with this book, but you are not done with healing or growing up. As long as we're alive, none of us ever is.

---

107   My mother is very sane, loving, and successful. People also tell me she's drop-dead gorgeous. She won the genetic lottery, but her sister was not so fortunate.

There is so much more to be done—with yourself, with other individuals, with your community, and out in the world.

This book is a beginning. It is not a grand solution or magic bullet. It's a first step into something much, much bigger.

Whether your body is Black, white, or otherwise, you and other members of your group need to care for yourselves, care for each other, and help one another mend and grow up. You will also need to create new culture.

I'm a therapist, not a futurist. I can't predict what these new cultures will look like—but they will need to be body-centered; they will need to focus on healing; and they will require us, over and over, to settle our bodies, confront ourselves, and metabolize our clean pain.

All of this will take time and effort. I don't know how much time. Maybe ten years. Maybe three generations. Either way, the time to begin is now.

At some point in this process, we'll all need to contend with hate. It's there, wrapped inside our trauma, and it's going to come out. After centuries of systematic violation—first of white European bodies, then of Black African and American bodies, how could there not be hate?

We can use the five anchors to accept that hate—in others and in ourselves—and then metabolize it and move through it.

We'll also need to deal with global shock. In 2017, many of us are already dealing with it, big time. At times you may feel strong sensations in your body: jolts, buzzing, twitching, tingling, trembling, or sudden crying. This is a normal part of healing. You are discharging energy.

You now have some understanding of trauma, some practice in settling your body, and some experience in using the five anchors, so you know what to do to help yourself move through this.

Don't try to stop or avoid what is happening. Settle into your body and let yourself fully feel those sensations, without analyzing them. Use the five anchors to metabolize the experience and move through it.

Remember that trauma is all about speed and reflexivity. Slow yourself down and pay attention to your body. Be curious about what is going on there. Lean into your body's experiences and sensations. Do the same with uncertainty.

Love and trust are not concepts or tactics. They are ways of being with someone, ways of being in the world, and ways of being in your body.

We experience love and trust in our bodies. For me to love and trust you, my body needs to sense that you deserve that love and trust. Yours will need to sense the same thing about me. This is visceral, not cognitive.

I wish we could all begin with trust and love for each other. But we can't. There has been too much damage to too many bodies for too many generations.

But we all *can* begin with respect, caring, and a willingness to help.

On that foundation, we African Americans can learn to love ourselves and each other. White people can do the same with other white folks. Police officers can do it with other police.

Eventually, maybe we'll all be able to come together. Mutual love and trust are waiting in the wings for a time when enough of us are ready. Until then, we can practice giving respect, caring, and assistance.

Once there's been widespread healing and growing up, fingers of love and trust can begin to reach out from one group to another—and then, slowly, start to intertwine.

—BODY PRACTICE—

Can you feel hope in your body? Excitement? Anticipation? Where do you sense it? Is it a release or expansion? A tightening born of eagerness? A rush of heat or energy?

What hopes accompany these sensations? The chance to continue to heal and live an ever-bigger, ever-deeper life? To help others mend and live bigger, deeper lives? To free the world from the shackles of white-body supremacy?

Congratulations. You're just where you need to be for what comes next.

RE-MEMBERINGS

- None of us is ever done with healing or growing up.

- You and members of your group need to care for yourselves, care for each other, and help one another grow up. African Americans can do this with other African Americans. White people can do it with other white people. Police can do it with other police.

- You and other members of your group also need to create new culture.

- As part of this process, each of us will need to contend with hate, which is wrapped inside our trauma. But we can use the five anchors to metabolize that hate and move through it.

- Over time, once there has been some widespread healing and growing up, fingers of love and trust can reach out from one group to another—and start to intertwine.

- We can each begin with respect, caring, and a willingness to help.

- The time to begin is now.

CHAPTER 24

THE RECKONING

"It's time for you to move, realizing that the thing you are seeking is also seeking you."

IYANLA VANZANT

"Everything will change. The only question is growing up or decaying."

NIKKI GIOVANNI

"People who shut their eyes to reality simply invite their own destruction, and anyone who insists on remaining in a state of innocence long after that innocence is dead, turns himself into a monster."

JAMES BALDWIN

"We as a nation must undergo a radical revolution of values. . . . When machines and computers, profit motives and property rights, are considered more important than people, the giant triplets of racism, extreme materialism, and militarism are incapable of being conquered."

MARTIN LUTHER KING, JR.

"What a world this will be when human possibilities are freed,
when we discover each other, when the stranger is no longer the
potential criminal and the certain inferior!"

W. E. B. DU BOIS

When European settlers first came to this country centuries ago, they brought a millennium of intergenerational and historical trauma with them, stored in the cells of their bodies. Today, this trauma continues to live on in the bodies of most Americans.

Most white immigrants to the New World didn't heal from their trauma. Instead, beginning a little over three centuries ago, they created the concepts of whiteness, of blackness (and redness and yellowness), and of white-body supremacy. Then they blew much of their trauma through the bodies of Africans and their descendants. This served to embed trauma in Black bodies, but it did nothing to mend the trauma in white ones. Much of our current culture—and most of our current cultural divides—are built around this trauma.

An African American elder said to me recently, "There is a root to the trauma tree, and what we see now is the fruit." That tree, which was planted roughly fifteen centuries ago, now casts a shadow across our entire nation. Today, many of us still feed each other its bitter, poisonous fruit.

None of us asked for this trauma. None of us deserves it. Yet none of us can avoid it. It is part of our personal and national histories. In many American bodies, the Civil War, or the American Revolution, or the Crusades, rages on.

Today we're at a reckoning. We Americans have an opportunity—and an obligation—to recognize the trauma embedded in our bodies; to accept and metabolize the clean pain of healing; and to move through and out of our trauma. This will enable us to mend our hearts and bodies—and to grow up.

If we do this, both as individuals and as a nation, America may be able to live up to W. E. B. Du Bois' vision: a country in which human

The Reckoning

possibilities are freed and we discover each other. If we don't, we will likely tear each other—and our country—to pieces. This second path— the path of destruction—is the one we are currently walking together.

This reckoning is not about rich versus poor, liberal versus conservative, nationalism versus globalism, Christians versus Muslims (and/or Jews), or any of the other ways in which our country is being pulled apart. It is not even about white versus non-white human beings. These divisions are all reflections of a much older and more elemental conflict.

That conflict is the battle for the bodies and souls of white Americans. This battle has been fueled by trauma as old as the Middle Ages, and it has been simmering in white American bodies since long before we became a nation. Now the heat has been turned up, and the conflict has reached critical mass.

This is a conflict that white Americans must heal in themselves, for themselves, and among themselves. We non-white Americans can support this healing, but it cannot be outsourced, either to us or anyone else.

Americans have reached a point of peril and possibility. We will either grow up or grow smaller. This trauma will either burst forth in an explosion of dirty pain, or provide the necessary energy and heat for white Americans to move through clean pain and heal. Only this second outcome will provide us with genuine safety.

As part of this reckoning, our bodies—especially our soul nerves— are being activated big time, in both painful and pleasurable ways. Our racialized trauma, and much of our other trauma as well, are routinely getting triggered. We need to fully sense our soul nerves' constriction and expansion; the pain, fear, hope, and dread; the sense of peril; and the sense of possibility.

To tolerate the discomfort of this activation, we all need to carefully observe ourselves, slow ourselves down, settle our bodies, and use the five anchors, especially when we are in difficult situations. This will be an ongoing challenge for each of us—but I believe we are up to the task. We can live out of the best parts of ourselves. This book can help us move forward in that direction.

For centuries, it was possible for white Americans to accept white-body supremacy without questioning it; to enjoy its privileges and to take them for granted; and to ignore or deny the ways in which white-body supremacy routinely harmed dark bodies. Those days are now over. If you're a white American, you can't look away anymore. You have to choose. You can move through clean pain and grow up. Or you can dive deep into dirty pain—and create much added misery for everyone, including your descendants and yourself.

This does not absolve us African Americans from addressing our own trauma. We, too, need to recognize our trauma; accept and metabolize our pain; mend our hearts and bodies; and grow up. Through this process, we can also fully reclaim our bodies, our resilience, and our place in America and the world.

I've focused this book mostly on America and written it primarily for people who live in that land—but there is nothing uniquely American about trauma. It is a part of normal human experience, and it affects almost every human body.

Similarly, white-body supremacy is not uniquely American. Like so much of American culture, it has been exported and embraced around the world. As we've seen, cultures and governments in Germany, Australia, South Africa, and elsewhere have studied American-style white-body supremacy and created their own variations abroad.

My hope is that this book will ultimately reach far beyond the US borders, and help people around the world to heal their trauma, live lives of resilience and purpose, and reclaim their rightful places in the human community.

*

I'm looking at a photograph of my grandmother, taken when I was about eight years old. She's in her kitchen, cooking for us, cutting vegetables. Her hands seem steady and sure; her body is calm and settled. I'm almost certain she's humming.

While we'd eat, she'd stand over us, touch the back of our heads, and ask, "Does that taste good?" We'd nod and say, "Yeah, grandma, it's good." And it *was* good. My mother could make a decent meal, but my grandmother could *cook*. The two women could each make the same dish and the results would taste completely different.

Back then, I always ate supper in a hurry, so I could go out and play with my friends. Usually, as I left the house, my grandmother would say to me, "Boy, you be careful, now." I knew she wanted my siblings and me to grow up successful and happy. But now I understand that the main thing she wanted was for us to be safe.

I feel the same way about my son Tezara. I want him to have a good life—but, right now, what I most want for him is safety. I want him to grow to adulthood unharmed and intact. I want him—and my grown daughter Brittney—to be able to trust rather than fear white Americans and police officers. I want them both to have what so many of their ancestors—and boys such as Tamir Rice, Trayvon Martin, and Emmett Till—were denied: the opportunity to fully inhabit their own bodies.

RE-MEMBERINGS

- We Americans have an opportunity—and an obligation—to recognize the trauma embedded in our bodies; to accept and metabolize the clean pain of healing; and to move through and out of our trauma. This will enable us to mend our hearts and bodies—and to grow up.

- If we do this, both as individuals and as a nation, America may become a country in which human possibilities are freed and we discover each other.

- If we don't, we will likely tear each other—and our country—to pieces.

- Today we're at a reckoning—a battle for the bodies and souls of white Americans.

- This battle has been fueled by trauma since the Middle Ages, and it has been simmering in white American bodies since long before we became a nation. Now it has reached critical mass.

- To tolerate the discomfort of transformation, we all need to carefully observe ourselves, slow ourselves down, settle our bodies, and use the five anchors, especially when we're in difficult situations.

- If you're a white American, you can't look away anymore. You have to choose. You can either choose clean pain and grow up, or choose dirty pain, increase the age-old trauma, and pass it on to others.

AFTERWORD

"Turn your wound into wisdom."
OPRAH WINFREY

As I write these words, I'm enveloped by two forms of urgency. *My Grandmother's Hands* goes to press in a few days; my immovable deadline is hours away. Yet I must write an Afterword I had no plan or intention to write. A unique moment in history is unfolding around me, around my city, and around the world. Six days ago, Justine Damond was shot dead. Her killer was Minneapolis police officer Mohamed Noor. Like the shootings of Philando Castile, Jamar Clark, and Matthew Hovland-Knase by law enforcement officers, this occurred just a few miles from my home.

The story of Damond's killing is achingly familiar: The police were called to investigate reports of a possible sexual assault behind Damond's home. A police car containing two officers drove up. Damond came out of the house—unarmed, in her pajamas—to speak with them. In what appears to have been a lizard-brain annihilation response, Noor shot Damond dead through the patrol car window. Both officers were wearing body cameras—in fact, every on-duty member of the Minneapolis Police Department normally does—but both cameras were turned off. So was the car's dash cam.

Today is July 21, 2017. As of today, Noor has not allowed the Bureau of Criminal Apprehension to interview him. However, both he and his fellow officer in the car, Matthew Harrity, quickly lawyered up. The lawyer for Harrity explained that it was "certainly reasonable" for Harrity to fear that they were the target of an ambush.[108] Or that, as the Minnesota Bureau of Criminal Apprehension "copsplained," one of the officers "was startled by a loud sound."

The killing of an American by an American police officer is not unusual. In fact, on average it takes place three times a day.[109] And the percentage of African American bodies that die at the hands of police is two and a half times that of white bodies.

For decades, the world has known that we Americans routinely eat our young—particularly our young with dark skin—in this way. Many people have grieved on our behalf and shaken their heads in disbelief. But very few have risen up in outrage. With Damond's death, all of this changes. The outrage is now directly in our American faces. This outrage is not only justified, but vocal, persistent, and worldwide. For Damond was not American, but Australian. Our "uniquely American" problem has now jumped the border. Our deadly national dysfunction has now become a problem for the world.

The Damond/Noor story unfolds by the hour, capturing much of the world's attention. For almost a week it has been the main news story on the entire continent of Australia. Millions of human beings around the world have expressed their horror and shock. The Prime Minister of Australia, Malcolm Turnbull, has publicly demanded answers.

Three other pertinent details: Damond was white. Her home is in a quiet, upper-middle-class, mostly white neighborhood in Minneapolis. Officer Noor is Black—a Somali American. Many of

---

108   It's clear where this line of reasoning is headed: Hannity and Noor may have each "feared for my life." Ostensibly, this fear is justified during any routine 911 call, because any such call might be an ambush. As we've seen, the "feared for my life" defense has been carefully developed, honed, and proven to lead to many, many acquittals. If Noor is found not guilty, then America will have knocked down the final barrier and authorized its police to shoot and kill anyone at any time, since any and all situations might set up an ambush. This will force every American to calculate the potential danger of asking for police intervention in any situation, and to weigh it against the potential benefit. African Americans and other people with dark skin must already make such calculations routinely.

109   The United States has about 321 million people. Of these, 1,000–1,500 are typically killed each year by police. By way of comparison, the combined populations of Germany, Holland, Japan, Australia, Norway, and the UK equal about 321 million. In 2011 (the most recent year for which data were available for all six countries), the combined number of people killed by police in these six countries was nineteen.

my fellow Minneapolitans are bewildered that this could happen in Damond's neighborhood. Yet for decades, people with dark skin, and organizations such as the NAACP, have been predicting just such an event, and have repeatedly urged police forces to take steps to prevent it. These urgings went largely unheeded.

As Shaun King noted—bluntly, accurately, and eloquently—on July 17, police brutality jumped not only a national border, but a racial fence:

> A few weeks ago, a buddy of mine told me, "Shaun—I don't think this country is ever really going to give a damn about police brutality until they see it destroying the lives of white families." I think he's right. That's the American way . . .

> Here's the thing—I think Eric Garner, who was choked to death by the NYPD three years ago today, is the perfect face of police brutality victims. So is Sandra Bland. So is Tamir Rice. So is Amadou Diallo. So is Rekia Boyd. So is Jordan Edwards. So is Philando Castile. But I'll be honest with you, I think a lot of well-meaning white people have looked at the most well-known cases of police brutality, and have seen a black problem that is simply unlikely to visit them like it is now visiting the family of Justine Damond.

> Maybe, just maybe, with the shooting death of Justine Damond, millions of white people, for the very first time, will now see a victim of police brutality, and see themselves.[110]

Annihilating Black bodies in the name of safety is often delusional and immoral. Of course, annihilating a body of *any* skin tone is equally delusional and immoral. Moving from "I saw a dark body and feared for my life, so I killed it" to "I saw an unfamiliar body and feared for my life, so I killed it" is not progress. We have simply blown our pain into a slightly larger gene pool. Actual progress would be fewer deaths at the hands of law enforcement professionals. That is what Campaign

---

110   Shaun King, "Police Brutality Jumped a Racial Fence with Minneapolis Cop Shooting of Justine Damond," *New York Daily News*, July 27, 2017, "http://www.nydailynews.com/news/national/king-police-brutality-jumped-racial-fence-minn-shooting-article-1.3332799.

Zero (joincampaignzero.org) is all about.

The trauma embedded in the bodies of American police is no longer a Black problem—or an American problem. It now affects the world. Who will be the next victim like Damond or Castile? You? Your partner? Your child? Nobody knows. What we do know is that these deaths will continue until we begin healing our trauma, individually and collectively. As individuals, as a culture, and as a country, we can no longer soothe ourselves by trying to blow our pain and trauma through the bodies of dark-skinned Americans. Or white-skinned Australians. Or individual police officers.[111]

Our habit of blaming the corpse is also no longer sustainable. "Eric Garner should have taken better care of himself." "Philando Castile shouldn't have reached for his license after Officer Yanez asked him for it." "Tamir Rice shouldn't have been playing with a toy gun in public." "Justine Damond shouldn't have walked so fast toward the police officers." "Terence Crutcher shouldn't have walked away from the police officer." "Charles Kinsey shouldn't have laid in the street with his hands up, explaining the situation calmly to the police officer." "Your child shouldn't have littered." "You should have known when you dialed 911 that the responding police officers would expect an ambush." "You should have made sure there were no loud sounds nearby." The world will no longer allow us these dodges.

Not hurting is no longer an option. We must face and feel soul-stirring pain. But this pain can be clean or dirty. We have a profound and historic opportunity. As the world watches and holds us accountable, we can choose clean pain. If we do, then the deaths of Justine Damond—and Philando Castile, and Tamir Rice, and countless other human beings whose lives were taken from them—may be partly redeemed. This book can help us make that choice, and to navigate the unknown waters into which we will need to sail.

---

111   Try to explain this to someone not from the United States: In June 2017, Jeronimo Yanez was found not guilty of killing Philando Castile. Yet after this "not guilty" verdict, Yanez's employer, the town of St. Anthony, Minnesota, paid Philando Castile's mother a wrongful-death settlement of nearly $3,000,000. The city also paid Yanez $48,500 for agreeing to leave the force. As for Castile's partner, Diamond Reynolds, with whom he lived—and her four-year-old daughter, whom Castile was helping raise—neither was reported to have received a penny. (During that same month, the city of Ferguson, MO, also paid an undisclosed sum as a wrongful-death settlement to the family of Michael Brown. The officer who killed Brown, Darren Wilson, was not charged with a crime.)

If, instead, we choose dirty pain, then Damond, Castile, Rice, and so many others will simply become names on an ever-growing list of corpses—dark and white, foreign and American—that will come to define our country.

*

Here is another choice we now must make: Will we ask, encourage, mentor, and expect our police officers to be full human beings—professionals who care for others *and* themselves? Will police officers' bosses, coworkers, and organizations support their health, happiness, empathy, and humanity? Or will we continue to treat law enforcement as a technical skill—like welding, but with guns and corpses instead of plasma torches?

If you want to become a physician, completing a bachelor's degree and medical school are not sufficient. You also have to complete a residency and an internship or fellowship. You're being coached and mentored and evaluated every step of the way. At all times, you're being evaluated by your teachers, other medical professionals, and patients. Only after years of successful clinical experience can you call yourself an MD. And you might never get there. If you don't have the requisite skills, knowledge, social intelligence, patience, stamina, and human compassion, you might wash out.

What if we took a similar approach to police work? Instead of just training future law enforcement professionals, have them complete residencies. Residents would have mentors who coach them, encourage them, observe them, look out for them, and hold them accountable. Each resident would also have to learn psychological first aid, some basic somatic healing techniques, and some mindfulness practices. They would learn de-escalation techniques and basic pastoral care. They would also be encouraged and mentored to care for their own bodies, minds, and souls.

Most important, what if our future police were given face-to-face, heart-to-heart, body-to-body experience with the people they hope to serve and protect? They would spend time—many weeks, if not many months—in community shops, parks, barber shops and beauty salons, and other meeting places, talking to folks, getting to know them and their families, listening to their cares and concerns and jokes and stories, and sharing some of their own.

Law enforcement professionals with this kind of experience are less prone to unnecessarily draw their guns—or squeeze the triggers. Their lizard brains aren't as quick to order an annihilation response. Because they know and care about the people in their communities, their bodies naturally know what to do: when to settle and when to activate; when to constrict and when to relax; and when to fight, flee, freeze, annihilate, or simply experience safety. This kind of wisdom simply cannot be trained into anyone. It requires person-to-person, heart-to-heart, body-to-body interaction.

Shortly after the Philando Castile and Justine Damond shootings, the police who fired the deadly shots went home, pulled the curtains, and lawyered up. What if, instead, they had reached out to the families of the people they shot, sat with them (out of uniform, of course), briefly expressed their own sorrow and regret, and listened mindfully as family members expressed their grief?

Three days after Justine Damond's death, Ilhan Omar, the Minnesota State Representative for a large portion of Minneapolis, published this comment:

> The current officer training program indoctrinates individuals of all races into a system that teaches them to act first, think later, and justify with fear. It's time we explore solutions beyond improved training and cameras to capture evidence. We need to look at a complete shift in the culture of the police department, away from the use of lethal force and deadly weapons.

On that same day, Richard Carlson, a retired public defender, published a piece in the Minneapolis *Star Tribune* that echoed Omar's concerns, and insisted that it is "the civilians who must be in control, not the police. These days it appears to be the opposite."

Those civilians are us. Let's get to work.

FIVE OPPORTUNITIES FOR HEALING AND MAKING ROOM FOR GROWTH

The healing of trauma, and the creating of room for growth in the nervous systems of our children and other human beings, does not only happen in therapists' offices. Our everyday lives present us with endless opportunities to heal—through the things we say and do, the harmful things we are able to *not* say and do, and the ways in which we treat ourselves and others. We all have the capacity to heal—and to create room for others to heal. Our relationships, communities, and circumstances all call us into this healing.

Life offers us five types of such opportunities. If you're fortunate, all five may be open to you. Most of us can practice at least the first three. Since you're reading these words, you're already practicing the first.

Opportunity #1: Healing on your own. You can read (and reread) this book and follow its guidance. More important, you can regularly practice some of the activities presented in this book—especially the five anchors in Chapter Twelve.

Opportunity #2: Healing with another trusted, caring person. This might be a friend, a partner, or a family member. You can talk with them about your experiences, your concerns, your family and ancestors, and/or your hopes for the future. They can listen and support you as you metabolize some of your trauma and move through it. You might listen and support them in their own healing, as well.

Opportunity #3: Healing in community. With other people you know and care about, you can practice some of the shared healing practices in this book. You might also ask a trusted community figure—such as an elder, a spiritual leader, or a community activist—to listen, support you, and offer their guidance.

Opportunity #4: Healing with the help of a body-focused healing professional. This might be a craniosacral healer, a massage therapist, an energy worker (such as a Reiki practitioner), an osteopath, a homeopath, or an acupuncturist.

Opportunity #5: Healing with the help of a trauma therapist. This is the deepest and most life-changing form of healing. Trauma therapists have tools and skills that most other therapists do not. Usually these include some combination of Somatic Experiencing (SE), Sensorimotor Psychotherapy (SP), Eye Movement Desensitization and Reprocessing (EMDR), neurofeedback, and/or emotion-focused therapy (also known as process-experiential therapy). You can find a good list of trauma therapists on the website of the Somatic Experiencing Trauma Institute at sepractitioner. membergrove.com.

The more opportunities you practice, the better. But each one is important—and each can help mend your trauma, create more room for future generations, and heal the world.

ACKNOWLEDGING MY CONTEMPORARIES

I first want to thank my mentors; I am grateful and privileged to stand on their shoulders.

Dr. David Schnarch is the author of the relationship books *Intimacy and Desire, Passionate Marriage,* and *Resurrecting Sex,* and the founder of the Crucible Institute (crucibletherapy.com). The concepts of clean and dirty pain, which inform much of this book, are based on his work. In addition, the five anchors are outgrowths of Dr. Schnarch's 4 Points of Balance.

The late Dr. James Maddock—professor emeritus at the University of Minnesota, and founder of the University of Minnesota Medical School's Program in Human Sexuality—also taught me a great deal. Dr. Maddock routinely combined constant kindness, generosity, and a complete refusal to tolerate bullshit. Doc Maddock began as a mentor and became an ancestor for me.

I am grateful to Dr. Ruth Morehouse, co-director of the Marriage and Family Health Center in Evergreen, Colorado, for her guidance and uncompromising integrity.

My thanks to Peter Levine and his Somatic Experiencing organization, as well as to the Minnesota Somatic Experiencing community, all of whom have helped me become an ever-more-effective therapist. I'd also like to give a special shout-out to Thea Lee and Tommy Woon, who established some of the earliest and most important connections between somatics and culture.

I owe much to my other mentors and elders: Dr. Oliver Williams of the University of Minnesota School of Social Work; Dr. Noel Larson of Meta Resources; Mary Azzahir, known to the many people who love her as Mother Atum; her husband, Seba Akhmed Azzahir; and Mahmoud El-Kati.

I offer my gratitude to former Police Chief Janeé Harteau, Acting Chief Medaria Arrandondo, former Assistant Chief Kris Arneson, and Commander Charlie Adams, all of the Minneapolis Police Department, as well as to my brother, police officer Christopher Mason.

I am deeply grateful for the love, presence, and support of my wife, Maria; my daughter, Brittney; and my son, Tezara.

Books, like human beings, grow up in community. This book would not be what it is without the efforts, insight, guidance, and provocative questions of Scott Edelstein, my longtime collaborator and literary agent. I'm also grateful for his friendship.

My thanks to the many talented people at Central Recovery Press, including Patrick Hughes, Valerie Killeen, Nancy Schenck, and, most of all, my editor, Eliza Tutellier, who was a profound advocate for the book from the moment she encountered it. I'm also grateful to Felicia Pruitt Brown, my graphic designer, who designed the somatic timeline on page 74 and the trauma pyramid on page 46.

Other folks shared their many talents to support this book, spread the word about it, and build community around it. Chaka Mkali provided his artistic guidance and support in multiple fields of expression. Brent Meyers contributed his social media savvy and expertise. Mychael Fisher coordinated all the many related visual projects. And an entire posse of visual, musical, and video artists created works that connected people's bodies and hearts to this book.

I'd also like to thank Susan Raffo, Janice Barbee, Margaret Baumgartner, Fen Jeffries, Repa Mekha, and Ariella Tilsen; my longtime friend US Congressman Keith Ellison; my important childhood friends Sandy Voss and Jodi Nowak; and my mother, Amanda Coleman-Mason.

My mentors, ancestors, and elders all held me accountable without holding me up for ridicule. They taught me to consistently act out of the best parts of myself. They encouraged me to grow up. I am deeply grateful to them all.

I'm especially grateful to my late maternal grandmother, Addie Coleman, whose loving presence infuses these pages, and without whom neither I nor this book would have been born.